Books by Ralph Keyes

WE, THE LONELY PEOPLE: Searching for Community
IS THERE LIFE AFTER HIGH SCHOOL?

Is There Life After High School?

Is There Life After High School?

RALPH KEYES

Little, Brown and Company — Boston – Toronto

Fifth Printing

T 06/76

The author is grateful to the following publishers and companies for permission to reprint previously copy-
righted materials:
   Cheerleader Supply Co., Inc., for the photograph of the cheerleader in the upper right-hand corner of
page 88 from the 1974 mail order catalog. Copyright © 1974 by Cheerleader Supply Company.
   Doubleday & Company Inc., and Jean Shepherd, for quotations from "Wanda Hickey's Night of Golden
Memories" from *Wanda Hickey's Night of Golden Memories and Other Disasters* by Jean Shepherd. Copyright © 1969
by HMH Publishing Company, Inc.
   Field Newspaper Syndicate, for the Mary Worth cartoon of December 1, 1974, by Saunders and Ernst,
copyright © 1974 by Field Enterprises Inc.; and for the Jules Feiffer cartoon of January 13, 1974, copyright
© 1974 by Jules Feiffer.
   Grove Press, Inc., for the Photograph "Gridiron Maidens" in the upper left-hand corner of page 88 from
Evergreen Review, No. 48, August 1967. Copyright © 1967 by Evergreen Review, Inc.
   National Lampoon Incorporated, for the cartoon "Gratuitous Unfulfilled Wish" by Doug Kenney, *National
Lampoon*, December 1971, copyright © 1971 by National Lampoon, Inc.; and for the cover of the *1964 High
School Yearbook* issue, May 1974, copyright © 1974 by National Lampoon, Inc.
   Penthouse International Ltd., for permission to include an anonymous letter published in *Penthouse*, February
1974. Copyright © 1974 by Penthouse International Ltd.
   Tree Publishing Company Inc., for excerpted lyrics from "Sidewalks of Chicago" by Dave Kirby.
Copyright © 1970 by Tree Publishing Co. Inc.
   Frank Zappa Music, Inc., for excerpted lyrics from "Status Back Baby" by Frank Zappa. Copyright © 1968
by Frank Zappa Music Inc. All rights reserved.

LIBRARY OF CONGRESS CATALOGING IN PUBLICATION DATA

Keyes, Ralph.
   Is there life after high school?

   Includes bibliographical references.
   1.   High school students — United States — Conduct
of life.   2.   High schools — United States.   3.   Social
values.   I.   Title.
LA229.K48   373.1   75-46572
ISBN 0-316-49130-6

Designed by Susan Windheim

*Published simultaneously in Canada
by Little, Brown & Company (Canada) Limited*

PRINTED IN THE UNITED STATES OF AMERICA

For Muriel

Foreword

This book is about memories of high school. One question it confronts with forthright evasion is whether the high school in memory still exists in fact. It may not. If only in dress and speech patterns (to say nothing of hallway violence), today's high school is different from the one I attended, and from the one people recalled for this book.

But if the high school of my book's title is yesterday's, I write as though it were alive today. Because it is alive: in our minds. High school lives on in memory, and memory can feel just as real as reality.

This doesn't mean adolescent memories are joyous. Whoever called high school "the best years of your life" must have started college at thirteen. Or grown up in Samoa. "My folks keep telling me these are the best years of my life," a sixteen-year-old writes Ann Landers. "If they are right, I hate to think what the rest of my life is going to be like." No, joy isn't the best word to describe most memories of high school. What they are is *intense*. Vivid. Filled with feeling. Whatever else may be said about this time, there's little doubt then of being ALIVE.

While teaching a course on adolescence at Prescott College, I had students suggest items under two headings: what contributes to status in high school, and what doesn't. A long list for Status wasn't hard to compile (cutting classes without getting caught, your walk, your talk), nor one for No Status (straight A's, going to swim meets, association with anyone doing any of the above). But when I tried to start a third list of things that didn't matter one way or the other, only silence was contributed. Finally, a young female voice muttered from the back row, "In high school, *nothing* didn't matter."

This class gave me an opportunity to compare my own high school memories with the more recent ones of college freshmen. Many of my students insisted that at the high schools from which they'd just graduated status is less hierarchical than it used to be. In other words, if you didn't make it in this crowd, you could make it in that one: if not as a soc, then as a freak; if not a jock, a preppie; and so forth.

But the one thing that hadn't changed was the power of status, no matter how defined. When I started to list "riding your bike to school" under No Status, several young voices cried out, "No! No!"

"Riding your bike to school can be *status*," one voice explained. "It just depends on what *kind* of bike."

High school changes; high school stays the same.

Although private and parochial schools come up occasionally in this book, I've concentrated on public schools. While adolescent memories are intense in any setting, the social mix of public high school gives it a distinctive flavor that I've tried to bring out in my book. I'm convinced that democracy takes its purest form in a public high school locker room where everyone's undressing for PE.

More names in this book than I would like are changed, as are other identifying details and the names of some schools — particularly in the chapter on reunions. Since high school is a sensitive topic, I've tried to treat it sensitively.

Acknowledgments

A book cannot be written without help, and this book is no exception.

Among those I would like to thank for their help are:

EARLY ENCOURAGEMENT: David Maxey, Ken Minyard

RESEARCH ASSISTANCE: Liz Fancher, Dick Harrington, Nicky Keyes

TECHNICAL ASSISTANCE: Phil Elsbree, Orienne Strode, Jim Cravens

LOAN OF YEARBOOKS: Wendy Blair, Karen Maynard, Lu Meredith, Terry Ranson, Fleur D'Amour Stark, Ken Wasserman

MANUSCRIPT CRITICISM: Tom Blair, Barbara Bodin, Barbara Houlton, Scot Morris, Dick Peacock, Joanne Pitts, Philomène Resnikoff, Byron Skinner, Jane Weisman Stein, Gay Swenson, and Charles J. O'Leary, Ph.D.

LITERARY CONTRIBUTIONS: Linda Boraz, Earl Burrows, Colin Campbell, Norm and Izetta Chambers, Tom Chapman, Bill Coulson, Steve Doyne, Jim Flanders, Tom Gillette, T George Harris, Gail Hay,

Pat Horn, Mal Karman, Steve Keyes, Connie Koenenn, Doug and Elsie Land, Bob and Marion Lee, Layne Longfellow, Marshall Lumsden, Dave McNeil, Janey Martin and her friend Mike, David Maxey, Elaine Pearson, Nancy Powers, Jo Reed, Philomène Resnikoff, Patt Schwab, Leslie Shelton, Pearl Sickles, Bob Smith, Jane Weisman Stein, Bill and Anne Stillwell, Jeannie Trounstine, Barbara Williams, Sam Wilson, John Wood, and a much longer list of people who helped me think high school through during casual conversations on the topic.

Particular thanks to: Butch Skinner for photographic help far beyond the call of neighborly duty; the San Diego Public Library, whose staff remained patient under my blizzard of magazine-request slips; and John and Shirley Worobec, for their patronage of the arts.

Although it is their job, both my agent Don Cutler and my editor Bill Phillips did far more than their job helping bring this book to life. Phillips is a good editor.

Finally, this book could not exist in its current form without the help and support of my best consultant, my wife Muriel.

As I guess it's necessary to say, anything good about this book is due in part to the above people; anything wrong is my responsibility alone.

Contents

High School Fever

A man may remember his childhood with pleasure, but where is one who does not wince at the memory of his adolescence?
— JOHN A. RICE

In his inaugural speech before Congress, President Gerald Ford made a confession.

"I'm here to confess," said Ford, "that in my first campaign for president — of my senior class at South High School — I headed the Progressive party ticket and I lost.

"Maybe that's why I became a Republican."

In Washington, William J. Schuiling watched the President's televised confession with consternation. "I was amazed," Schuiling recalls, "absolutely amazed that this little incident would be any part of his mind."

William Schuiling is the man who beat Ford in high school. Schuiling today is an investment banker. His office is within view of the White House. On one wall Gerald Ford's picture is inscribed "with appreciation for our long and close friendship." Beneath this picture, not long after Ford's speech, Schuiling gave his version of their contest in Grand Rapids forty-three years before.

"I had been approached," he recalls, "by a friend named Thad Williams, who suggested that I give it a try. And I was *aware* of the fact that Jerry Ford had a running start because he was captain of the championship football team, he'd been an all-city center for three years in a row, and uh . . ."

Popular?

"Oh, yeah." Schuiling smiled and leaned forward over his

desk. Tall and balding, he resembles Jack Benny. "But you see Jerry had a few close friends while I had many, many friendly acquaintances." The banker leaned back, hands clasped behind his head.

"So I thought my root system was stronger than his."

Unlike his opponent, Bill Schuiling was not an athlete. His constituency came from places like the Y Club and Zoological Society, some of whose members got together with him for a strategy-planning picnic in the fall of 1930.

"Let's see, there was Thad Williams." Schuiling ticked off on his fingers. "And a girl, I think her name was Carol Tully. And Burt Salisbury.

"That evening, while roasting our wienies and so forth —" Schuiling raised his palm in the air "— no beer! that was *unthinkable!* — we thought we would gain an advantage by immediately assuming the name of the Republican party — the reason being that we were from a Republican community.

"This left Jerry at a disadvantage and he picked the name of the Progressive party. Now the Republican party platform seems rather trite today, but it was very important then." Schuiling paused, with a sheepish grin.

What was it?

"Rings and pins before Christmas."

Rings and pins before Christmas?

"Rings and pins before Christmas.

"You see we were seniors and we thought this would be a way of encouraging our parents to buy our rings and pins for us for Christmas. Very few of us had rings, so we were *very* anxious to get them."

On this platform, and with the added promise of two dances and a spring picnic, Bill Schuiling's Republicans beat Jerry Ford's Progressives.

"But I don't think the best man won," Schuiling is quick to add. "I just outplayed him. I got to more of the, the, uh . . ."

The banker pondered his words. ". . . the student who was not *involved* in many things, who liked some *attention* — and I think they realized that the *Varsity Club* would not be appointed as committee chairman and that they would all have an opportunity to participate."

Did that happen?

"Yessir! Yessir!"

How did Jerry Ford take the defeat?

"Well, he was the first one over to congratulate me. But apparently it made a lasting impression on him, because he mentions it from time to time. And I don't believe ever in the history of an inaugural was such an insignificant personal situation brought out."

Do you remember by how much you won?

"Yes, I do." Schuiling again leaned over his desk. "But I'm not gonna tell you. Because it was a very, very comfortable margin."

Do you remember the actual count?

"Yeah." His voice rose. "It was a *very* comfortable margin."

Why don't you just tell me?

Schuiling settled back in his chair, his face taking on a Buddha-like resolve. "You'll just have to go ask the President and get the figure, but I know what it is."

Is it something you've remembered over the years, or did you look it up?

"Oh, I didn't have to look it up. It's a figure that just stuck with me for some reason."

High school, for some reason, just sticks with us. Somehow those three or four years can in retrospect feel like thirty — embarrassing though this may be to admit outside the privacy of reverie.

For years I had no idea this was true of anyone but me. Of me it was obvious. I was hopelessly mired in a quicksand of adolescent memories — reliving for years that fight with Carl Malone, and wanting still to tell Lynn Blanchard I'm sorry I stopped talking to her.

At a time when I should have been pondering mortgage payments and the balance of payments, what I seemed to prefer thinking about was a slumber party Pete Kreile and I were invited to. Except the hostess's parents found out and decided not to leave town. Suppose they hadn't found out? Suppose they had left town and their daughters to us? What then?

This is the infection that tormented my mind long after maturity was supposed to have set in. Graduation, it seemed, in my case didn't take.

I feared this affliction was some exotic malady, an obscure high school fever contracted in the hallways by me and me alone.

Symptoms of this fever include:
— shortness of breath when seeing an old classmate;
— heart palpitations upon walking onto a dance floor, or when confronted with anything resembling a test;
— hot cheeks while reviewing loves of the past;
— pulse quickening at any sound like a locker door slamming;
— neurotic obsession with how I'm coming across: elation when feeling popular, despair at feeling any other way;
— inability to focus on another person without imagining him as he was in high school;
— trembling hands at the mere thought of high school, stiffness of tongue trying to talk about it;
— panic upon receiving a reunion notice.

Though I fear this high school fever may be chronic, its symptoms have declined somewhat over time. And in the years since it's been possible to talk about high school without stammering, I've discovered that other people exhibit symptoms remarkably like my own.

I noticed this first among those friends who grew unusually

alert when I finally was able to gasp out a memory or two from high school. At parties people generally scan the room over my right shoulder, but not when this topic comes up. At the mere mention of high school other eyes snap back to mine. Then, as pupils dilate, eyes seem to reach inside as if trying to grab hold not of my memories so much as something the memories set in motion. Then cheeks flush a bit. Finally my listener's mouth matches mine — high school memory for high school memory and often stammer for stammer.

Not only friends, but people I meet at social gatherings, those sitting next to me on the bus, or celebrities being interviewed seem to suffer something akin to high school fever. Mia Farrow, for example, hasn't forgotten the time every girl but her was asked to dance, nor Charles Schulz the yearbook staff that rejected his every cartoon. Warren Beatty constantly brings up the ten football scholarships he turned down, reminding us of his high school heroics even as he ridicules them.

When I asked Dory Previn what she remembered about high school, the first thing that came to the singer's mind was a part she didn't get in the class play.

"I played the maid in *Don't Take My Penny*," Dory recalled. "Needless to say I was not the lead."

Do you remember who was?

"Hazel Croft."

You remember her name?

Dory laughed. "Oh ho — do I ever!"

It turns out that I'm not alone in remembering high school so vividly. In fact, I'm about as alone as frightened people at a sock hop. High school is a popular topic of contemplation among Americans. And our fascination with this time of life shapes in fundamental ways both the adults we become and the society we share.

In recent years especially, as we've lined up for *American Graffiti*, watched "Happy Days" on television and made *Memoirs of an Ex-Prom Queen* a best-seller, America has become sort of an ongoing high school festival. Even much of what passes for 50s nostalgia is really just writers in their thirties and forties reminiscing about high school.

Once you grow alert to the impact of high school on this society it registers like blips on a radar screen. American politics, for example, could not be as we know it had participants not learned to poll their popularity so they can get elected as freshmen to Congress, and enter its Class of '76.

Our very vocabulary relies on terms learned in hallways — "stuck-up," for example, "pep rally" and "pretty as a prom queen." For such words to make any sense, we must have shared the experience in which they were born. And we have. Within this century, high school has become perhaps our most universal experience as Americans, one endured today by over ninety percent of the population. Thus, when Rhoda says, "My hands haven't sweated so much since I tried out for cheerleader," I know just what she means. I can feel the drops on my palms.

Long after the last strain of "Mood Indigo" at the prom (assuming we were there), it remains possible to perceive the world in terms of what men played high school football, which women led cheers, and who led a life only of bitter rejection.

When given actual data we're delighted. What adult is beyond a lift upon hearing Ali MacGraw confess she never had a date during high school, or when finding out that the young Henry Kissinger is recalled by one classmate as "a little fatso"? Such information brings people into focus, and can be an enormous comfort.

The only problem is, much as we value such data, it's not polite to ask for it. An implicit protocol of this society is that if you don't ask me what I was like in high school, I won't ask you.

But we do ask, silently, inside the privacy of our minds. And we speculate about each other as adolescents, often with cunning accuracy. "What you have to remember about Henry," a colleague once said of our secretary of state, "is that he's the kid nobody would eat lunch with."

Noticing how common such speculation is, and how volatile high school memories can be, finally led me to wonder: suppose someone took to asking out loud what we often wonder in silence? Questions such as, "What were you like in high school?" "Were you popular?" "How did you feel about your body?" "What do you suppose your classmates were saying about you?"

These are not questions to which one gets a simple yes or no answer. Those struggling to respond are soon caught up in a flood of memories long dammed by adult propriety — dates, dances, fights, slights. The memories are always personal, and unusually animated. Masks carefully constructed over the years crumble after a few moments of adolescent reverie. Bodies squirm, and voices change.

For the past two years I've watched this process again and again — first in amazement, then fascination, and finally in resignation — as I've posed questions about high school in conversation, over the air, and during formal interviews. Anywhere this seems inappropriate, which is everywhere. While asking about adolescent memories I've been rude at reunions from a fifth to a fiftieth, and in interviews with people ranging from Art Linkletter to porno star George McDonald.

Early in my search I called Robert Logue, who works for Arizona's Highway Department in Phoenix. I wanted to know how it felt to beat Richard Nixon for senior class president in 1930. After I asked, there was a long pause at the other end of the line. Then a man's voice replied, "That was *student body* president."

It did not take many such experiences to convince me that high school fever had infected others. The malady was not exotic. It was just the opposite: an epidemic.

But epidemic as this fever may be, the plague is a discreet one. Documenting high school fever calls for the determination of a

Salk, and the patience of a Pasteur. Asking people to describe their symptoms I've been cut off, put down, and lied to ignominiously. At times I was reduced to shivering frustration, not knowing why I didn't choose a topic easier to investigate than high school memories. Watergate, say.

Because what seems like an innocent inquiry into events of long ago more often is heard as an invitation for a little friendly torture.

"Was I a cheerleader?" responded one woman who wasn't. "That's like asking was I a person."

Inhibitions about this topic are of two basic strains. First, and most common, is a reluctance to reopen the thousand cuts one may have suffered during high school. The second inhibition is exhibited by those who enjoyed their high school years, the rare ones who felt popular and successful and enjoy reliving the triumph — yet are chagrined to admit this.

But even if people are more reluctant to start talking about high school than almost any topic I've ever asked about, they also don't stop once started. Like water backed up for years behind a dam, once the floodgates open at all, a trickle quickly becomes a river of high school memories bursting through.

Winding down after an hour or two, those reliving their high school years will come up for air, look around sheepishly, then say something like, "You know, this is a *fascinating* topic."

The fascination, of course, is themselves. They and their memories of high school. There may be no more interesting time of life.

Based on my own experience, interviews, and related readings, I've found that:

a) high school is the source of indelible memories,

b) these memories focus on comparison of status, and

c) status comparisons continue long after graduation, in a society shaped fundamentally by high school.

In the Hallways of Your Mind

High school isn't a time and a place. It's a state of mind.
— FRANK ZAPPA

Memories Are Made of This

As the guest on a Los Angeles radio show, I asked, "Is there life after high school?" In response the switchboard lit up like a pinball machine as callers competed for time on the air to tell their adolescent tales.

One call came from a great-grandmother who said she still likes to get out her yearbook from half a century ago, and read over margin notes about dates: who she went with, where, and what they did.

A recent graduate called to complain that his class vice-presidency had little value now, and a twenty-six-year-old bragged about the fight he'd won eight years before.

Finally, a man named Luke called, a 1939 graduate who told about his recurring dreams of high school. The dreams were vivid, Luke said, actual memories of horsing around in class, throwing spitballs, and winning a fight in his senior year. Even though he'd get out of bed and try to walk them off, the dreams kept right on coming — every week or so.

Luke, it turned out, had been a star athlete in high school, the winner of eight out of nine possible letters — "which is hard in the St. Louis system," he assured us. Now retired and in his fifties, by his own admission Luke had done little of consequence as an adult. "My life's been pretty mediocre since high school," said Luke.

"You know that question you asked — 'Is there life after high school?'

"Well, in my case there isn't."

Ken Minyard, the show's host, was at first uncertain if this topic had substance. But as the show proceeded, Minyard himself began to be invaded by memories of his own Oklahoma high school days two decades before. Ken remembered in particular a guy dunking him in a pool, and said that to this day if anyone tries in the slightest way to push him around, he feels the very same rage he felt in that pool.

What impressed Ken more was that he still remembered the name of his high school tormentor — both names, first and last. He felt odd, and a little embarrassed, that such trivia should stick in his mind.

In fact, Ken is not odd at all. At Ohio Wesleyan University several hundred subjects were recently tested on their recall of high school classmates. Graduates fifteen years out of high school could identify by name ninety percent of their classmates' pictures, and even those nearing their fortieth or fiftieth reunion recognized seventy-five percent of classmates' faces. Although prompting with yearbook pictures produced the best results, the researchers found that recent graduates usually could name several dozen classmates off the top of their head, while older subjects remembered nineteen names on the average without prompting.

In my own interviewing, I've found it common that people will remember a roll call of high school classmates' names and talk of these old acquaintances as if they were next-door neighbors today. "This guy," or "that girl," are not phrases we use to convey high school memories. What we say is, "So Ellen Markowitz reached down and grabbed my . . ." or "and right there in class Jim Oates began to . . ."

But names are just the most prominent detail sticking out in high school memories. I've also been told, down to the taffeta slip, what was once worn to a prom, and the precise phrases used to tell off Faye Clemens. Cheers from games are commonly remembered word for word, and can today be recited not just by ex-cheerleaders but by those who were listening in the crowd.

Two things I find people remember with uncommon accuracy are how many times their picture appeared in the yearbook and exactly what was written under their senior picture. One woman who couldn't recall every word of the caption did remember its meter. "The first line was dah dah dah dah, dah dah dah — something about my heart. 'Gay and carefree all the while,' I think it ended."

Just as interesting as what people *do* recall from high school is what they *don't* — like education, the supposed reason for gathering. An occasional inspiring teacher may stand out in the memory, but rarely anything that went on in a classroom beyond passing notes.

The one place where academic memories do show up is in dreams. Dreams set in high school seem unusually common, and one dream in particular: showing up unprepared for a big test.*

The dream next most often recalled has to do with a locker which won't open, usually because the dreamer has forgotten its combination.

But none of these standouts from high school memory — the dreams, the names, the prom dresses, or the yearbook captions — can convey the feelings with which they're described: the way voices crack, hands grab the air, and eyes dart wildly around the room as people talk about their high school years.

It's as if the adolescent within never dies, that inside each of

* A 1940 Harvard graduate once wrote to its *Magazine* that he'd had such a nightmare repeatedly since graduation from college. This letter was followed by sixty more from correspondents, aged twenty-two to sixty-five, who reported similar dreams.

us lies a high school kid napping. This kid may sleep for years without waking, and lull us into believing we've grown up. Then someone will nudge him awake with a rude question. Or we'll catch a whiff of brownies baking and be cut again by that snub in Home Ec. Or hearing Johnny Mathis sing "The Twelfth of Never" will float us right to the sofa where Carla Rollins first let us touch her breast. Even a single glimpse of *Happy Days* on TV may be enough to take us helplessly back to all the clanging lockers in the hallways of our mind.

Finding the teenager within alive and kicking still can be exciting. It also is embarrassing. The single word I've heard most often used to describe the feeling of looking back on high school is "embarrassed."

After explaining in great detail why he only got two letters rather than three in his senior year (because of missing baseball practice) one forty-five-year-old ex-jock told me, "I'm embarrassed about not getting that letter. But what embarrasses me more is that I'm even talking about it."

Most embarrassing of all is how easy it is to recall now what mattered most then: status.

Status on My Mind

Pop Quiz

Directions: A list of social situations follow. Some contribute to one's status in high school, others don't. Indicate situations that are high status with a T for "True," those that are low status with an F for "False."

1. _____ Show up at the most popular hamburger drive-in at 10 P.M. on a Saturday night with your parents.
2. _____ Be put in charge of yearbook picture captions.

3. _____ Forget your locker combination so a janitor has to come open it as the halls are full between classes.

4. _____ Arrive late to class often, but always with a flurry and comment that makes the class laugh and the teacher smile.

5. _____ Your mother is elected president of the PTA.

6. _____ When you raise your hand in class, a big, round, dark mark is clearly visible around the armpit.

7. _____ Play piccolo in the band.

8. _____ On Slave Day, bidding is loud and long when you come on the block.

9. _____ When not at McDonald's, always sit at the crowded second table from the northwest corner of the cafeteria.

10. _____ Consistently be seated in class several minutes before the bell rings.

11. _____ Break your leg skiing and walk around school for a month in a cast covered by autographs.

12. _____ Earn a letter sweater, but wear it only occasionally.

13. _____ Carry a briefcase in the hallways, usually fat with papers.

14. _____ Show up late to an important party.

15. _____ Make Honor Society your junior year.

16. _____ Ride your bike to school and park it next to the main door as the first bell rings and your classmates stream in.

17. _____ When you cruise the drive-in on Saturday night, there's lots of honking and waving.

18. _____ A girl with a small gold megaphone hanging around her neck asks for the answer on a test, and you refuse because "it would be wrong."

19. _____ Be assigned to 11R English, the "R" standing for "Remedial."

20. _____ Flakes of Clearasil fall from your face to the floor as you walk down the hallway.

Special Status Section for Women Only

1. _____ 30 AA
2. _____ pierced ears
3. _____ anklets
4. _____ cashmere sweaters
5. _____ A rumor circulates that you went all the way.

Special Status Section for Men Only

1. _____ Your letter reads "Mgr."
2. _____ '57 Chevy
3. _____ Chess Club
4. _____ chest hair
5. _____ Future Farmers

Answers:

Men Only	Women Only
1. F	1. F
2. T	2. F
3. F	3. F
4. T	4. T
5. F	5. F

1. F	6. F	11. T	16. F
2. T	7. F	12. T	17. T
3. F	8. T	13. F	18. F
4. T	9. T	14. T	19. F
5. F	10. F	15. F	20. F

Long after graduation it's possible to recall one's adolescent social standing with the precision of a Social Register editor. In response to the question "Were you popular in high school?" I hadn't expected such a common reply to be "Which year?" I then would be given a detailed breakdown of where the respondent stood in the pecking order year by year ("Now in my sophomore year I was. . . . But then by my junior year . . ."), or even semester by semester ("So by the first half of my senior year...").

Dory Previn said that during no year did she feel especially popular at her New Jersey high school. Recently, however, she's seen some old classmates who remember her as popular. This always surprises today's singer-songwriter. What Dory remembers feeling was mostly inadequate — crooked-toothed, curly-haired, and bad in schoolwork compared to those who had "straight hair, straight teeth, and straight As."

Dory Previn today is a delightful-looking lady with an extraordinary helmet of orange hair over a freckled mobile face that can shift from pathos to boisterous good humor with just a second's change of gears.

One of her more vivid high school memories is of the prom she didn't attend. Dory had been invited. The last possible week a guy asked her. "I'm sure he must have asked several other people," she recalls, "but I was thrilled out of my mind that he'd asked me."

Then the invitation was withdrawn. Just before the prom Dory's suitor came up to her in the hall and said he'd heard she was making fun of him ("I think he said another girl, who evidently liked the same boy, told him that") and the date was off.

How did you feel?

"Oh," said Dory looking pained. "I was heartbroken! I was, like, so grateful to him for having asked me he will never know. But I couldn't admit it, I couldn't say, 'Hey, listen, I'm really grateful. *Please* don't ever think I put you down. If anyone said that it just simply isn't true. I'm damned grateful that I finally got an invitation.'

"But I couldn't have said that in my own defense in those days because I was pretending it wasn't so terrific when I was really ecstatic."

When she thinks about walking around the halls of her high school, Dory mostly remembers how firmly she kept her head bent to the floor, hoping no one would notice her freckles. "Flyspecks" the other kids called them, and Dory railed at whoever it was that spattered a paintbrush across her face.

What she craved, more than anything, was braces. "Rich kids had braces." Dory explains, "I was too poor." Also Sara Gordon had braces. Sara was the classmate Dory Previn envied most — the girl who was as pretty as Dory felt plain, Jewish instead of Catholic, and rich enough to afford braces.

"Sara had the most wonderful buck teeth," Dory remembers, "and for a long time, while she was wearing the braces, I used to imitate her — sticking out my top lip as though I had buck teeth too." Dory stuck her lip out to demonstrate, then laughed and blushed nearly enough to hide her freckles.

No less than officers of the military or members of primitive tribes did we compare the outer signs of status. At a time when bodies seemed to change daily, physical appearance was the basis for comparison. Through artful dress we could sometimes conceal our shame. But then there was always PE. And showers. Because of the comparisons being made within, locker rooms are a torture chamber in the memory. For guys this was where the truth came out about pubic hair and penis size. Girls, before showering, had to remove their various falsies.

Chests were the focal if not the only point of female comparison. Breast size was the basic medium of exchange, the gold to which all other currency was relative. And woe to the pauper with but two small nuggets.

Yet while the unluckiest women recall stuffing their bras with Kleenex and trying to get out of PE, girls at the other extreme were binding their chests in a desperate effort to squelch an abundance of riches. High school is simply not a time when you want to stand out in any way. Actress Dyan Cannon recalls being so embarrassed by a forward-looking bosom that she stuffed oranges in her bra at night hoping to hold down the swelling.

While bodies were at the heart of comparison, a listing could continue for pages of signals people remember looking for to sort each other out — everything from sweater brand to books in hand — anything to peg our classmates and compare them with ourselves.

A successful magazine editor two decades beyond high school told me in painful detail how as an adolescent she was desperate to get tuberculosis and sympathy as did one member of her class. The woman also made a connection between the suicide of a guy's father and his getting elected class president. She prayed some similar tragedy might befall her so people would like her better.

Recently, this editor was invited to a dinner party with a classmate who had outranked her in the status sweepstakes. She turned the invitation down because, as she told me, "I have *not* forgotten."

As the most tribal experience many of us will ever have, high school must be memorable. Never again are we ranked so precisely by those around us, and on so many scales. Through the popularity polls of our classmates, and their inexperience at tact, daily feedback was conveyed about how we were coming across. Such merciless judgment is not easily forgotten, the last time of life we know just where we stand in the scrutinizing eyes around us.

What high school has become, in fact and in memory, is a self-contained community, a tribe with its own special rituals and status systems. High schools are commonly farthest from your home of any school attended, large buildings, sealed off by a fence. The society within, as sociologist Edgar Friedenberg points out, is so insular that it even has its own means of telling time — by period rather than the clock (as in: "I'll meet you after fourth period").

In recent decades high school has evolved into a tribal gathering where teenaged Americans act out their puberty rights and wrongs, improvising paths through the stage of life when feelings bubble over most freely, undammed by adult masks. The clang of lockers was tom-toms to our ears as we gathered in high school, the cafeteria our central stewpot. Within we were united by ritual and contest, by pep rallies and homecoming, and by the purchase of a class ring. And always the contests, the jousting for position as beauty queens or class officers, members of the team, and inspectors of the uniform.

In so status-conscious an environment, even something seemingly so innocent as nicknames takes on desperate significance: a precise barometer of one's social standing.

In the first place, you had to count enough to be given a nickname. A nickname means you're noticed. It means you're included.

What I thought was an innocent question, "Did you have a nickname in high school?" most commonly provoked the response: "No. But I would have liked one."

"I really wanted a nickname," one woman told me, "because I thought that having one would make me seem more popular. Consequently I went around giving nicknames to everyone else in hopes someone would give me one, but no one ever did."

A nickname is not something you can give yourself. Others must bestow it upon you. Even a nickname you don't care for means classmates have recognized your presence, which isn't a bad thing to have recognized.

Those lucky enough to have nicknames could rely on them as a subtle but accurate gauge of status and its evolving nature. Raquel Welch, for example, as a young teenager was known as "Birdlegs" because of her long, skinny legs. In high school this was first changed to "Rocky," then "Hotrocks" — "after the equipment arrived."

More than two decades before he produced the Coleman Report on school equality, sociologist James Coleman was known as "Dopey" to his football teammates at Manual High in Louisville. "This nickname was very strategic," he recalls, "because if you're a good student on the football team, you're subject to suspicion from the other players. So I acted in ways that would negate the image of me as a kind of distant intellectual. I acted very much as a buffoon. So I got this nickname 'Dopey.' "

Coleman, who retains the chunky, flat-nosed look of a football player, later earned a Ph.D. at Columbia. He then undertook a major study of status in the American high school, interviewing several thousand students in ten midwestern high schools on topics such as how one got into the leading crowd, and whether it was higher status to date a football player or an honor student.

The surest path into the leading crowd, Coleman found, was athletic ability. The high school social systems revolved around teams and honored most those who excelled athletically. Cheerleader for girls was the only status to compare, but the prestige of this job varied more from school to school than did the prestige of being an athlete.

After sports, paths to the social center depended on the school. What helped in one setting might hurt in another. Good grades were a source of pride in some high schools, shame in others. Family standing counted far more in older towns than in newer subdivisions. Being in the band was played up only in a school without football.

But what *was* consistent to all high schools was the controlling force of status itself, no matter how distributed. Prestige, Coleman found, was the basic medium of exchange within high school. "The adolescent society," he writes in his book of that title, "has little material rewards to dispense, so that its system of rewards is reflected almost directly in the distribution of status."

James Coleman told me that the American high school interested him as a sociologist because it is "the closest thing to a real social system that exists in our society, the closest thing to a closed social system."

What I like about Dr. Coleman's approach to high school is

that he took seriously what we thought about at the time: who's got the status.

What neither he, nor anyone else I know of, has ever studied seriously is the lasting impact of this struggle for status on our adult lives, as we continue to hold postures struck by lockers long ago.

High School, U.S.A.

Somehow years, even decades, after graduation, no categories for making sense of the world seem to improve on the ones we learned in high school. "She's still queen of the hop," we'll say, or "a real cheerleader-type."

A vulgarian to Americans is one who uses "locker-room language."

Then there's that completely untranslatable concept, "high school mentality."

"He's got a high school mentality, know what I mean?"

Of course I know. I went to high school. And since most of us have, using such terms makes it likely we'll be understood from Boston to Burbank.

Midterm

Directions: On the left are descriptions of prominent Americans that have appeared in the press. On the right is a list of possible people so described. For each description, select the person actually described.

1. She was pretty and blonde and energetic and, as we used to say in high school, popular.

    a. Jacqueline Onassis
    b. Phyllis Diller
    c. Alice Cooper
    d. Barbara Howar

2. . . . she was not beautiful in either the hip-swinging or prom queen sense. . . .

a. Marilyn Monroe
b. Barbra Streisand
c. Valerie Perrine
d. Mean Mary Jean

3. Onstage she sometimes projects the air of a spoiled, slightly heartless prom queen. . . .

a. Lily Tomlin
b. Karen Carpenter
c. Moms Mabley
d. Gloria Steinem

4. In many ways, she reminds you of the girl you necked with in the back seat after Friday-night football games.

a. Ingrid Superstar (Andy Warhol's stable)
b. Dale Evans
c. Julie Eisenhower
d. Indira Gandhi

5. . . . she has the waggish air of a Norman Rockwell cheerleader. . . .

a. Bella Abzug
b. Chris Evert
c. Cybill Shepherd
d. Bette Midler

6. Her style is pretty much what you might expect from the giddiest girl in the 11th grade.

a. Erica Jong
b. Tatum O'Neal
c. Joanie Mitchell
d. Agatha Christie

7. He was the class Fat Boy, somehow, without being fat.

a. Orson Welles
b. Gerald Ford
c. Richard Nixon
d. Robert Redford

8. . . . he looks like the well-bred right guard on some winning high school football team. . . .

a. Euell Gibbons
b. Truman Capote
c. Marlon Brando
d. Warren Beatty

9. He is a high school quarterback.

a. O. J. Simpson
b. Omar Sharif
c. Fran Tarkenton
d. Woody Allen

10. Like a prom king in a high
school gym, _____
nodded to the subjects
trotting back and forth
before his throne.

    a. Henry VIII
    b. Abbie Hoffman
    c. Buck Owens
    d. Lyndon Johnson

11. _____, whose mous-
tache looks perennially like
a paste-on job for a role in
the high school operetta.

    a. Burt Reynolds
    b. Sen. Hugh Scott
    c. Telly Savalas
    d. Walter Cronkite

12. At 50 [he] is the same
gawky, overgrown Irish
bookworm-turned-class
clown.

    a. Steve Allen
    b. Carroll O'Connor
    c. Don Rickles
    d. William Westmore-
       land

Answers:

12. a	6. a
11. b	5. c
10. d	4. a
9. c	3. b
8. d	2. b
7. c	1. d

Just as it consumed our adolescent minds and clogs the hallways of memory, status dominates the high school concepts that
we rely on to communicate as adults. "Cheerleader-type" has
an obvious status attached, as does "big dumb jock." Or (God
forbid) someone might be "the kind of person who always had
his hand up in class."

Since our social standing as adults may never be defined so precisely as it was during adolescence, after graduation we simply fall back on high school concepts to make sense of each other. Howard Cosell comes right into focus as an undersized kid hovering around the jocks, whimpering "Hey you guys," just as Don Meredith was clearly on the inside, yelling "Get lost!"

After completing *The Graduate*, Dustin Hoffman told reporters that his co-star Katherine Ross was the kind of girl who never paid attention to him in high school.

Asked her opinion of two fellow models (Cybill Shepherd and Cheryl Tiegs), Lauren Hutton called them "all-American cheerleaders," adding, "I was never able to make it as a cheerleader."

But since high school itself is so all-American, such notions only make sense in the culture that spawned them. Much that I'm writing about — the intensity of adolescence and its durability in the memory — characterizes any culture. What's peculiar to America is high school as the setting of such memories, high school and its odd concepts. Try to talk about "making out" or "majorettes" in Great Britain. You might as well speak Swahili.

When Frank Zappa's album *Absolutely Free* was released in London, the rock 'n' roll musician had to prepare a glossary of high school terms for a local underground paper, defining such concepts as "cheerleader" and "pom-pom." Zappa told me about this soon after returning from a concert tour abroad, when the problem was fresh in his mind. "One of the weird things about going to Europe," he explains, "is that you start talking about high school–type things and it doesn't mean anything.

"How can you describe a paper pom-pom and its manufacture — or its sexual significance — to somebody in Vienna?"

Zappa's early work is rich with the pom-poms, cheerleaders, and jocks he had to contend with at his central California high school in the late 50s. One of the singer's more vivid high school memories is of an assembly where teachers were doing humorous skits. Zappa and a buddy were cutting up in back, which made the cheerleaders and lettermen angry. "They were getting very disturbed at our comments," he recalls, "so when they finally got up to do their routine — I can't remember whether it was to salute the flag or sing the school song or some stupid thing — Dede Watson, a cheerleader, said 'Now we will all stand and do this and blah, blah — and you too, Frank Zappa.'

"So everybody turned around and went 'ooohhh,' like that, and I just sat there. And while they were standing up and I was still sitting down I screamed out, 'Well fuck you Dede Watson!' as loud as I could. In those days you couldn't say 'fuck you' to anybody, let alone a cheerleader, and she burst into tears and they carried her off. It was the ultimate blasphemy."

During a short stint in college, Zappa approached his sociology professor with the idea of studying high school's social system. The teacher was discouraging. How could one make a study without a degree? "So I said, 'Fuck that,'" Zappa recalls. "I didn't feel like sitting around and waiting for someone to approve my ability to ascertain the working of the social structures.

"So I didn't become a sociologist."

What Zappa did become was a rock 'n' roll musician, putting his analysis of high school to tune:

I blew some status at the high school
I used to think that it was my school
I was the king of every school activity
But that's no more, oh mama what will come of me?

The other night we painted posters
They played some records by the Coasters
A bunch of pom-pom girls looked down their nose at me
They had painted tons of posters, I had painted three
ooooooh

I hear those secret whispers everywhere I go
My school spirit's at an all-time low
     "Status Back Baby," © FRANK ZAPPA, *BMI*

"That was for Dede Watson and the girls," says Zappa.

Many such songs grew out of Frank Zappa's postcollege experience playing beer bars in Pomona: "Everybody in there was somebody who was too large to go to high school," he explains, "but they were still strictly from high school. You'd see them in there, they're working at the hardware store now, but high school is where they're coming from. They're still thinking about cars, that whole thing.

"High school isn't a time and a place," he concludes. "It's a state of mind."

I'm not sure this is what the founders of universal secondary education had in mind, but it's what they got by requiring high school as an experience in common. For most of us grade school was more neighborhood-based, and even military service was sex-segregated (both points pre-1970). The high school years are the only ones many of us ever spend with a social and economic cross section of our peers. Therefore, when meeting as strangers, groping for some common ground beyond the *Tonight Show* — high school is an obvious choice. "I felt kind of a senior-prom nervousness — know what I mean?"

Of course. I went to high school.

Such dependence on adolescent metaphors is not as frivolous as it may sound. This being so universal an experience, information about what we were like back then helps make us understandable to each other now. Trying to make sense of a stranger, especially one in the public eye, is far easier once you're in command of their high school background. I may not know what it's like to be a Hollywood star, or how politicians behave in Washington, but I do know about high school.

Just to get it out of the way early, I'm going to list here, after extensive research, my best information about where a cross section of public personalities stood in high school.* This is not to sneer, expose, or even chuckle knowingly, because I'm too vulnerable about my own standing back then (not high enough). But since we speculate all the time anyway, I think we ought at least to be accurate, and get adolescent identities out into the open — with celebrities and with ourselves.

Jocks	*Cheerleaders*	*Student Government*
Warren Beatty	Ann-Margret	Warren Beatty
Bill Blass	Dyan Cannon	Johnny Carson
James Caan	Eydie Gormé	Peter Falk
Alice Cooper	Patty Hearst	Hugh Hefner
James Dickey	Vicki Lawrence	Bowie Kuhn
Bill Graham	Eleanor McGovern	Ali McGraw
Dennis Hopper	Cybill Shepherd	Bette Midler
Arthur Miller	Dinah Shore	Ed Muskie
Robert Redford	Carly Simon	Pat Paulsen
Jason Robards	Lily Tomlin	Philip Roth
John Wayne	Raquel Welch	John Updike

Thespians	*Debate*	*Newspaper*
David Carradine	Mia Farrow	Alice Cooper
Johnny Carson	Dennis Hopper	Howard Cosell
John Denver	Art Linkletter	Hugh Hefner
Kirk Douglas	Eleanor McGovern	Ann Landers
Charlton Heston	George McGovern	Philip Roth
Cliff Robertson	Richard Nixon	Jerry Rubin
Katherine Ross	John Wayne	John Updike
Naomi Sims	William Westmoreland	Abigail Van Buren
Robert Young		Kurt Vonnegut

Yearbook	*Band*	*Pep Club*
Steve Allen	Jean Seberg	Johnny Carson
Hugh Hefner	Frank Zappa	

* A cautionary note. Since some of this information is by self-report of those on the list, and since high school is right up there with sex and salary as a topic of candor, this list should not be considered definitive.

Honor Roll

Helen Gurley Brown
Betty Friedan
Henry Kissinger
Ann Landers
Art Linkletter
Shirley MacLaine
George McGovern
Eleanor McGovern
Rex Reed
Barbra Streisand
Abigail Van Buren

Hoody

Merle Haggard
George Lucas
Sal Mineo
Michael Parks
Elvis Presley
Robert Redford
O. J. Simpson
Rod Taylor
Hunter Thompson

Dis-Honor Roll

Woody Allen
H. R. Haldeman
Michael Landon
Arthur Miller
Gregory Peck
Burt Reynolds
Charles Schulz
O. J. Simpson
Gay Talese
Joseph Wambaugh

Wallflowers
(self-described)

Joan Baez
Erma Bombeck
Mia Farrow
Betty Friedan
Lauren Hutton
Ali MacGraw
Joan Rivers
Buffy St. Marie
Barbra Streisand

Miscellaneous

Wittiest: Bea Arthur
Best Eyes: Lauren Hutton
Biggest Grind: William Proxmire
(also Most Energetic and
Biggest Sponger)
Most Attractive: Cybill Shepherd
Most Popular Boy: Walt Frazier
(also Most Athletic)

Class Clown

Steve Allen
Johnny Carson
Dustin Hoffman
Bette Midler
Carrie Snodgrass
Jonathan Winters

Women Tall &
Men Small

Woody Allen
Bea Arthur
Burt Bacharach
Dick Cavett
Lauren Hutton
George Lucas
Shirley MacLaine
Kim Novak
Paul Simon

Dropouts

Harry Belafonte
Cher Bono
James Garner
Gene Hackman
Merle Haggard
Dean Martin
Bill Mauldin
Elaine May
Rod McKuen
Steve McQueen
Al Pacino
Frank Sinatra

Youth Sits in Judgment

rm Hall   Pat Paulsen   Dick Sh
LIGHTWEIGHT BASKETBALL

STUDENT COUNCIL OFFICERS, FALL SEMESTER. *Standing:* E. Wasilewski, Treas.; J. Brophy, First Vice-Pres. *Seated:* M. Dulen, Second Vice-Pres.; E. Biowski, Sec.; H. Hefner, Pres.

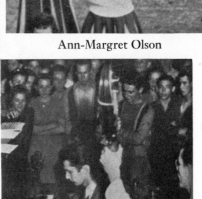

Ann-Margret Olson

DRAMATIC CLUB BOARD
First Row: Miller, Dodds, Engelhard. *Second Row:* Heston, Berlin.

Linkletter

If it's boogie-woogie you're looking for, you've come to the right place. Steve Allen's your best bet, and just to show you, he gives a demonstration.

This is information we love to get. Knowing what a person was like in high school can make, or seem to make, everything fall into place.

This is one of the reasons yearbooks have become a basic work of reference in American society. A staple of celebrity profiles is pictures and data from the subject's yearbook. When someone discovered that the inscription under Martha Mitchell's annual picture read:

> *I love its gentle warble*
> *I love its gentle flow*
> *I love to wind my tongue up*
> *And I love to let it go*

the press was delighted. Of course! That's it! We knew all along. And what better confirmation than a high school yearbook?

Since high school is such an enrolling experience in this society, yearbooks are its register — an annotated list of those who belong. Marilyn Monroe, who did not graduate from high school and was sensitive about it, at age twenty-nine had a photographer shoot her portrait as it might have appeared in an annual.

To the casual eye, yearbooks may look only like a scrapbook of bad photographs and worse prose. This is misleading. What an annual resembles more is one's driver's license or Social Security card — a symbol of full participation in American society.

Except yearbooks are more indelible.

A Social Security card can be burned and a driver's license let expire. You can change your name, quit your job, leave your family, and flee to Samoa — but someone can always look up your yearbook. When a woman wrote Ann Landers bemoaning the fact that her mother-in-law had passed away unphotographed due to sensitivity about a big nose, Ann said that was nonsense: "Have you thought about her high school yearbook?"

One woman with whom I talked said that as a freshman ten

years before she realized that her only source of immortality would be the yearbook. So she diligently set about building a legacy of seeming success. Part of the strategy was to accumulate a long list of activities to be placed under her picture. But more important was joining the yearbook staff, then maneuvering to write her own picture caption. She couldn't bear the thought of "leaving such a crucially important task to someone on the yearbook staff.

"Some of my recollections of the politics of yearbook writing," this woman concluded, "make the Nixon administration pale by comparison."

Most of us took no such preventive action and may not like the way we appear in our annual. In fact, we may not like the way we appeared during high school at all. The yearbook is just a painful reminder. This document may revive old memories we'd rather let die, record forever a status we didn't like, and be too painfully available to others who want to find out what we were like in high school.

For such reasons annuals get hidden beneath underwear in the bureau drawer, carefully censored with scissors, or thrown away in the dead of night. In these more activist times, some yearbooks have had to be recalled and defended against libel suits. Annuals get treated every way but casually. Yearbooks are not commonly lost, and they rarely show up in secondhand stores.

For all that trauma, high school annuals are not good predictors of destiny. They may have been right about Martha Mitchell's mouth, but Eydie Gormé's yearbook emphasized her cheerleading, before adding, "sings a little too." Dwight Eisenhower's high school annual had him becoming a history professor at Yale, his brother Edgar a two-term President of the United States. Ed Muskie was also spotted as a future President by his yearbook, as was Mel Brooks.

The real question is not whether yearbooks predict well, but whether high school does. Since we do remember high school so vividly, and continue to deal with each other through its concepts — particularly status — the inevitable question follows: are these concepts indelible, or can they be changed?

Need we be who we were in high school or can we be different?

Is there life after high school?

As the Tables Turn

I have in the past year encountered several people with whom
I went to high school, and whose backgrounds were more than
similar — yet I am amazed, more and more as time goes on,
that so many of my fellow students failed to achieve what we
expected they would — and that so very many who seemed
rather drab have turned out to be such vital people.
                              — LETTER TO *Project Talent News*

Robert Logue was late for our appointment. Actually, Logue had forgotten about it and almost went to shoot a game of pool. But he was tired and decided instead to come home. There he found me waiting in his driveway, enjoying the sweet, blossomy smell of citrus on a spring evening four months before Richard Nixon resigned the presidency.

One of the first things I wanted to know after we went in the house was whether Logue figured his classmate would go so far.

"No," he replied. "I don't think anybody did."

What did you think he might become?

"Thought he might be a hard-working lawyer."

So what do you suppose propelled him?

"I can't answer that."

Have you ever fantasized about being President of the United States?

Logue shook his head sharply. "God, I sure wouldn't want to be President — take all the headaches you have to take."

Robert Logue is not given to flights of oratory. A compact man, he looks rather like a craggy Garry Moore. Beneath close-cropped hair Logue's face is deeply furrowed, and his dark eyes focus on you intently as his lips open frugally to dispense their occasional words.

Just the summer before, Mr. and Mrs. Logue had cut short a European vacation to attend his forty-second high school class

1   2   3   4

5   6   7   8

9   10   11   12

13   14   15   16

A. MARTHA E. BEALL (Mitchell)
Glee Club '34, '35, '36; Band Maid '36; Student Council '36, '37.
"I love its gentle warble,
I love its gentle flow,
I love to wind my tongue up,
And I love to let it go."

B. VONNEGUT, KURT, JR.

C. GLORIA MARIE STEINEM
"Glo," . . . hit Western with a bang . . . a gal of many talents . . . humorous and alluring . . . smart and stylish . . . enjoys dancing and cooking.

D. ELDRED GREGORY PECK
St. Johns Military Academy. Adv. Glee, Boy's Hi Jinx, Class B Football, Interclass Football, Interclass Baseball. State.

E. LEONTYNE PRICE

F. FITZGERALD, ROY II (Hudson, Rock)
° Winnetka: Swimming 1; Geography Club 2; Navy.

G. RAQUEL TEJADA (Welch)
Cheerleader 11; Class Council 12; Veep 12; C.S.F. 11, 12; Drama Club 10, 11, 12; Girls' League Girl of the Week, chrm. 12; Jazz Club 12; Mariners 12; N.F.L. 10, 12; Rally co-chrm. 12; Sr. Play chrm. 12; Majors: Speech, Drama; Career: Actress; Future: College; Born on 9/5/40

H. MELVIN KAMINSKY (Brooks)
111 Lee Avenue
Class Day Committee; Senior Council; Dean's Assistant; Fencing Team.
Kaminsky – To be President of the U. S.

I. PRESLEY, ELVIS ARON
Major: Shop, History, English
Activities: R.O.T.C., Biology Club, English Club, History Club, Speech Club.

J. ZAPPA, FRANK

K. ARTHUR GORDON LINKLETTER
"Art"
Woodrow Wilson Junior High.
Timalathean, 3, 4; Ex-Committee, 4; Treasurer Senior B, 4; Senior A Cabinet, 4; Class B Basketball; Debate Team, 4.
Take trip around world.

L. HUGH HEFNER
Popular "Hef" cartoons, writes songs and plays . . . goes for jive, plaid shirts, corduroys . . . Student Council, Student Court, Green Curtain Players, As We Like It, Track, Choral Society.

M. ANN-MARGRET OLSON

N. GENE ALEC LITTLER
History, Mathematics Majors; Varsity L 11, 12; Track 11, 12; Basketball 11, 12; Golf 11, 12.

O. JANIS JOPLIN
Art Club – 59–60; FNA – 58–59; FTA – 57–58; GRA – 57–58; Slide Rule Club – 58–59; "B" Average Award – 57–59.

P. GORME, EDITH
125 East 168th St.
Cheer Leader, Bond Show, Councilman. Co-captain of the cheering squad, sings a little too, but the one she likes the best of all is the guy in Navy Blue.

ANSWERS

16. F	12. P	8. E	4. G
15. A	11. L	7. I	3. N
14. D	10. C	6. B	2. M
13. H	9. J	5. O	1. K

reunion. They had a very good time. "Of course Dick wasn't there," he said, "though he did send a nice note." Logue hasn't seen his former classmate since they graduated from Whittier High in 1930. Occasionally they've corresponded. He did try to look up Nixon once in New York in 1963. But the future President was out of town. In Spain, Logue thought.

I wondered if he were eager to see the President.

"Not especially. Maybe if I were back in Washington. It's been going on forty-three years. I don't know.

"I understand he's coming here to Phoenix. I think in May. But I imagine he'll be pretty busy."

We sat in silence for a time. Then Robert Logue asked, "Would you like to see a picture of Dick in high school?"

I said I would, and he went to look for his yearbook, leaving me alone in their living room. This is dominated by a large color console television. On one wall a needlepoint reads: "DEAR HOUSE We're really very small. Just big enough for LOVE that's all."

Logue returned, holding open in both hands a thin blue book called the *Cardinal & White*. "I wonder what they said was gonna happen with Nixon in the prediction?" he said, flipping through pages blue with inscriptions. "I'm sure they didn't say he was gonna be President." Reaching the prophecy, Logue chuckled while reading it over, then handed the yearbook to me. For Dick Nixon the annual predicted: "He sponsors the [Los Angeles] Times Oratorical Contests, which are still going strong."

Stuck inside the yearbook was a faded red tag with a string on it that read, "STOP Think and Vote BOB LOGUE Pres. of Student Body."

This tag marked the page to which Logue now pointed, saying "Here's one I'm sort of proud of." His finger rested on a dark-haired, smoother-faced picture of himself in shorts and numbered jersey clutching a basketball with both hands. "Capt. Bob Logue," the caption read. "Forward. Southern California Champs."

I wondered if he got his yearbook out often to look it over.

"Not often," Logue replied.

Did you like high school?

"Oh yeah. Real well."

Any best memory?

"By far the best one was winning the student body presidency. I did a pretty good job. I held student body meetings once a week."

Leaving UCLA two years shy of a degree in economics, Robert Logue ended up in Winnemucca, Nevada. There he ran an auto supply store for twenty-eight years before moving to Phoenix. Following a fling at real estate, Logue joined the Arizona Highway Department's relocation division, for which he today works as an appraiser.

"It's turned out to be a real good job," he said, fingering the cork tip of a Kool, then lighting it.

I wondered if he liked his life.

"Oh yeah!" was the quick reply.

Ever wish it were different?

"Like what?" Logue pressed his lips together and stared at me from deep behind those wide, dark eyes. Finally he turned and gestured toward the backyard. "Sometimes I wish we didn't have the pool out there. The kids enjoy it, but it's still their dad who has to clean it up."

The hour had grown late, and Bob Logue went off to chat with his wife, who was watching TV in a back room, leaving me alone with his yearbook.

"Dear Bob," read one inscription. "You were a great success as a Student Body President and no foolin'." "I hope you'll have lots of successes and fun," said another. A third: "Bob: I hope you make as good out of High School as you did in High School."

Richard Nixon's stern young face was pictured next to that of President Bob Logue's in his consolation job of student body general manager. By the picture Nixon had written: "I have gone

43

to 2 different schools and have had 4 different Student Body Presidents and, no kiddin' Bob, you are the best I have *ever had*. Really, Bob, you surely have made a big success this year, in everything you have done. (continued at Senior Picture)"

By Nixon's senior picture the inscription proceeded. "(continued from page 2) you know I've always been crazy about athletics, etc. but I have never been able to go out. You have certainly done your part in that line. Very few athletes have been able to combine good grades, high office, and athletics — but you sure have (continued on page 153)"

Page 153 had Nixon's picture as a Constitutional Orator, and his continued inscription. "(continued from senior picture) Thanks a lot for helping me this year at the gate and in everything you could. Boy, I've sure appreciated it. Remember me Bob, not as an orator, scholar or anything but just old Dick Nixon, member of the Student Body. Thanx — lots of love an kisses.

Dick Nixon

p.s. Stay away from Blondes."

Logue returned to the room as I looked through the yearbook and settled quietly back in his easy chair. I commented that people seemed to think he had done a good job as student body president. Logue nearly smiled. "Well, maybe I did, I don't know. I got through it.

"I think it gave me a little self-confidence."

How would you compare your life today to President Nixon's?

"Frankly, I think I've got a better life than he does. I think he's got what he wants. But I don't think he's happy." Logue shrugged. "He might be. I don't know."

Are you?

Logue nodded. "Oh yeah." He looked off beyond the TV. "I've got a good family life. I'm financially independent. I can do what I want, when I want to. No debts or anything."

Logue leaned back in his chair, hands folded over chest.

From the back room we could hear the late evening news. President Nixon had agreed to pay over $400,000 in four years' back taxes. As this information drifted through the room, Bob Logue shook his head slowly and went "Whew!" A Republican and long-time Nixon supporter, Logue felt the President's tax omission constituted mostly bad judgment.

"But a hundred thousand dollars a year does seem like a big mistake," he added upon reflection. Then Logue turned to me.

"You know, you see Nixon on TV and he has no gray hairs. Our birthdays are nine days apart. When I see him on TV, I say to my wife, 'I don't know how he does it.'

"She says, 'I do!' "

We sat in silence some more. Robert Logue's face rested in one hand and looked beyond mine. His right leg jiggled in its perch over the left. Finally he broke the silence.

"I think if he comes down here in May, I'll try to see him — if he's not too busy."

The way Richard Nixon and Robert Logue switched roles after high school may seem out of the ordinary. It's not. Because the tables do turn in adulthood as high school's kings come down from the mountain while losers of student body presidencies win those of the United States.

High school can be a vivid memory. We may act as adults like it never ended. But few of us are happy with who we were back then. So instead of acting out the parts assigned us by our classmates, we just as commonly *re*act against them, and try to be who we weren't in our teens.

For this reason one of the crueler things you can tell an old classmate at a reunion is, "You haven't changed a bit."

"My God!" the response can be to such an observation. "Don't you realize that the only reason I've come back is to show off how much (check one: __lighter __heavier __taller __quieter __more talkative __better dressed __blonder __fuller-busted __more famous __smarter __sharper all around) I've become?"

This wish to be different from our high school selves is what makes us throw away yearbooks, hide them in closets, or cut out our picture within. It's why we can be so desperate to rehash adolescent memories even as we fear them.

The fear is that high school's social structure will be cast in concrete: that the cleats of football players may remain forever on our necks as blood-lusty cheerleaders scream them on.

Even when reality intrudes, this fear persists. Kurt Vonnegut once endorsed a friend's foreboding that life thereafter is simply a replay of high school. But the truth may lie in the opposite direction. Because it's not high school that shapes us so much as the way we remember it. If the memories aren't what we'd like them to be, we won't want to relive high school so much as reverse it.

In Dan Wakefield's novel *Going All the Way*, Sonny Burns, a pudgy little loser at Shortley High, later runs into former all-everything Gunner Casselman as both return from the Korean War. Burns, having been an information officer during the war, examines Casselman's chestful of combat decorations with "the sinking feeling that maybe indeed all of life would turn out to be like high school, the Gunners continuing to be heroes, him going quietly on collecting the boring Good Conduct Medals of life."

But in Wakefield's novel, as in reality, rather than play out their roles from high school, both characters struggle heroically to trade parts. "Look," Gunner tells Sonny soon after they meet,

you saw it at Shortley. All that social-climbing shit. The rod system, the jock stuff. You were one of the quiet ones, you just sat back and observed. Watched us run around chasing our tails, a bunch of green-asses. You were a detached observer.

Sonny shifted uneasily and took a gulp of beer. "Well, sort of," he said.

The truth was he had been a detached observer because he was never asked to be an active participant. . . .

47

Sonny then spends the rest of the book taking savoir-faire lessons from Gunner while his ex-jock mentor tries to blur that identity with a beard and by taking up painting.

This theme of tables turning after high school is not one with which Americans become easily bored.

Within recent television seasons: Maude has been visited by a plain high school chum who is showing off her face-lift and success as an executive; Rhoda's bridal shower has turned into a little reunion of high school classmates, including an obnoxious ex–prom queen who is "amazed" at how attractive Rhoda has become; and Edith Bunker has attended her twenty-fifth reunion, where to Archie's delight the slim, golden-haired hero of her dreams has lost hair and gained weight.

Underdogs are not the only ones eager to be different after high school. Topdogs have their own wish to switch roles: former jocks trying to prove they're not dumb and ex-cheerleaders sensitive about seeming rah-rah. Just as high school's lowly are hoping as adults to win some of the status denied them at the time, the postpopular set can be struggling every bit as hard to develop the independence and sophistication they lacked as high school heroes.

Psychiatrist Daniel Offer is following up a group of students he studied in high school some years ago, and has found that those who want to tell him they've changed come from both directions. "A kid who was shy and not outgoing might be eager to report having tried marijuana," Dr. Offer reports, "while an extroverted football player would tell us he was more shy and withdrawn now."

I once asked a former football captain, who now wears hair to his shoulders and won't eat meat, how he would feel if I entered a crowd of his current friends and said, "Hey, Stan. I haven't seen you since you used to run out on the field after the coin was flipped. How's it been going?" Stan looked appalled at this thought. He replied, "I'd try to think of something to say right away which would let people know I've changed."

I've changed. Like a litany, this phrase is repeated by people willing to discuss their high school memories only after assuring me that they're different now, they've changed.

I once caused a woman to flee from my presence simply by asking if she'd ever been a pom-pom girl. "Is it that obvious?" she asked making her way across the room. Turning around at the door, she added "I'd like to think I've changed!" Then she walked out.

But is all that struggle necessary to reverse high school roles? Or is it inevitable anyway that the tables will turn?

In fact, mobility up and down may be more the rule than the exception after high school. In many ways life thereafter is not so much a continuation as the mirrored reflection of high school. Our most prominent citizens aren't those who excelled at the time so much as those who didn't. Only after graduation do they have the opportunity to move up — to say nothing of the motivation.

Just as Richard Nixon may have spent the better part of his life after high school campaigning for student body president, his 1972 opponent George McGovern could also have been struggling against the caption under his yearbook picture, which read: "For a debater, he's a nice kid." A shy introvert in high school, McGovern went on to be elected president of his class three years out of four in college. He also admits that enrolling in his college air corps, then becoming a bomber pilot during World War II, was in no small part to refute the taunt of a high school gym teacher who'd called him a coward. "That cut me more than anything anybody has ever said to me," the South Dakota senator has recalled.

In his biography of Franklin Roosevelt, who did not do well at Groton ("I always felt hopelessly out of things," the President recalled), John Gunther hypothesized that those who did do well were rote-steppers who marched off into obscurity after graduation. "As a matter of fact," writes Gunther,

49

the boys who were the best "Grotties" usually turned out to be non-entities later; boys who hated Groton did much better. The explanation of this lies in the fact that the boys who became successes were not conformists; hence they were apt to be excluded from the compact group that made the core of each class. . . . A great many people, even including presidents, have overcompensated in later life for slights and slurs undergone in school days.

President Harry S Truman wore thick glasses as a boy, fled from fights, and was admittedly not very popular. Nor was he the best student in his class. This honor went to Charlie Ross, valedictorian of their class and editor of its yearbook. At graduation, Ross was given a big kiss by the students' favorite teacher, Miss Tillie Brown. Truman and his classmates protested this favoritism. Miss Tillie stood firm. When the rest of them earned a kiss, she said, they'd get one.

After becoming President of the United States more than four decades later, Harry Truman hired Charlie Ross as his press secretary. The first person they called to tell about it was Miss Tillie Brown. "How about that kiss I never got?" President Truman asked his old teacher. "Have I done something worthwhile enough to rate it now?"

Quite commonly those who are accomplished as adults point (and point often) to some adolescent humiliation that preceded their later triumph, and may have contributed to it. Actress Sandy Duncan says that being seventh out of six elected cheerleaders both crushed her and turned her attention to a career on stage. Before campaigning successfully for mayor of Los Angeles, Tom Bradley talked in a speech about being defeated for president of his senior class, and said his adult political ambition could be traced from that defeat.

Without necessarily drawing such a direct connection, other adults we consider glamorous today often describe feeling just the opposite in high school. For example:

Isaac Hayes. At Memphis's Manassas High the singer remembers being "a perfect example of failure." Squeaky-voiced and shabbily dressed, Hayes says that girls gambled their status by being seen with him, while guys ridiculed his late-changing voice and called him a sissy. Only after his voice changed and he won a talent contest late in high school did today's singer feel anything other than rejected.

Lauren Hutton. A decade before she appeared on a record number of *Vogue* covers, model Lauren Hutton recalls being "extremely unpopular" in high school. Tall, small-busted, and with a funny gap between her teeth, Hutton says she learned by cunning to compensate for her lack of natural gifts. But she still refers regularly to not making cheerleader in high school, and the fact that her prom date had to be arranged by a teacher. Hutton also has described more than once the time her falsies were discovered by a classmate and shown around. Of her high school experience overall, Lauren Hutton says: "I really knew despair."

Dustin Hoffman. As a high school student in Los Angeles, Dustin Hoffman recalls being short of body and long of nose. He also had acne and braces. What he didn't have was hair on his chest. Relegated to playing class clown, Hoffman dreamed of being bigger, tougher, and better off with girls. He lifted weights to this end and fantasized a lot. But nothing worked. Today Hoffman dwells constantly on pains left over from high school. When his name began appearing on theater marquees, the movie star complained: "Why couldn't this have happened to me when I was sixteen and needed it?"

To our delighted surprise, things do change after high school. If there's a single report I've most often been given about ex-classmates it's that they didn't turn out as expected. "Do you know," a woman told me at her twenty-fifth reunion, "the girl who was Most Likely to Succeed in this class now works in a drugstore." The woman grinned. A trim, blond, and vivacious proprietor of a beauty salon, the woman remembered mostly being fat in high school, "Fat and dull.

"And you know," she continued, "people here look at you like they don't know who you are, and you're glad they don't.

"I think there's more to people twenty-five years later," the beautician concluded. "At eighteen you're only a potential."

"Yeah," added her husband. "I'd hate to be voted most popular in my class."

At the same reunion a participant's wife who was once a cheerleader told me of seeing recently the football star she'd almost married. Now he was selling furniture for his father-in-law back in Michigan. "Super guy," she said, "and you gotta love him. But they fall apart." The man she did marry had been a nerd in high school, the kind of quiet nonentity she wouldn't have spoken to, let alone married, had they been classmates. Today he's a highly successful attorney.

Recently the ex-cheerleader had been to her own reunion in Michigan and found herself dancing most often with guys she didn't know existed at the time. She was impressed overall that "the athletes, the superstars, the supermen weren't super any more.

"Maybe they didn't have the tenacity," she speculated. "It's the little guy that hasn't had that last spurt of growth that's trying, that has the stick-to-it-iveness."

I've heard any number of alternative suggestions to explain turnarounds after high school, theories based on everything from hormones to Jung. But no one seems quite sure why this should be. Dr. Jack Block, a psychologist specializing in human development, began his book *Lives Through Time*:

It is an instructive, somewhat wry experience to attend a high school reunion twenty years after one's graduation. . . . the formerly lissome and lithe may now be pudgy and stiff; the great adolescent dreams of glamour and omnipotence largely have been deflated by reality. . . .

Although many friends from adolescence have become the kind of person implicitly anticipated long before, others have not. The class literary esthete went into public relations work. Why? The tense, big-boned, not really attractive girl at seventeen is now, two decades later, a sophisticated, intellectual, sex-radiating woman, while the classically pert and pretty cheerleader of yesteryear is several times divorced and older, yet less changed than she should be. Why?

After looking at research bearing on this question, and talking with those who have studied it, an explanation suggests itself: role reversal after high school has less to do with any change in personality than the simple change of environment.

Study after study has shown that there is seldom much difference in *behavior* between adolescence and adulthood. This finding has been reported often, and in no uncertain terms. A second look at one group of students thirteen years beyond high school reports their "remarkable persistence of personality trends." After fifteen years another study concluded: "A striking feature of this investigation was the evidence for the persistence of behavior patterns over a decade and a half." After analyzing data on a group observed from birth through late adulthood, Jack Block himself reported that their "unity or consistency of personality is compellingly apparent. . . ."

This means that we're probably stuck for life with the behavior we displayed in high school. If chattery then, we'll most likely be talkative now. Self-assured as teens, we'll appear on top of things later. A study comparing one group of physically mature high school boys with another group who took longer to develop found that fifteen years later the first group still acted more sure of themselves, even though their physical advantage had declined over time.

For those who want life to be different after high school, this is discouraging news.

But here is encouraging news: although our *behavior* may not change after high school, the *setting* does. What succeeds in school won't work later on. Physical gifts, looks, a winning way and easy smile — except for the odd Paul Newman or Ann-Margret — such qualities won't get you two seconds on the evening news. On the other hand, those qualities that can lose you status in high school — aggressiveness, imagination, and an independent turn of mind — may be just the qualities needed to make it in a larger setting where performance counts more than style. No study I've read, or researcher with whom I've talked, has found any correlation between high status in high school and later achievement as an adult.

To the contrary, one report on 351 graduates eight years later found no relationship whatever between success in high school and later vocational success. "The impact of an active social schedule in high school does not necessarily result in long-term gains," concluded this report. "Some of the high school wall-flowers are now leading very active social lives, and some of the sociometric queens of the prom now have little social interaction outside their own family.

"A study of the 20 socially most popular and prominent members of the senior class," the report continued, "showed that this group did not maintain a relative advantage or success in either social or other areas of young adult performance when compared with a matched group of socially non-prominent peers."

After following up on a group of high school graduates at age thirty, another researcher found that although "many of our most mature and competent adults had severely troubled and confusing childhoods and adolescences. . . . Many of our highly successful children and adolescents have failed to achieve their potential."

In other words, things do change after high school and roles can reverse — radically. This is not because the humans themselves change. Our basic personality is probably set long before high school. What does change is the context. What works in high school just won't work later on. And vice-versa.

Something important to keep in mind is how very eccentric an environment high school is. What happens within bears little relationship to what happens without. High school is too insular, too inbred, too focused on its own peculiar rituals to prepare people for life thereafter. Robert Logue, the more successful politician in high school, could not continue in government and didn't want to. Richard Nixon, the serious-minded orator, proved more hungry over time.

"Adolescent social systems," writes sociologist Lloyd Temme, "reward with prestige achievements that bear little relation to those expected of a man later in life. . . . As a result, adolescents are ill-equipped to deal with their entry into adulthood, and tend to fall back on their high school achievements as an important part of their lives. . . ."

Temme, who is affiliated with Washington's Bureau of Social Research, has during the past five years begun an ambitious follow-up of high school graduates in their subsequent careers. After tracking down eighty-five percent of the 9,000 students James Coleman studied in 1957, Temme administered questionnaires about their life since and is now tabulating results.

Lloyd Temme and I arranged to meet at The Class Reunion Restaurant near Bill Schuiling's office in Washington. The Class Reunion, a popular journalists' hangout, says "Welcome Back" on its front window. Inside, the restaurant is decorated with megaphones, trophies, and a set of old yearbooks over the bar. The owner/maitre d' introduces himself at the door as "senior class president."

Really? I asked while waiting for Temme. Were you really president of your class?

His smile faded. "No, not really. I wasn't even an officer."

What were you?

"Oh," said the maitre d', who had short graying hair and the affable manner of a fraternity president, "I lettered in track. And I was out for football."

Letter?

"Nah, I got injured."

55

Temme arrived and we went upstairs to eat. As we walked off, the maitre d' handed me one of his business cards. After his name it read SENIOR CLASS PRESIDENT.

As we looked over the menu (on which appetizers were listed as "Freshman," daily specials "Sophomores," and entrees "Juniors"), Temme told me about his project. Though just beginning to analyze by computer the thousands of responses to his questionnaire, the bearded young sociologist does have some preliminary reactions. "If you're an early bloomer, you're an early dier" is one such reaction. "I kept getting that impression from telephone interviews. The leading crowd members more or less died at graduation. Because high school was the high point of their lives, they get hit pretty hard later on."

Over lunch, my Class of '52 (Coquilles St. Jacques) and his Class of '47 (Irish Cut Prime Beef), Temme added that in contrast with leading crowd members, he could sense that those who went on to do interesting things as adults had not been at their high school's social center. By example he mentioned a woman who'd been unattractive and not popular when Coleman made his study, then returned to her tenth reunion as a New York model.

But, ever the careful researcher, Temme is quick to add that his hypothesis has not been confirmed statistically. And based on his early analysis Temme says it's important to distinguish between those who were at the bottom of the social ladder and those who stood on the "second tier," one rung below the top. Those lower in the pecking order get used to being dumped on over time, he speculates, and are less resentful of it. But those on the second tier aren't accustomed to being excluded and resent it bitterly. Adults from the second rung don't lose this resentment after graduation. One way Temme has discovered this is his experience at parties. When asked what he did, the sociologist used to say that he was doing a follow-up study of high school students fifteen years after graduation. "But as soon as I'd talk about what's happening to the leading crowd," Temme reports with a dry laugh, "I got pressed and pressed and pressed. People wanted me as a scientist to confirm what they believe — that leading crowd members die at graduation. The people that most wanted to do this were usually from the second rung.

"Now I just tell people I'm studying occupational achievement."

Temme — who assured me he was not in the leading crowd himself — believes that high school, even more than college, is "the most pervasive influence of a person's past.

"I think the rest of our lives are spent making up for what we did or didn't do in high school."

I don't want to go off the deep end with this notion of tables turning. Some of us as adults continue to be who we were in high school, sometimes even successfully. Saying roles inevitably reverse does not account for the Friedman twins, Eppie and Popo, who wrote a gossip column for the Central High paper in Sioux City, Iowa, and today are Abby Van Buren and Ann Landers. The role reversal theory overlooks baseball commissioner Bowie Kuhn, who was voted Most Likely to Succeed, and Donald Rumsfeld, who went from being vice-president of his class to President Ford's assistant.

But such cases must be exceptional, simply because there are fewer openings at the top of life than within high school. A big noise from high school who wants to continue being heard must find new instruments to play.

Peter Falk, for example, says that after being a multiletter athlete, senior class president, and honor student at Ossining High in New York he lasted seven weeks at Hamilton College. "In Ossining I'd been Mr. Wheel," the actor has explained, "and I was looking for college to be a continuation of high school. Instead it was guys hitting books.

"I tended to retire and went into a period where I looked down on all college activities."

This is not an uncommon syndrome according to Dr. Robert

Lawrence, assistant vice-chancellor of the University of California at Irvine. Dr. Lawrence for years has kept tabs on student leaders in college — who becomes one, and why. He's found that high school's success stories commonly quit trying in college. In one freshman class Lawrence studied at Irvine, of the thirty-five student body presidents from high school who were enrolled, few remained active in college. Those who did become wheels in college for the most part didn't get rolling until high school ended. (Dr. Lawrence's interest is also personal. Elected to nothing at Beverly Hills High, he later became president of his college student body.)

If a frustration to high school's insiders, college is open casting for the left-outs — a brand-new ball game, resurrection from the dead, a chance to retread and become who you weren't allowed to be earlier.

College is where Francis Ford Coppola, the retiring teenager loner, became a widely discussed play director. It's where Eva Marie Saint, after failing to make her senior class play in high school, won not only drama leads but election as the freshman Dream Girl, May Queen, and Sweater Queen.

College for Art Linkletter was everything high school was not. At San Diego State Linkletter was president of men and the intra-fraternity council, captain of the basketball team, and an all-conference swimmer — a big guy physically and socially, popular with guys, desired by girls. In high school he had been just the opposite: a shrimp of a kid without status or car, who could only make the B basketball team, and who won friends by doing their homework. In fact, says Linkletter (who was young due to skipping a couple of grades), he was so undersized in high school that he usually got cast as a kid in plays.

In his senior year, they finally gave him a break and let him play the detective in a mystery play. "I had one of the key roles," Linkletter recalls, "but in the first scene I forgot some of my lines and I jumped and went to the closing and suddenly the whole damned play was over. I had given the lines as to who was guilty and it was done. When I came off, they said, 'Why did you do that?' I said, 'Why did I do what?' They said, 'You went from page three to page twenty-eight and it's all over. There is nothing more we can do. The play is done.' "

Linkletter shook his head with remembered mortification. "That was an awful experience. I flunked. I got an F in Dramatics." Then he looked directly at me beneath highly arched brows. "And do you know I've never been a good actor since. I've been in movies and plays, but I'm not a good actor. I'm good at being me."

Art Linkletter in person is quite close to his broadcast image: ruddy, good-natured, and with eyebrows always in motion. He is also rather large physically for someone who remembers having once been so small.

What Linkletter remembers most vividly about his 1926 to 1929 tenure at San Diego High is frustration: frustration about his size; frustration at not making teams; frustration at not being a hit with the girls; and frustration about not feeling popular overall — or even noticed. When I asked how a classmate might describe him at the time Linkletter's first response was, "They probably would have said, 'Oh, he's a grind.' Or else, 'I don't know, I never noticed him before.' By the time I was a senior they would have said, 'Oh, he's that kid who debates,' because I was a good speaker and captain of the debating team in high school."

Then he smiled at a happier memory. "On the other hand, if you'd have asked a girl that question, she might very well have said, 'He's one of the best damn dancers in town,' because I really applied myself."

This was at a ballroom downtown where Linkletter went at fourteen to learn the latest steps — sometimes dime-a-dance. Of those who taught him to dance, Linkletter says, "God, they were the best teachers in the world — I used to be able to pivot in both directions, reverse and go both ways all the way around the whole floor without stopping. So then when I went to school dances, I would finally get a dance with somebody and they could see I was doing stuff that the other kids didn't even know about. Then girls would come around and say, 'How about a dance?' "

And all this evolved from being turned down so often, "the only reason I would take the ego-beating to go down to a ballroom and take a worse beating for a while."

Such cunning and persistence at age fourteen honed the young Linkletter's competitive edge. He thinks this might have happened anyway, had he been big and popular. But having to compensate for being so young and small forced him to be resourceful at a younger age. Linkletter has written of his "obstacle course to success," those problems such as poverty, being frail, and learning he was adopted, which made him "want to be somebody as my way of striking back at having been rejected."

"Really," he told me, "most of my memories of high school are of work and overcoming handicaps. While that probably didn't make it as happy a place for me as it might have been, I now recognize that it gave me my first hard, competitive edge."

Today Art Linkletter gets down his old yearbook from time to time, turns to his senior picture, and cringes. "I look at it — I was such a childish-looking boy, so thin and so light, so skinny, so immature."

I wondered if any of that feeling didn't persist today, like the formerly fat person, say, who loses weight but still feels heavy.

"Oh, no," he replied quickly. "I have no hang-ups, none at all. I don't feel — none of those early days had any traumatic impact — because everything has been so great since. Forty-five years of success, of unbroken success, wipes out the three, four, or five years when you realized first that you were really nothing much — didn't get much done."

Four years behind Art Linkletter at San Diego High, a classmate of his wife-to-be, was an angular, painfully shy rail of a boy named Gregory Peck. Mrs. Linkletter, according to her husband, remembers Peck only as exceedingly bashful, not impressive in any way — not someone you ever heard about.

Peck himself has talked in later years about the pain of succeeding at nothing during high school. He did not make good as an actor, nor at sports, or in romance. Once he entered some lyrics in the school song contest, then froze trying to sing them for the glee club. "I was gangly, tall, and all bone," Peck has said of himself at the time. "I seemed to want to sleep a lot."

Three decades after graduating from high school, Gregory Peck returned home for the local premiere of *To Kill a Mockingbird*, the film that eventually won him an Oscar. Walking into the Spreckels Theater lobby, Peck spotted a familiar face. Pointing a finger at this gentleman, he exclaimed: "YOU! *You* are the one who beat me out for the lead in the senior play!"

The man at whom Peck's finger was pointed was Richard Lustig, an accountant who still lives in San Diego. "Yes, I remember the incident," Lustig said when we met seventeen years later. "Greg had come to the theater to bolster the box office. I was in the lobby, and he came up the aisle and then he saw me and said, 'You're the guy who beat me for the lead in the senior class play.' "

Lustig smiled without parting his lips. "It's ludicrous really, my claim to fame."

Robust in build with a full moustache and bushy sideburns, Dick Lustig says that even if the actor hasn't forgotten, he honestly does not remember competing with Gregory Peck for the lead of *Oh, Wilbur*. He does remember Peck in general as "very shy, a tall, bashful, gawky guy — very awkward in his movements. Back in high school he was all voice and no body."

Someone whose success surprised you?

"Oh yes. Very definitely. If anyone was least likely to succeed Greg was definitely it. He would be the last person I would have thought would make it."

Were you envious of Peck's success?

"Yes," Lustig replied, after a moment's hesitation. "I guess in my case there's a certain amount of jealousy. I have to be honest. As each picture came out I'd shake my head and say, 'This can't last.' "

The accountant shook his head. "I think the whole class was stunned."

As you watched his rise, did you think it might have been you?

Lustig seemed a little perplexed by the question. "I tell you, I, uh — I could have, uh — yes and no.

"There's nothing he has done that I know I couldn't do."

He fell silent and looked off around the study where we sat. On one wall was a painted portrait of a younger Dick Lustig, thinner of body and thicker of hair, with a pipe clenched in his teeth. Lustig then looked back again. "You know these are hard questions you're asking.

"But to answer your question, ah, sometimes I wonder . . ." He looked off once more.

After excelling at public speaking in high school and working after school at a theater, Dick Lustig went to Hollywood immediately upon graduating in 1933. But within months his flame was sputtering. Checking in with every major studio, Lustig was called back only by one — for minor roles and menial chores. Then the studios were shut down by a labor dispute. Soon the eighteen-year-old movie aspirant was washing dishes in a restaurant and wondering what in the hell he was doing in Hollywood.

In February of '34 he hopped a freighter. At sea, with time to think, Lustig decided to study accounting. Today he is a successful independent accountant in San Diego.

I wondered if he had any regrets about not sticking with Hollywood.

"Regrets?" Lustig replied. "No, I don't think so." He looked at me brightly. "I still do acting in town. I played the Old Globe

[San Diego's Shakespearean theater] for many years, and other little groups. I've directed in town."

At this Lustig rose and walked over to a shelf of his study, then returned with a bulging scrapbook. "Look at this," he said. "I have every program for every play I've been in."

We spent the rest of the evening poring through this scrapbook, which was fat with programs listing Richard Lustig's name in various sizes of type; clippings of play notices, yellower at the beginning, whiter toward the end; and one article on slick paper from a 1953 issue of his college fraternity magazine which was headlined COAST ALUMNUS APPEARS WITH HOLLYWOOD STARS.

"When I was in the La Jolla Playhouse," Lustig explained, looking up from the scrapbook, "I was in two plays with Howard Duff and Ida Lupino. I had a solid offer to travel to Germany and do a film with them. But I had to turn it down because I couldn't take time away from the office."

Mixed in with the scrapbook's programs and clips were telegrams with messages such as DARLING! BE SMASHING. LOVE, JANE, and DEAR DADDY: WE KNOW YOU'LL LIGHT UP THE PLAY. NANCY, JEFF & STEVE.

"My wife, my kids," Lustig smiled. "They'd send me a telegram before every performance. Some were like these." Lustig chuckled and pointed to a telegram which read THE LUSTIG DID IT AGAIN. SIDNEY SKOLSKY, and another saying A SCINTILLATING PERSONALITY. BROOKS ATKINSON.

He then riffled the last few pages saying, "One place here it said, 'It wouldn't be a summer in La Jolla without you,' but I can't find it."

Finally Lustig put the scrapbook aside and said, "You know even now some pros say they envy me. I have an awful lot of friends — a lot of clients in entertainment — and let me tell you, some of their lives are miserable. Not knowing what's coming tomorrow and so on.

"So in answer to your earlier question, no, I don't regret it. I've got the best of both worlds."

Compared with the hundred or so classmates who attended his fortieth reunion, Lustig says he feels good about the way his life turned out.

"I always felt it would be great to be famous," he explained, "to come back to my high school as the man who had made it.

"Now I realize that's ridiculous. That the men who have made it might not really be the men who have made it. The men who really made it might be in the audience."

Like Robert Logue, Richard Lustig illustrates the other side of role reversal. It's not that either man is worse off than his more famous counterpart or even that they'd wish their lives had been different. But their roles did change, as did those of Richard Nixon and Gregory Peck. Which men are better off is largely a matter of taste.

This is a problem inherent in any attempt to evaluate lives after graduation, including this book. How does one measure success? Salary? Prestige? Personal happiness?

Is a hard-driving millionaire with two ulcers and a divorce more successful than a carpenter with two mortgages and a happy marriage?

For this reason I've largely ignored the ambiguous concept of "success" in favor of the more functional one of public recognition to illustrate role reversal after high school. On the simple scale of public recognition, it's obvious that adults who won acclaim in high school can't continue to win attention on the same basis as adults. Behavior leading to status in high school may lead only to frustration later on, because the need for recognition can stay constant even as the means of achieving it grow obsolete. Just as "outies," those who felt excluded, may be struggling as adults for the status they didn't get in high school, "innies," those who hoarded the status, are confronted after graduation with a frustrating encore problem.

Looking Back on a Great Future

The Levi's that I'm wearing have been good to me
They just won't admit they're growing old
Though my shirt's made contact with the gutter,
Now and then
At least it keeps my body from the cold
The good folks back home in Harlan County
Can't see what success has done to me
Would you believe the kids in Harlan High School
Voted me "Most Likely to Succeed"?
Now I'm walking on the sidewalks of Chicago
If I buy the bread, I can't afford the wine
Now I'm walking on the sidewalks of Chicago
Wishing I had lived some other time.
    — DAVE KIRBY, "Sidewalks of Chicago,"
       Copyright © 1970, Tree Pub., Inc.,
       as sung by Merle Haggard

One thing I'd heard innies do for an encore is pornography. As an outie sensitive to such things, my antennae have always quivered when hearing that one erotic actress in high school had been Most Likely to Succeed, or that before copulating on a trapeze in *Behind the Green Door*, Marilyn Chambers once led cheers, while her co-star George S. McDonald had been a multi-letter athlete and president of his student body.

Green Door co-producer Art Mitchell remembers Marilyn Chambers as a cheerleader-type.

"Not in the same rah-rah sense as the old days," he explains, "but strong, out front, an exhibitionist. She was that then, and she's still that now — only she's singing out on the stage, instead of in front of the student body."

A lot of the actresses he's worked with are cheerleader types, Mitchell adds, and the men tend to be athletic. This seems to help their confidence in performing. Slim and balding, with all the raunchiness of an assistant Methodist minister, Art Mitchell and his brother Jim have been making erotic movies since the late 1960s. He says their film group now employs several high school classmates, including an ex–class president who does their advertising and a film editor who was once an all-state athlete and "everybody's hero."

The day Art Mitchell told me this in his second-story office, the Mitchell Brothers' O'Farrell Theater below was showing

High School Fantasies on a double bill with *Wild Campus*, starring George S. McDonald.

When it comes to getting an erection and holding it, Mitchell says McDonald is the champ. In five years of making porno movies he's seen nothing to match George McDonald. "In a tree, upside down, it doesn't matter. Never does he fail to get it up."

And it's not just a matter of physical prowess. Mitchell finds that McDonald is also good at back-set politics and helps keep people mellow. He thinks this might reflect the actor's background as a student leader.

"Like in *Sodom and Gomorrah*," the producer says of their latest epic, "we had a new girl who'd never been in a film. We had a fuck scene in a tree and George was really good working with her, keeping her calm. This was new for her — different, outside, and you've got the crew around. He was a steadying influence. Kind of showed his experience."

George McDonald himself remembers the tree episode as trying. Not only was the girl new, but everybody below seemed to be giving different directions.

"There I am," he explains, "up in a tree naked, trying to maintain an erection, and seven guys below with their clothes on are telling me different ways to do it. And the girl's going, 'Oh, ah — what's happening?'

"But when you've found you can do it, calming down while everybody's putting maximum pressure on you — then you get strength. And it picks up from there."

The evening before he told me this in his Sausalito apartment, I'd seen George McDonald in *Wild Campus*. On screen he displayed an impressively easy manner, in and out of bed. McDonald had a way of holding books with both hands behind him while shuffling his feet and flashing an aw-shucks smile.

Porno's first male superstar says his ability to perform grows out of adolescent experiences — on the football field, while running for office, and making speeches from an auditorium stage.

"It all began in high school," he explains, "where I got my confidence to get up in front of people. That's what I'm doing now. And people are looking up at me. They're always looking up."

Soon after we began talking, George McDonald asked if I'd like to see his yearbook. He thinks this could be his longest-owned possession. His picture, he told me while fetching the annual from a shelf, appears within twenty-two times.

"I did a lot of shit," McDonald said, riffling the book's pages. "Here I am on the yearbook staff. I'm in a lot of these clubs too. The Key Club. Even the ads — here's one for the radio station."

Covered neatly in clear plastic, the yearbook in McDonald's hands was dated 1966 — his junior year of high school in Fresno. McDonald explained that he valued this more than his senior annual because he'd gotten so many more people to sign it as a means of building political support. By his senior year there was nothing left to run for so he didn't bother much with signatures.

Turning the book toward me, McDonald pointed to pictures of himself as head of the student court, on the wrestling team, and running track. A full-body shot of him with short hair, smiling, in a suit and tie, illustrated his student council presidency. There was no football picture for him that year, because he couldn't play for lack of a parent's signature. An orphan, McDonald was between foster homes.

"I always held office, was in clubs," McDonald said. "I didn't have any family, so I made up for it in school."

Many of the yearbook's inscriptions congratulated its owner on being elected student body president, a post McDonald says he held concurrently with his senior class presidency. He remembers running for both jobs unopposed because "no one would challenge me for anything I did."

I wondered what he thought his classmates were saying about him when he wasn't around.

"Stuck-up." McDonald replied, "Egotistical. I was mostly known as egotistical. 'Oh, he's on an ego trip,' they'd say, 'he knows that he's the best baseball player in the valley and he's living that moment because ten years from now he's going to be fat and run a gas station.' "

Do you really think that's what they were saying?

"Sure. But I didn't give a shit what anybody said because I was in control.

"I was set up to be the all-American boy, and I'm not there today. Now I'm blowing them out on the screen."

Not long after graduating from high school, George McDonald went with a friend to the O'Farrell Theater. He remembers being both put off and intrigued by what he saw on screen. "The girl looked good," he explains, "the film looked good, and the cash looked good. Everything looked good, but the guy couldn't get it up. I said jokingly I could do it better than that. I took it as a challenge."

Answering a Mitchell Brothers ad in the *Berkeley Barb*, McDonald soon was on the verge of making his first porno movie. The anticipation scared him. Would he be able to do it? Could he get it up? And hold it?

He could, it turned out, and did, and has. "What a flash," today's porno veteran recalls of that first experience. "What a rush."

McDonald says that after fifty-one succeeding films his "biggest rush yet" was being recognized on a street in Singapore by an American who'd seen him in *Green Door*. But he finds it increasingly common to be recognized by strangers, recognized and admired. "I feel like people come up to me with respect," he explains: "They're all sort of flashed out by it. Wow, the recognition. They saw the act. They never expected to see the flash.

"And I'm in control because I've done it, they've seen it, and I have to be reckoned with. It's always them looking up at me."

Like George McDonald, every innie faces a dilemma after high school.

70

What to do for an encore? How to hold the center stage, once both stage and center have shifted?

Acclaim at a young age can be addicting. Once hooked in high school, the adolescent aristocracy naturally hopes for a lifetime to continue the good times. But to stay on center stage, innies must quickly learn new routines. Or, like George McDonald, they can find a setting comparable to high school in which to perform.

Most innies do neither and face only frustration in their quest for a post–high school encore.

A friend nearing forty has told me often what a burden it is to have been cheerleader captain, football queen and president of her senior class. She calls this past her Myth of Sisyphus — a dazzling youthful record she can't hope to match as an adult.

But the ex-cheerleader keeps trying anyway, keeps pushing uphill her boulder of expectations.

She says it's exhausting.

Far from being a boost, high expectations can prove a burden. Early triumph can make it harder, not easier, to hold the center. Those who succeed too young learn only a self-assurance that continues long after they have anything to be self-assured about. Especially when their triumph is irrelevant to any setting other than high school.

In *Rubyfruit Jungle*, Rita Mae Brown chronicles a lesbian named Molly who was president of Fort Lauderdale High's student council, governor of Girl's State, and so generally involved in activities that they take up her weekend. "When I was handed my diploma," recalls Molly, "I received a standing ovation from my constituency and a hug from Mr. Beers [the principal]. When the noise ebbed, he said in the humming microphone, 'There's our governor in twenty years.' "

But only a handful of student council presidents can hope to live in a governor's mansion, just as a tiny fraction of high school's football players ever make it to the pros, and even fewer cheerleaders. More get to dribble out the glory for a while in college, but eventually, like Biff Loman, every high school hero must struggle with how to take hold. This task is harder for having once been so easy. Ears accustomed to the roar of crowds can ring with the silence of graduation. Those anointed in high school can feel doubly weak as the ex-anointed. Their fall from the peak is extra jarring because innies have much further to fall.

A participant in a drug rehabilitation program once told me one bonus of his status was that finally nothing more was expected of him. Most Likely to Succeed just five years before, only now did he feel relieved of that burden. Since he'd fallen so low, all hopes for him finally had been taken off his back.

The innies' path after high school in many ways is harder than that of outies. While the peasantry beyond the castle walls grew tough as they huddled around fires plotting during long, cold nights of rejection, the royalty within grew bloated by carousing. With their court dispersed by graduation, the lords and ladies of high school must stand alone and wonder where the party went.

Innies face a tortuous obstacle course once forced from the castle. Their ego has been swelled by meaningless rewards. Then they are hobbled with expectations while prancing across the drawbridge. Stumbling quickly on the irrelevance of early triumph, innies fall face to the ground where they are kicked around and taunted by peasants wielding stereotypes such as "big dumb jock," and "cheerleader-type."

The one asset that innies are allowed to carry from the castle — like the single suitcase of a refugee — is self-confidence. Since adolescence is a time of such self-doubt, if your behavior is endorsed at that time, the award of self-confidence may be won for a lifetime.

James Coleman says that for years he could tell with unerring accuracy whether women he met had belonged to their high school's leading crowd. "I'd meet a woman at a party," explains the sociologist, "thirty-five years old or some age like that, and I'd try to predict it, and nearly every time I'd come out right.

There is a certain degree of extreme self-assurance that arises from being in the center of the leading crowd in high school that I think a girl gets no other way and stays with her."

But such self-confidence can be wildly inappropriate after adolescence, relevant to no setting other than high school or one just as eccentric.

I've been struck in recent years by how often innies show up at the heart of radical movements. David Harris, for example, before leading resistance to the draft, was a three-year football star in high school. Fugs founder and sometime Yippie Ed Sanders not only played football but was president of his class and a member of the student council. Then there's Rennie Davis, who went from leading his student body to leading the antiwar movement before coming to rest at the feet of the Guru Maharaj Ji.

Among those Symbionese Liberation Army members shot by Los Angeles police was Angela Atwood. Seven years before "Angel" Atwood had been head cheerleader at Manchester Regional High School in New Jersey. A classmate later wrote an essay about her called "Cheerleader for a Revolution," in which he speculated that Angel was seeking the same attention and same clarity of values in the SLA that she had known in high school. "Angel always liked the spotlight," her father was quoted as saying.

One of America's crueler hoaxes is the delusion perpetrated on innies that high school heroics can continue. And we always seem so startled to discover this isn't the case. In Tennessee Williams's *The Glass Menagerie*, the narrator says of his fellow warehouse clerk Jim O'Connor:

In high school Jim was a hero. He seemed to move in a continual spotlight. He was a star in basketball, captain of the debating club, president of the senior class. . . . He was shooting with such velocity through his adolescence that you would logically expect him to arrive at nothing short of the White House by the time he was thirty. But Jim apparently ran into more interference after his graduation

73

from Soldan. His speed had definitely slowed. Six years after high school he was holding a job that wasn't much better than mine.

Such tales usually are told with a tone of surprise (to say nothing of delight); but the decline and fall of high school's elite should not be so surprising. The notion that those who do well in adolescence will continue doing well is based on a misconception: that early success leads to later success. It could be the other way around.

Following up on a group of 166 high school graduates at age thirty, psychologist Jean MacFarlane and her colleagues were surprised by their findings. "Our theoretical expectations were . . . rudely jarred," she reports, "by the adult status of a number of our subjects who early had had easy and confidence-inducing lives. As children and adolescents, they . . . were the adulated images of success. Included among these were boy athletes and good-looking, socially skillful girls. One sees among them at age thirty a high proportion of brittle, discontented, and puzzled adults whose high potentialities have not been actualized, at least as of now."

Dr. MacFarlane did not know what to make of this finding, nor of their discovery that many troubled, unsuccessful adolescents matured so remarkably as adults. She speculated that early pain may induce growth, while young success delays it.

It could be the innies' very hope to continue the good times after high school that most prevents them from doing so. Erik Erikson says the task of establishing adult identity consists of moving successfully from one life stage to the next. Of the eight stages he identifies, adolescence is both the hardest to get through and the most important in determining adult identity. The danger here can lie more in a temptation to linger than in any desire to flee.

It's not that innies can't discover an encore, that they can't win acclaim in life as well as high school. Rather, it's that early triumph makes it harder, not easier. Talking with ex-innies who have not come to tragic ends, or even frustrating ones, and hearing them describe the comparable rewards of career and family — I believe them. But I also notice how even is their tone while describing life after high school compared with the sparkle of eyes and lilt to a voice recalling the roar of a crowd.

I once spent a morning at the Reverend Jesse Jackson's Operation Breadbasket service in Chicago, where hundreds of participants hung on his every word. Standing before this group on a stage, Reverend Jackson clutched a microphone and led them in chanting, "I am — somebody!"

> *I may be poor*
> *But I am*
> *Somebody!*
> *I may be uneducated*
> *But I am*
> *Somebody!*
> *I may be unskilled*
> *But I am*
> *Somebody!*
> *I may be on dope*
> *I may have lost hope*
> *But I am*
> *Somebody!*

Certainly this work is comparable to status in high school, and of greater social significance. But afterward, when the Reverend Jackson took a few seconds away from the worshipers tugging at his sleeve, his face softened with a slight smile when I asked about how he remembered high school. "Those were great years," said the Reverend Jackson. "I played football, basketball, baseball. I was president of the student body.

"Great years."

To understand more clearly the innies' encore problem, consider what won them acclaim in the first place. For those blessed with the necessary qualities, high school status is not hard to achieve. But you've got to have the qualities — a smile, a style, and enough changes of outfit. Physical gifts are basic. One study compared sixteen larger-sized high school boys with the same number of smaller ones. In general, the more generously endowed displayed greater self-confidence, seemed to talk less, and would show up late to parties. Among their number two were elected president of their student body, one president of the boy's club, and several were chosen committee chairmen.

The smaller boys by contrast seemed to chatter and scurry about more. They were on time for parties. The highest status any of them achieved was a class vice-presidency.

For girls, this syndrome is more likely to be reversed, with excess size being penalized and petite-to-average size rewarded.

In either case status grows directly from physique.

Though paths into the social center vary with the school, one currency is universal: athletic ability. A primary reason for this is that sports is the purest source of attention available in high school: the roar of a crowd, fuzzy behind the glare of lights; all eyes upon the captain as he elects to kick or receive; everyone rising to cheer an especially good play; reporters crowding around to take down a young athlete's words, and sometimes pressing a microphone to his lips.

"My God!" Willie Loman says of his son Biff in *Death of a Salesman*. "Remember how they used to follow him around in high school? When he smiled at one of them their faces lit up. When he walked down the street. . . ."

In a small town, not just the school's attention but that of the entire community is focused on high school athletes. One reason football is so statusy a sport, and to a lesser extent basketball, is that they're commonly played at night when the whole town can come.

Although he was the first freshman in his small-town high

school to letter, one man told me the honor was nearly worth-less because the letter read only T for track. Track meets were held in the afternoon and few people came to watch. The man said his best memory is not of a race he won, but one he didn't. This was during the one meet that was held at night. The exhila-ration of being cheered by townspeople was greater than actually winning. "To this day," says the ex-trackman, "I remember one guy in particular yelling 'Come on Sammy! You can do it Sammy!' I only took second or third, but just hearing that crowd, that guy yell my name, had to be my biggest moment in high school."

The only girls' status to compare with an athlete's is cheer-leader. As women remember high school, cheerleader was top of the line. After cheerleader there just wasn't much to which a girl could aspire. Beauty queen was one-shot. Majorettes were low-class. There was the band, if you were into baggy slacks and a policeman's hat. Or yearbook editor or class secretary, which weren't bad, but weren't cheerleader.

In her painfully authentic novel *The Cheerleader*, Ruth Doan MacDougall describes the ecstasy of Snowy, whose name had just been posted as a varsity cheerleader.

Throughout the day, instead of saying hi, the kids said "Congratula-tions!" and it was the most blissful day of her life. . . . She wanted to be one of those fabulous Varsity cheerleaders cheering at a game that mattered, for boys who mattered, the crowd caring passionately, and she herself one of those who led them.
  . . . She didn't notice the girls who were leaving silently, some of them crying.

Snowy's sophisticated, cynical friend Bev makes a point of not trying out for cheerleader. Later she confesses,

"Remember when I decided not to go out for cheering?"
"Yes. You said you couldn't stand being lame."
"Did I? Well, that wasn't the reason. I absolutely couldn't face the

tryouts. What if I didn't make it? Everyone would know I'd tried out and hadn't made it. So if I never tried out, maybe I could seem above it all. I'm not. Nobody is."

Years later, grown women can remember in excruciating detail the setting where they tried out for cheerleader — the room, what color it was painted, who was there, and the expression on their faces. They also remember vividly how it felt when their name wasn't posted the next day. "Crushed," "defeated," and "humiliated" are some of the words used to describe this feeling.

Those whose names *were* posted use a different set of phrases. "The world opened up" is one way I've heard making cheerleader described, "the beginning of my exciting life" and "people looking up at me."

On the face of it, leading cheers seems rather an absurd occupation. But consider the rewards: you're part of a tiny elite, five to ten girls; you get first crack at the athletes, on the sidelines and on the bus home after the game; on a good night thousands of people respond to every lift of your arm; and on Fridays you can wear your uniform to school.

In *Rubyfruit Jungle*, Molly describes the one member of her threesome who led cheers. "Carolyn was captain of the cheerleaders," says Molly, "and she usually showed up in the lunchroom in her uniform with blue tassels on her white boots. Connie and I scoffed at such a thing as cheerleading, but Carolyn was the social leader of the school because of it."

With her own success in the political sphere, together with these two friends Molly feels at the very center of their high school. "We concocted one scheme after another," she says, "and soon the whole school, two thousand strong, began to hang on our every action, word, look. The power was overwhelming."

Power is central to innie status. Finding this out has been rather a surprise to me. I always thought status in high school had to do with being well liked, and liking yourself. Actually, it's nothing of the sort. In memory, at least, innies didn't feel better liked than anyone else. If anything they felt less well regarded and more unknown because of their lofty social position.

"I felt people liked me only because of my apparent status," a former cheerleader told me, "not because of me."

To the delighted surprise of an outie who assumed all innies lived a life of daily ecstasy, I've found this refrain common: nobody knew me, I was a phony, and didn't feel like I really had friends. When I would ask how they thought classmates perceived them, yesterday's leading crowd members would come up regularly with terms such as "stuck-up," "egotistical," and "snobby."

An ex–football star, for example, figured a classmate would probably say of him, "Joe high school. Quarterback. Stuck-up. Knows he's important. Not too easy to make friends with if you're not on the football team."

Even within their own crowd, innies don't remember feeling secure. What they do remember is holding on for dear status and scrutinizing each other like soldiers on parade for the slightest deviation as a cause for disciplinary action. Innies didn't feel liked, and often didn't like each other. That isn't what status is all about. What it's about is power.

A sense of control, of being at the center of things is what emerges most vividly in the memory of innies: the floodlights seeking them out as they ran out on the field; the crowd roaring at the raise of their pom-poms; classmates squirming when they read what's written under their yearbook picture; student council members waiting to be called on to speak.

Such power mattered mostly for the status sweepstakes among classmates, but not exclusively. Teachers could also be disciplined by powerful innies. "The teacher who is not involved in the student activity program," one educator concluded after studying the situation, "will be less sensitive to the status differentiation of the informal system. . . . Lacking the personal influence of association he may risk conflict with the politically potent informal student group."

In reaching for the handles of power, discrimination was important. The obvious spots weren't always the right ones. The right ones were those where status could be awarded or withheld directly. Being in charge of captions for the yearbook was more important than running the whole operation. Editing the paper counted for less than writing a gossip column and mentioning the right people.

The feeling of being an innie is aristocratic. To those at the center, high school's status system feels like the natural order of things. To an eye looking out from within, the great mass of outies is a bit blurred. Innies are not scornful of the peasantry so much as ignorant of them. At best they take occasional pity and toss an outie a smile like a crust of bread. The attitude is more indifferent than oppressive, not Stalin herding opponents into labor camps so much as Marie Antoinette crushing peasants beneath her carriage wheels because she doesn't recognize their existence.

"At times," an ex-innie explains, "it felt like there was only me and three or four others in the whole school."

But as with any aristocracy, the status of innies is more by anointment than reward. Innieness has nothing to do with ability. It's a confirmation of givens — physical gifts, coming from the right family, being able to afford a car, and the right clothes. These are among the tickets of admission to high school's inner circle.

What does not help one get inside is competence. If anything, too much talent is suspect. Innies know this. And knowing their status is more bestowed than earned, they feel no pride in its attainment.

When describing their high school triumphs, innies invariably discount them. A homecoming queen from Missouri assured me the honor was only awarded her because she happened to be dating the football captain. One from New York says she got elected only because junior high kids got to vote and she was nice to them. And a Most Likely to Succeed from Sacramento remains convinced to this day — a decade later — that someone stuffed her ballot box.

In interviews with innies, I've heard a litany of self-ridicule based on the feeling that it's so "simple" to make it in high school — a joke really. "As far as I could tell," one two-letter athlete and class officer told me, "we were just laughing at the whole thing." He did not, the man told me, feel popular. He felt like a con.

Had I read my Edgar Friedenberg earlier, finding all this out might not have been so surprising. While interviewing high school students for his book *The Vanishing Adolescent*, the sociologist found that "Thomas," a high-status football captain and judge of the student court, also displayed some of the least self-regard of any student interviewed. Compared with less recognized classmates, Friedenberg found that "Thomas has very little love for himself — far less than the school has for him. . . .

"This boy is no egotist. He has one of the weakest egos in the sample.

"About all Thomas knows about Thomas is that he is good at sports, loves sports and depends on success in sports for his self-esteem."

Given the weak foundation of their self-regard in high school, is it any wonder innies later face such an encore problem?

Regularly I've heard from latter-day innies how achieving that status compensated for unhappiness at home. But, paradoxically, a price of entry into the leading crowd was covering up the very anxieties that made them so eager to belong in the first place.

"I thought I was the most unhappy person in my class," an ex-cheerleader tells me. (She being the one whose yearbook called her "gay and carefree all the while.") "I was tortured. I walked around a whole lot with either butterflies or lead in my stomach."

Innies must keep a tighter lid on things. They have more to

lose by opening up. Warren Beatty remembers himself at the time as "a cheerful hypocrite."

In the human sense, looking so put-together on the outside can make it that much harder to ventilate inner feelings and share experiences that might cause a chink in the armor. A former football star told me that one of his more memorable experiences in high school was defecating in his pants after tackling somebody hard during an opening kickoff. He played out the game without changing his uniform. Later, on the bus going home, he tried to tell a friend what had happened. "You're kidding!" the friend said incredulously.

"Yeah," the first guy replied quickly. "I'm kidding."

Innieness can be a prison.

Once released from the chains of their status, innies often feel a relief the rest of us may have trouble understanding. At last they can be friends with anyone. Innie after innie has told me what a blessing it was to graduate from high school and be able to choose friends by preference rather than social standing. Sometimes they even go so far as to marry the kind of creep they wouldn't have noticed, let alone gone out with, during high school.

But it can take more than graduation to release innies from the prison of their status. Even after high school innies are handicapped by the stereotypes we hang on them as a sort of penalty, a few thumbtacks thrown underfoot for looking so put-together when the rest of us felt so distraught.

"Big dumb jock" is one such stereotype. The has-been high school athlete is a stock figure, almost a cliché of American literature. John Updike has made sort of a speciality of this character, particularly as Rabbit Angstrom, the ex–basketball star first sketched in a poem and short story, then featured in two novels. Reduced to selling gadgets at the five and dime, Rabbit hungers not just for the acclaim but the transcendence he last felt on a high school basketball court. "It *was* great," he says of those days. "It's a fact. I mean I'm not much good for anything now, but I really was good at that."

A variation of this character shows up in the writing of Philip Roth, F. Scott Fitzgerald, Irwin Shaw, Larry McMurtry, Dan Wakefield, Frederick Exley, and Arthur Miller, among others. Jason Miller put not just one but four frustrated ex-jocks on stage in *That Championship Season*, and Tennessee Williams has portrayed him not only as Jim O'Connor, but as Brick in *Cat on a Hot Tin Roof*, who, according to his sister, "never carried a thing in his life but a football or a highball."

The companion stereotype reserved for those who once waved pom-poms is "cheerleader-type." If anything this label is more handicapping than "big dumb jock." I know of no more provocative question one can ask a grown woman than "Were you a cheerleader?"

Replies to such an inquiry are instant, agitated, and heartfelt.

One set of responses is of the "Hell no!" variety. "Not me!" such women say. "No way!" This reply is from women who either tried out for cheerleader and didn't make it, or, like Bev, begged the issue by not trying out.

"A lot of my identity derived from *not* being a cheerleader, *not* being the type," one woman explained, "so I didn't even try out."

Then she thought about that for a few seconds, and added, "Of course there was always the fantasy that some day, maybe. . . ."

The second type of response to "Were you a cheerleader?" is just as immediate, and equally fierce, but relies on phrases like, "Why did you ask me that?" "What a question!" and "Do I look like one?"

This reaction, of course, comes from women who once led cheers. For a long time such responses puzzled me. Why, I wondered, should such a high-status past be a source of so much sensitivity in the present?

Finally it got through to me: the ex-cheerleaders' defensiveness had little to do with having once led cheers. About this achievement former pom-pom girls tend to be bashfully proud. (If you think old cheerleaders don't like to go through their routines, serve one too much liquor at a party.)

No, having been a cheerleader in the past is a much less touchy subject than being a "cheerleader type" in the present. When asked, "Were you a cheerleader?" what an ex-cheerleader hears is: "You seem like the cheerleader type."

I once posed this question to a vivacious college teacher. "What made you say that?" she responded. "Why did you say that? Do I seem like a cheerleader?"

Then she calmed down and admitted yes, she had once been a cheerleader, but found this often was embarrassing to admit. "My embarrassment," she explained, "is that it's a very superficial thing. The outer image has to do with cutesy, superficial things. So I react against it. Like people would think, 'Oh, how could she? How could she go for such a superficial thing?'

"I don't tell too many people, because they say things like, 'Oh, she's a cheerleader-type.'"

All of which made me wonder: just what is a cheerleader type?

The answers to this question can be contradictory. On some points there's consensus: sparkle, enthusiasm, and plenty of spunk. Blond comes up a lot, and a big smile. But some people say straight hair, while others think curly. Goody-goody is mentioned by many, but just as many agree with Frank Zappa, that "deep down every cheerleader in school was a closet nymphomaniac. They all wanted to be lustful pervs. Somewhere in the deep reaches of their consciousness they all wanted to go out there and cavort like all the weird people did."

In search of a more precise definition of "cheerleader type," I attended a summer cheerleader camp on a college campus. Here four hundred and fifty bouncing, screaming, jumping, and cartwheeling cheerleaders had gathered for two weeks to sharpen their skills.

"Are we the best?"

"OK!"

"Are we the best?"

Clap. "Hey!" Clap. "Yes!" Stamp, stamp, stamp.

The big practice field was dotted with clumps of five to ten girls all yelling like the crowd at a public hanging, and waving their arms in unison.

"You bit off — more than you can chew!"

"Because your eyes are too big!" (hands around eyes)

"For your tummy, too!" (hands on stomach)

A petite, but full-breasted black cheerleader walked by so I popped her my question: what's a cheerleader type? She thought for a second, smiled, then did a little Tina Turner jiggle and said, "Oh, you mean bouncy. They're jouncy and they're bouncy and they've got a lot of spunk." She laughed while explaining this to me in a voice hoarse from yelling.

Are you a cheerleader-type?

"I guess so." Still smiling, she again did her shimmy, fists moving in and out like pistons. "I like to move around."

Another cheerleader, who was listening in on our conversation, interrupted in her own hoarse voice to say: "You can't type people like that! You feel all cheerleaders are goofy and like to mess around. But some people are goofy and like to mess around and aren't cheerleaders."

"Well," replied the first cheerleader, "we like to mess around and have fun, and wear goofy outfits like this." She wore a yellow T-shirt with a turtle on it and the words SLOWPOKE, PH, ROSANNE, and OUT OF SIGHT.

"At school," she added growing a little more serious, "it seems like it's plastered on your forehead that you're a cheerleader. There's four thousand kids at my school and when you sign annuals, people come up and say, 'Rosanne! Rosanne! Sign my annual!' and I don't even know who they are."

Rosanne had to return to her cheers, so I joined the camp's directress as she observed the girls' routines. A pert ex-tumbler, she replied "Attitude" when I asked what makes a good cheerleader.

"A good attitude that radiates from within and without — that sparkles in your eyes. If you've ever worked with cheerleaders you can just see the sparkle in their eyes. If they haven't got it. . . ."

She turned to survey the mob before us, then singled out a girls who wasn't smiling. "Look. That one girl over there is seventeen and has the lines of a forty-year-old. Crabby. That's negativeness.

"Watch her — that's what a cheerleader does *not* want to be. Watch her face, how often she pouts." I watched. The girl looked thoughtful.

The directress turned and looked directly at me for the first time. "I have two boys, and I've tried to tell them, 'Don't get upset over little things.' My younger son is rather negative on some things — I don't know why. I don't try to dig too deep.

"You dig too deep and you kind of get confused."

From every corner of the field the girls now converged into one jumping, clapping mob, yelling, "Let's go, let's go — leeeet's go!"

> *Hey now people*
> *You ain't cool*
> *You ain't got the spirit*
> *And that ain't good*
> *You ain't bad and you ain't mean*
> *You can't even make the scene*
> *You ain't bad and you ain't cool*
> *All you are is one big fool!*
>
> *How do you feel?*
> *SATISFIED!!*

Sometimes ex-cheerleaders try to deny that their status amounted to much. One woman went so far as to tell me that to her it was just a "free ride to the game."

A free ride to the game! I know women — mature women and sophisticated — who would gladly write that statement in large letters on poster paper, then cut the words out letter by letter and stuff them down a megaphone impaled in the ex-cheerleader's throat.

A free ride to the game!

Cheerleader is not a subject about which one wants to be blasé. The identity carries too much weight as an archetype, a cultural touchstone. It is difficult to overestimate the weight put on "cheerleader" as a source of status in high school and in the adult culture populated by its graduates.

In his book *Scoring*, Dan Greenburg reminds us often that the flaxen-haired Pepsi girl who for a time shared his bed had been a cheerleader not just in high school but also in college. At one point Greenburg refers to her "beautiful blonde cheerleaderliness."

Once you begin noticing, cheerleaders leap out from every point of the landscape — off the pages of *Esquire* and *Seventeen*, from Air Force recruitment billboards, ads for Skin Bracer, and on Corn Flakes packages. Here their presence is innocent enough, heavy on the cute and perky angle.

But in *Portnoy's Complaint*, Alexander Portnoy's adolescent wish-fulfillment is a sexually acrobatic cheerleader-type (my term) named Monkey. In his earlier novel *When She Was Good*, Philip Roth wrote in a real cheerleader also named Monkey, Monkey Littlefield, who interests his main character: "She was small and had dark bangs and for a short girl she had a terrific figure. . . . with these terrifically developed muscles in her legs, and that she was a bigshot cheerleader didn't faze him. . . . What was a cheerleader, anyway, but a girl who was an extrovert?"

"A cock teaser for sure."

This is how one woman describes herself and fellow cheerleaders at a Texas high school in the mid-sixties.

"We knew damn well what we were doing with those crotch

Kellogg's
CORN FLAKES

PACIFIC OUTDOOR

Come as you are.

Call Air Force. 800-44

Yes, we have pom-pons and everything else for
cheerleaders and pep clubs!
Sweaters / Skirts / Jumpers / Vests / Emblems / Pom-Pon Shakers /
Shoes / Tights / Books / Jewelry and Awards / Slogan Ribbons /
Buttons / Pennants / Beanies / Megaphones / T-Shirts, etc.

- RE-LIVE YOUR
CHILDHOOD FANTASIES!

TEENAGE x
CHEERLEADER

NO ONE UNDER 18 ADMITTED

RATED X

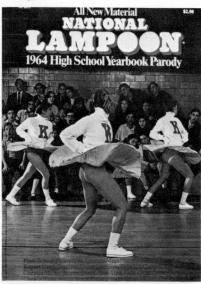

All New Material $2.50
NATIONAL
LAMPOON
1964 High School Yearbook Parody

They gave their all for the team

The
Swinging
Cheerleaders

R

Not all the playing
was on the football
field!

shots," she explained. "The cunt shots, the kicks — we really dug that. We made up so many cheers to expose ourselves. We all knew. We didn't admit it, but everybody who could put in a kick or show their ass in a cheer they made up, it was immediately giggled over and accepted.

"It's like guys in high school are so horny. So with the pompoms and lifting your skirt, it's like you're a big fucking sexual image. But it's like 'I'm pure because I'm here in a sweater.'

"It's cock teasing."

The woman telling me this has since graduated into stripping and acting in porno films. With her the day we talked was a former male cheerleader from Minneapolis who also does erotic dancing and movie-making. The two agreed that exhibitionism linked their pre- and postgraduate careers, exhibitionism and a taste for crowd control. "The biggest point about being a cheerleader," explained the man, "is imagining that you're standing in front of two hundred thousand people and you go like this" — he raised his arm — "and two hundred thousand people go 'YOU!'"

"What a rush!"

She agreed. "When you're cheerleading," the stripper added, "you can almost control the crowd. They put you there. It's like you're a demigod. I still do that on stage. You can keep their attention just like you did then.

"I would have killed to be a cheerleader," she concluded. "I was known to kick and trip people at tryouts." The high point of her life till now, the woman told me, was making all-city cheerleader while captain of her squad senior year.

Though neither ex-cheerleader had kept a yearbook, I later got his through a former classmate. While not pictured within seventy-five times as he'd told me, the guy was there often — kicking high as a cheerleader, looking efficient as class vice-president, and smiling broadly as Most School Spirited.

Corroborating the woman's story proved more difficult. In fact, it proved impossible. Calls to her city and further investigation turned up no one at the woman's high school by that name or self-description as a cheerleader/student council secretary/ homecoming court member/Lady Macbeth in the class play/or anything else she'd told me. Curiosity finally drove me to her hometown where vigorous yearbook research, rummaging at local high schools, and talks with the local citizenry never fully confirmed who my stripper was, but indisputably revealed who she *wasn't:* a cheerleader, student council secretary, homecoming court member, or Lady Macbeth in the class play. Zip. She was an outie. Here I thought the lady was telling me the tale of an innie with an encore problem. What I really had been hearing all along was a fellow outie with an active imagination and an ingenious approach to revenge.

Don't Get Popular, Get Even

Breathes there a man with soul so dead who never to himself has said: "Someday I'm going to show them"?

— RICHARD REEVES

Be prepared to discuss and evaluate in class the following information:

All the arrogance you read about stems from those days in high school. It all stems from a desire to be nobody's fool again. . . . it's conceivable that thirty million people will read your article, and I have let them know I'm something.

— BOBBY DARIN

I am totally motivated by it — I call it revenge.

— NORA EPHRON

I think for a long time there was an element in everything I did of "I'll-get-you-you-bastards."

— MIKE NICHOLS

Someday, so help me, I'll be so famous none of you will ever be able to touch me again.

— RONA BARRETT

If they don't like me, some day they'll learn to respect me.

— BETTY FRIEDAN

'Cause I was a Jewish girl growing up in a Samoan neighborhood . . . I left . . . and, you know, the old story about "I'll show *them*" . . . I really felt that way and I had a lot of anger built up from those years.

— BETTE MIDLER

Man those people hurt me. It makes me happy to know I'm making it and that they're still back there, plumbers and all, just like they were.

— JANIS JOPLIN

If I had been a really good-looking kid, I would have been popular with my classmates, I would have been smooth with the girls, I would have starting scoring at about age fourteen, I would have been a big fraternity guy in college, and I would have wound up selling Olds-mobiles. For sure I wouldn't have had the bitterness and the fierce ambition I've needed in order to become a successful freelance writer.

— DAN GREENBURG

I'd love to do something about all those football players I used to envy in high school. What's with them? They sell insurance and send their kids for karate lessons every Saturday.

— ROBERT BLAKE

Thank God for the athletes and their rejection. Without them there would have been no emotional need and. . . . I'd be a crackerjack salesman in the garment district.

— MEL BROOKS

Twinkle, twinkle superstar
To those who said you'd not go far
You showed them guts, you showed them nerve
Now, show them by the Scotch you serve.

— JOHNNIE WALKER

Sam Keen is a successful author. So far he has published five original books and a collection of magazine articles. Keen also lectures around the country for comfortable fees. Strikingly handsome as he pushes past forty, Keen has a head of thick dark hair, the lithe body of an athlete, and a resonant baritone voice. Women say Sam has sex appeal.

But Sam Keen says it wasn't always so. In fact, says the author, not until his thirties did he find women liked the way he looked. Back in his Wilmington, Delaware, high school it was just the opposite. There he recalls being a ninety-eight-pound weakling who wore cowboy boots, couldn't make teams, never had a date, and — to the ridicule of his classmates — refused to buy an activity ticket. Sam says he felt so unattractive at the time that if a good-looking girl paid him any attention, he figured she must have syphilis or some other social disease.

It was not until college, then while doing a Divinity Ph.D. at Harvard, that Keen began his metamorphosis. Larger by now, he took up wrestling, and later became a surfer. Sam says today he feels good about his body, satisfied with his achievements in life, and delighted about being attractive to women.

But when Keen goes home to Wilmington, and sees a former classmate approaching on the street — he crosses to the other side. "My whole impulse about high school," he explains, "is to get as far away from it as possible. I can't imagine anything, even old age, being as painful as high school."

Would you go back to a reunion?

"Hell no! They'd have to pay me a thousand dollars." Sam's voice takes on an uncharacteristic petulance. "They're all working for Bell Telephone now, and I'm *glad*. They peaked out during the high school Thanksgiving game.

"As far as I'm concerned, nothing too bad can happen to a high school athlete."

Don't you feel any compassion for such people?

"Hell no. They got what they deserve. My attitude toward high school heroes is that vengeance is too good to be left to the Lord."

One of the least recognized wars being waged in this country is that between innies and outies. Presumably our hostilities ceased with high school graduation. In fact this is just when the war heats up.

Most of the struggle is one-way, felt, initiated, and waged by a ragtag revolutionary army of high school rejects peppering away at the stolid innie Redcoats who just stand in formation, rarely returning any fire and wondering what all the commotion is about.

Leading crowd members aren't so much hostile to the existence of the lower orders as ignorant: in high school and out. And for this ignorance they will pay.

"You can't get away with this shit forever!" plain Beverly Katz screams at pretty Sasha Davis in *Memoirs of an Ex-Prom Queen*. "Someday you'll pay!" But Sasha Davis doesn't seem quite sure where all that fury comes from.

High school's innies will never know how desperately they're hated and envied by outies, and how long the resentment smolders. Nor do they realize how resourceful we can be in our continuing guerrilla warfare. Do they know that *Main Street* is considered a classic of our struggle, the outies' *Das Kapital?* Have they any idea why we make movies like *American Graffiti* with class presidents who end up selling insurance?

And have they listened, *really* listened to Janis Ian's song "At Seventeen" — the song about girls with ravaged faces, who lack social graces and learn early that love is meant for "high school girls with clear-skinned smiles/who married young, and then retired" — compared with those who grow up to write songs like "At Seventeen"?

Rock 'n' roll belongs to us. It's a field we control utterly. Frank Zappa says he's never met an innie playing his brand of music, "people who used to take their white bucks seriously." He does admit to the possibility of exceptions. The only thing close to an exception I've ever found is Alice Cooper, who ran track at Cortez High in Phoenix and won a trophy at the Lettermen's Talent Show.

Even so put-together a figure as John Denver makes no secret of a lust to show his classmates back in Fort Worth, the ones who used to call him "four eyes." During a TV special, Denver once took the opportunity to thumb his nose at a girl named Marcia who had made fun of his hair back in high school, and wouldn't go out with him.

One reason rock 'n' roll is so strategic to our side is that it's such an effective tool for organizing. Janis Joplin, a martyred heroine of our struggle, never missed an opportunity to strike back at her Port Arthur classmates, the ones who had called her "pig" and threw things at her in the hallways. When Janis went back to her tenth reunion ("just to jam it up their asses"), she took a lot of us with her. "She represented me," wrote one fan in Chicago, "who didn't go to the Senior prom and was never elected to anything. All the outcasts who didn't fit into the closed society that is the American high school knew she was one of us. . . ."

The girl continued:

Her beauty and creativity said *no* to all those teachers who had ignored us, all those football heroes who wouldn't date us, all those cheerleaders who seemed to own the world. Well, the teachers are retired, wrinkled old people now, and the footballers are beginning to get thin hair and paunches, and their cheerleader wives, shapeless and irritable, are screaming at their kids. They and their kind are only moons, reflecting the light of artificiality and never giving forth the life-force of the sun. And Janis was a comet, a life-force, a light in our darkening world, a beautiful person, and she was Ours.

Here is how the sides break down: we give the innies all of pro sports and its cheerleaders; we concede them the military, insurance agencies, PE departments, and heavy equipment. Politics and show business are divided zones, but we write everybody's lines because outies control America's means of communication. We write the speeches, publish the books, produce the movies, make the music, do the research, report for the papers, and comment on sports.

Also we *own* the teams.

Our war takes several forms, and its most effective weapons are not always the most apparent. Howard Cosell, for example, though one of us, is a bit of an embarrassment with his strident determination to take the world's jocks down a peg or two. More to our liking was Lyndon Johnson, the scrawny nonathlete who, according to his brother Sam, in high school weighed "less than a girl cheerleader." Lyndon later got off that classic line about Gerald Ford having played football too long without a helmet. This remark has stuck to Ford like tar and feathers. For such devastating subtlety LBJ deserved a medal, something like an Award for Meritorious Service in Maintenance of the Big Dumb Jock Stereotype. And add a Pom-Pom Cluster for his additional observation that Ford had trouble walking and chewing gum at the same time. This sort of takedown advanced our cause immeasurably, and Lyndon Johnson is sorely missed.

But many have stepped forward to grasp his fallen banner, because we are a numerous army and talented. After all, far more girls *didn't* make cheerleader than did, and only eleven guys can play football at a time. Also, there is nothing less likely to win you status in high school than talent.

Some of our best people have infiltrated advertising agencies and made these a tool of revenge. "How's your love life?" we ask the head cheerleader for Ultra-Brite. "How's my love life? Rah-rah-rah," we have her reply.

"How's your love life?"

"Rah-rah. . . . I'm available."

Teaching is a field shared by innies, but we tell them how to do it. Our strategy here is to take over the colleges of education, control research, and write all the books about how to teach high school. In these books we never take seriously any of the values innies used to keep us down. "Popularity" is a topic we're very condescending about and brush under the heading of "Peer Relations." Sports generally get ridiculed, and activities such as cheerleading and homecoming are reduced to "Student Culture: Ceremony and Ritual."

For strategic reasons, our best efforts are concentrated in the nation's means of communication: publishing, the media, and film.

We produce the movies these days, having worked into positions to boss around ex-jocks such as Redford, Reynolds, and Caan in addition to Ann-Margret and Raquel Welch who once led cheers and now follow us.

When director Mike Nichols said there's an element in everything he does of "I'll-get-you-you-bastards," the bastards he referred to were those tormentors who seemed to outnumber his admirers in high school. One guy in particular used to hold Nichols's head under water, then stand on it. Years later, when Nichols was doing comedy in a nightclub, this guy came up to him after a show, tapped his famous classmate on the shoulder, and said, "You don't remember me, but. . . ."

It was as if Nichols had been waiting fifteen years for that moment. "I said, 'I remember you very well. Your name is so-and-so and you are a shit. What are you doing now?'"

"I'm selling used cars," said the tormentor.

"I'm so glad," said Nichols.

Authors mostly are us. Larry McMurtry, who, according to the principal of his Texas high school, "was not accepted by the majority of his classmates," later inscribed a classmate's copy of *The Last Picture Show* "Revenge is sweet."

One reason ex-jocks look so ridiculous in print is that so few of them know how to write. We do. And books can be a perfect tool of retribution. Philip Roth, who's written an alcoholic ex–high school baseball star into one novel and a moronic jock into another, later wrote in *My Life as a Man:* "In early adolescence, I underwent daily school-yard humiliation (at the time it seemed there could be none worse) because of my physical timidity and hopelessness at all sports."

Except for playwrights Arthur Miller and Jason Miller, those who write of the ex-jock seem not to have been one themselves. John Updike, a friend says, might have been Rabbit Angstrom had he only been a better basketball player. In one of his autobiographical Olinger stories, Updike's narrator says of himself and a companion: "We were about the same height and had the same

99

degree of athletic incompetence and the same curious lack of whatever force it was that aroused loyalty and compliance in beautiful girls."

Tennessee Williams, while growing up Tommy Williams in St. Louis, suffered the aftereffects of childhood diphtheria. His mother had kept him in bed and away from other children, which the playwright says left him "delicate and sissified." In early adolescence, gangs of children followed the slight boy home, yelling "Sissy!" At University City High, Williams kept to himself and had little to do with his fellow students. Writing became his solace, his path of escape.

"I discovered writing," the playwright has said, "as an escape from a world of reality in which I felt acutely uncomfortable. It immediately became my place of retreat, my cave, my refuge.

"From what? From being called a sissy by the neighborhood kids. . . ."

The elite division of our communications brigade, the struggle's Green Berets, are those who control America's press.

The *National Lampoon* is a key outpost of this division, the front lines, as it were, in the war against high school's innies. Here is gathered a talented group of hard-core outies who have made the *Lampoon* a propaganda sheet for our side. Within its pages PE teachers get dumped on by birds overhead, sex education classes use live models, and Nancy Reagan advises on Dating Dos and Don'ts. Then there is the savage *Lampoon* yearbook parody, with its pantyless cheerleader twirling on the cover and an anal introduction by Principal Humphrey C. Cornholt.

Is the *National Lampoon* bent on revenge?

"Absolutely," says Executive Editor P. J. O'Rourke. "It sure is, especially [senior editor and co-founder] Doug Kenney and me. Doug's been trading on it a lot longer.

"Most people here frankly were geeks. Which has a lot to do with being a good humorist. You can't fight with your fists, so you fight with your mouth. [Contributing Editor] Chris Miller

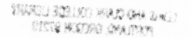

and I come the closest to having had normal lives, though neither of us was really popular."

P. J. O'Rourke has an open, friendly face with long, light brown hair. The day we talked in the *Lampoon*'s Manhattan office suite, O'Rourke wore Levi's, a pearl-buttoned work shirt, black garrison belt, and high-heeled saddle shoes.

The *Lampoon*'s editor recalls being an active social climber at the two high schools he attended, Toledo's DeVilbis High, '61–'62, then Oak Park in Illinois, '62–'64, finally transferring back to graduate from DeVilbis in 1965. O'Rourke says he started out kind of greasy as a freshman, then tried to become a jock at Oak Park, "which didn't work out because I'm a terrible athlete."

He remembers that at Oak Park there was a basic dress requirement for in people: white Levi's, madras shirt, ¾-inch belt of brown leather with a round buckle, penny loafers (preferably Bass Weejuns), and light socks. Before returning to DeVilbis for his senior year, O'Rourke was depressed about being no more a social success than he was and made a vow. "I vowed to myself not to try to make friends," he recalls. "I wasn't gonna care; fuck it. A real adolescent vow. I said to hell with it, I'm gonna wear dark socks.

"Well it turns out that at DeVilbis dark socks were really in — Levi's, madras shirt, and dark socks." O'Rourke's face broke out in a grin. "Three girls fell in love with me the first day, and I had this marvelous senior year — pledged an illegal fraternity, had a lot of dates, etc. Not a smashing social success, but better than before."

Even while part of it, O'Rourke says he was fascinated by high school's folkways and "detected the tribal atmosphere early on — as a sophomore — even though it didn't make me feel any better." He calls high school "the only place where you could set an Evelyn Waugh novel. Such a strict social code. If you wear the wrong socks, you've had it."

In analyzing high school's social structure, O'Rourke makes a fundamental distinction between geeks, or wonks, who were so far into the woodwork they couldn't see out, and those like himself who weren't really popular but at least knew what was going on. Most of the *Lampoon* staff are in the former category, he says, "writers, artists of all kinds — the great fraternity of high school geeks. We've discussed that a lot around here. I don't feel that way so much, but I do recognize that the outsiders from high school are gathered at the *Lampoon*."

O'Rourke took instantly to the innie-outie breakdown while emphasizing his conviction that it's important to distinguish between those outies who *knew* they were out, and those who didn't — the wonks. "Kissinger's clearly a wonk," he explains, "and a lot of kids who went to West Point were wonks.

"But Larry Kroger *knows* he isn't in. That's pretty clearly me."

O'Rourke turned around and pulled a copy of the *Lampoon*'s yearbook parody off the shelf behind him. Flipping to the senior pictures, he started reading the activity list for Larry Kroger (the yearbook's mythical owner): "Yeah, you see Track 2,3,4 because I could always stay on the track team. Like me, Kroger's nowhere, but not so nowhere as people you didn't even know existed. Like Penelope Cuntz: Good listener . . . attractive smile . . . shy type . . . pleasant grin . . . still waters run deep . . . a smile for all . . . 'Excuse me' . . . cheerful smile . . . attentive listener . . . quietly silent . . . a real cute smile."

O'Rourke laughed aloud as he read this, then pointed to Penelope's picture, saying, "She just didn't exist. I wonder what ever happened to those kids who didn't exist? The girls are probably total recluses, the guys hot-rodders."

P.J. leafed some more, pointing out that the layout of Dacron, Ohio, is that of Toledo, its streets named after presidents in the same way. Some yearbook ads come from Corngate Shopping Center, much like Toledo's Westgate Shopping Center.

"I even used my grandmother's maiden name for his mother's maiden name," he added, "I listed my grade school as his. Yeah, here: I used my home address as the school's." O'Rourke then held the book up and pointed to the school's paper, *The Prism*. "This *was* the DeVilbis high school paper," he said. "That was the *real* name." He continued leafing the book, chuckling to himself as he went. "Yeah, this was to a large extent an act of revenge by Doug and me on the world of high school."

One way you know that the *National Lampoon* is unmistakably US is when *The New York Times Magazine* runs an article reporting that "the Lampooners . . . are getting back at their adolescent years. . . ."

This sort of coverage is what makes journalism central to outie strategy. By reporting each other a lot, we're working hand in hand to build a better world, one just the opposite of that which excluded us in high school. When Janis Joplin went back to show up the classmates at her reunion, we covered the event like a political convention. In reporting on movement sisters like Janis, or Bette Midler or Barbra Streisand, we always give them plenty of room to settle old scores — after which we suggest that things are changing. Writing about Streisand, for example, Gloria Steinem says of the big-nosed actress: "In a world of snub-nosed American cheerleaders, she was clearly a misfit." Then Steinem adds, "Barbra Streisand has changed the bland, pugnosed American ideal, probably forever."

By saying this, Steinem helps make it happen. For this reason control of the print media is basic to our struggle.

"They are outsiders by nature," David Halberstam has said of Washington reporters. "The ones who did not run for high school class president and who were not Most Likely to Succeed."

Halberstam's colleague Gay Talese says this is true of him to a certain degree, though he denies being bent on revenge or even clearly being an outie. But based on the evidence, we claim Talese for our side.

This highly successful author once said of himself in high school: "I was not a good student. I was not an outstanding athlete. And I was not very much of anything, but one thing I could do was report. At the age of fifteen, in a town that had one weekly newspaper, I was describing the Siegfrieds of the city, the star athletes who on Saturday morning would walk down the main street in their red jackets and have all the old men come out of the barbershops waving at them as they passed, wishing them well in the great battle at two in the afternoon. I was looking at life from the press box. . . ."

This was what I asked Talese about when we met in his town-house on Manhattan's East Side. Somewhat taller than I'd expected, though quite slim, Gay Talese has an intense presence. His compressed mouth smiles economically, and wide, dark eyes lock on his listener like a searchlight as he talks.

Talese remembers being quiet at Ocean City High in New Jersey, quite shy and not sexually active. He thought his classmates might say about him, "He's a nice guy. Good listener. Dresses well."

But Talese didn't belong. He had no nickname. ("Gay was enough.") Girls did not compete for his attention. He wrote about others but never was written about. "I wasn't a group man," Talese explains. "Wasn't a joiner. I was always moving around, looking in on things.

"I never was part of the crowd, though I had credentials to walk in and out as I had all my life and do to this day."

Gay Talese says the biggest thing setting him apart was his father, a tailor, the son of an Italian immigrant and not your average Ocean City resident. "He looked different," Talese explains. "He wore a big red moustache, to my eternal embarrassment. Nobody wore moustaches at that time.

"So if you have a father who's very different, dogmatic, a very good dresser but wearing double-breasted suits at a time when no one else is, and has this red moustache — you feel different. Even if I had been able to blend in I don't think I could have because I was very much shaped by him."

Do you wish it had been otherwise?

"Oh yeah. In high school you don't want to be different. Especially in the forties. In this town you didn't want to be different and I didn't want to have a father who was different. But I had no choice. And eventually I got comfortable with it."

Being on the outside of things is often cited as an occupational hazard of journalism. What's less considered is how much being an outsider can be the cause of becoming a reporter, more than the effect.

Nora Ephron is among the few journalists I've seen write about this possibility. In a collection of her articles Ephron compared reporting with being a "wallflower at the orgy," the book's title. As a confirmed outsider, she speculated that an orgy for her would probably be just like the dances of her early teens, "only instead of people walking past me and rejecting me, they would be stepping over my naked body and rejecting me."

In an interview within *Wallflower*, she and Mike Nichols spent several paragraphs comparing notes on their mutual hunger for revenge.

In her later review without sympathy of Alix Kates Shulman's *Memoirs of an Ex–Prom Queen*, Ephron displayed a remarkable indifference to the problems of women who had once been beauty queens.

Nora Ephron's maiden column for *Esquire* was about the shaping influence of breast size in female adolescence and her own deficiency in this area. Here she reported the contention of some big-bosomed friends that their life was more miserable. "I have thought about their remarks," Ephron concluded, "tried to put myself in their place, considered their point of view.

"I think they are full of shit."

When I asked if there were a self she'd rather have been in

high school, Nora Ephron replied immediately, "Oh sure. Beautiful. Feminine. Popular with the boys, popular with the girls."

And your body?

Ephron grinned. "Just more of everything."

Nora Ephron in person is not quite so unendowed as one might expect from her self-description. Trim, erect — her mouth breaks open often in a wide, even seductive smile. And her breasts, while not munificent, are unmistakably there. They fit her frame. But arguing the point would be rather like saying, "Well, you don't *seem* short, Mr. Napoleon"; because Nora Ephron says her sense of herself has less to do with current realities than how she felt at fifteen.

"The one thing I would like to get across about my whole feeling regarding high school," said Ephron early in our conversation, "is how I was when I was fifteen. Gawky. Always a hem hanging down, or strap loose, or a pimple on my chin. I never knew what to do with my hair. I was a mess. And I still carry that fifteen-year-old girl around now. A piece of me still believes I'm the girl nobody dances with."

At Beverly Hills High, Nora Ephron was a junior class cheerleader. According to her this resembled not even remotely a real cheerleader. She thought about trying out for varsity. She also thought about being a child movie star. She attempted neither. "I knew my level," Ephron explains. "I was a terrible cheerleader. It's something I phased myself out of not to be rejected."

Nora Ephron does remember running for office, constantly, and always losing. She recalls with a tempered smile finally getting to be Girls' Athletic Association president and editor of the school paper. What Nora didn't get was popular. At least not as popular as she wanted. Nora Ephron remembers having two sets of friends in high school: smart and dumb. The dumb ones of course were the friends she wanted more of. After years of desperation Ephron finally snared a dumb boyfriend and began to feel more popular. This was after concluding that not raising her hand in class might help. She was right. The lower stayed her hand, the higher went her status. "It made a tremendous difference," Ephron recalls.

You got asked out more?

"Oh yeah. Instantly." She grimaced.

"I realize the kind of patheticness of it: a) that I stopped raising my hand, b) that I felt I had to, and c) that it worked.

"Occasionally I'll meet someone today — usually a stockbroker — who is so unspeakably dumb that I can't believe it. Good-looking and dumb. And I'll realize that if I were in high school I'd be miserable because he wouldn't ask me out.

"That is one reason why the revenge thing isn't really satisfying. Just as we don't ever lose the fifteen-year-old person, they don't either. They're always the student body president."

At one time Ephron felt her driving motivation was a thirst for revenge. Today she feels more circumspect, partly less angry in general, and partly just resigned to the futility of it all. Because what to her feels like revenge may to innies feel like just more of the same.

Ephron says this insight first dawned on her a few years after she got out of high school. While working at a good newspaper job in New York, having seen her by-line in national magazines, she went back to Los Angeles and looked up some old classmates from Beverly High. Nora smiles at the memory of one. "She had in the cupboard one of those jars of peanut butter mixed up with jelly and I was so pleased. I had this job in New York and everything.

"But all they could say was, 'Well, aren't you married now?' That was when I realized there was to be no revenge. After a while what one understands is that you never get revenge on their terms. They always have a way to feel superior to me — they have children, I don't. They're married, I'm not."

By now, Ephron says, she feels beyond her earlier vengefulness while recognizing it won't ever go away entirely and will always be a source of energy. "One of the reasons I was so driven was to get people to notice me," she explains. "But I hope that what

I'm doing at this point in my life I'm doing for myself and not for them. Because I don't want to be friends with them anymore. I don't want them to ask me to dance. I don't want to be them. I know what they're doing, and it's just awful! I want to be me.

"But I still carry around that hopelessly funny fifteen-year-old person who crawls out of me and onto the typewriter keys and in other ways."

Nora looked around the white walls of her apartment as she said this. A typewriter surrounded by paper stacks was in the far room. Then she looked back and grinned.

"Do you know that to this day when the mood seizes me I can do the entire Beverly Hills High School pom-pom routine, even though I was never a pom-pom girl.

"Tiada —

"Tiada —

"Tiada —

"I wrote about that recently in *Esquire*."

Before leaving, I asked Nora Ephron if she thinks she'd be a journalist today had she been more popular in high school. "I doubt it," Nora replied. "I don't think I would have been a writer. Art Buchwald says he's never known a writer with a happy childhood."

The hunger for revenge after high school is like a prisoner's vow: after release time may dull one's appetite, but vengeance is sought anyway to give meaning to past suffering. The vows we made then were desperate. How else could we endure? If today is a misery, what alternative does one have to pledging a better tomorrow?

Rejection in high school just hurts. Snubs cut deeper at that time than any suffered as adults. To soothe the wounds, we could only plot.

The other side will never know how early is planted the dream of revenge, nor how surely planned during adolescence. For those from a small town, this dream can take in not only one's high school, but the entire community surrounding it.

In her novel *Lives of Girls and Women*, Alice Munro describes a plain, literary-minded teenager walking with her male kindred spirit, a scientific sort, and

as we walked over the trestle a car full of people from our class passed underneath, hooting at us, and I did have a vision, as if from outside, of how strange this was — Jerry contemplating and welcoming a future that would annihilate Jubilee and life in it, and I myself planning secretly to turn it into black fable and tie it up in my novel, and the town, the people who really were the town, just hooting car horns — to mock anybody walking, not riding, on a Sunday afternoon — and never knowing what danger they were in from us.

If nothing is more elating for an adolescent than the worship of an entire community, no humiliation cuts deeper than their scorn. Subjected to such degradation, talented refugees like Munro, or Larry McMurtry, or Sinclair Lewis must vanquish not just their high school but the whole town it serves.

In other cases, those hungry for revenge content themselves simply with their school. A young Los Angeles radio producer, seven years escaped from a small high school in Ohio where she felt universally hated, told me she'll return to that school only when they have a special day in her honor. She's working to make it happen.

"The feeling of 'I'm gonna show you' is the foundation of my success so far," the producer explained. "The day's gonna come when I'll return home and they're gonna have a 'Marty Thomas Day.' And I'm gonna say, 'Fuck you!'"

Larry King, a writer, is more limited in focus, though every bit as vengeful. King says he'll be satisfied with nothing less than a written apology from the Class of '46, which he then plans to reject.

In the most focused of cases, a single classmate may be the one against whom revenge is dreamed of, and sometimes achieved. A college vice-president told me with table-banging glee about his quarterback tormentor who now reads gas meters. "Gas meters!" the vice-president exclaimed with a broad grin. "Can you dig it? He's the guy who knocks on my parents' door and asks if he can go down in the basement to read their meter!"

A final dream of retribution is that directed at a teacher. High school teachers seldom appear in this book because they seldom appear in people's memories. An odd inspirational teacher is remembered by some, but just as often a hated excuse of an educator is singled out as a target of vengeance.

When I asked Michael O'Donoghue, formerly with the *Lampoon*, whether he had any desire for revenge, the writer first replied, "No, I don't wanna go back and rub cheese graters over their faces."

Then he thought a moment. "A few people maybe. . . ."

Then he thought a moment more. "There's one vice-principal I'd like to get alone with a cheese grater."

PE teachers in particular loom large in the black schemes of outies. Sam Keen says had he been Stalin, his first purge would have been of high school PE teachers.

Burt Prelutsky has a more particular target: the tennis coach of Fairfax High. Prelutsky is a hard-core outie who writes a column for the *Los Angeles Times* and is not averse to using his column as a tool of revenge. In the case of his tennis coach, he wrote in anguished detail how the guy kept giving second chances to a flashier player named Ralph, even when Prelutsky won their challenge matches. The columnist added that ever since then he hadn't been crazy about guys named Ralph, either.

Burt swore he hadn't meant to include me in that observation the day we met for lunch to discuss his role in the journalists' brigade of our outies' army. He did recall beating Ralph and earning his spot on the team as "not just a physical victory, a game victory, but a victory against hypocrisy and injustice. I beat not just a good player but a coach bending the rules so Ralph could be on the team. And when I got to write that column, I got back at him, the SOB."

Burt Prelutsky is not a large person. After grievances from high school, the rights of short people is one of his favorite column themes. Prelutsky does point out that his 5'7" today is a vast improvement over the 5'1" with which he started high school.

Other than being short, Prelutsky remembers being a klutz in high school, not knowing how to dance, having no dates, and getting just so-so grades. Tennis was his only success. But even there his team nickname was "Boom-Boom," in recognition of a feeble serve.

One of Burt's more vivid high school memories is of getting beat up after sixth period PE. It was raining that day, and everyone was down in the cellar before school taking off their jackets. Some guy stole his buddy's jacket, but Burt chased him down and got the coat back. Later, after PE, the thief jumped Prelutsky and hit him in the kidneys.

"After that," the columnist recalls, "I fantasized waiting with a baseball bat for him to come home on Friday night, or getting him with a zip gun. I used to go to sleep at night envisioning ways to kill him without being found out. A month later he got kicked out of school. I always wish I had killed him. Anyone that shitty doesn't grow up. They just get older."

Burt chewed his hamburger in silence for a moment, staring off into space. Then he mumbled, "I'd still like to kill him. Just thinking about him. . . ."

Then there was only silence.

I don't want to leave you with the impression that Burt Prelutsky is driven only by a dream of revenge, and uses the public record exclusively to settle old scores. In a movie review of *Up the Down Staircase*, the writer even took several paragraphs to throw bouquets at his old high school English teacher, Miss Lamb.

He also turns his column over regularly to fellow outies so they can plead their own cause. Phil Spector, for example, four years before making his first million as a rock 'n' roll magnate, was a classmate of Prelutsky's at Fairfax High. There, the columnist says, Spector was by informal consensus considered "least likely to succeed." Ten years later Spector showed up at his tenth class reunion in a Rolls-Royce with two bodyguards. Prelutsky asked why he'd done so, and reported Spector's reply: "Just to show up — to show them up.

"They all came over and all of a sudden wanted to talk to me. And I asked them to talk to me as much as they had in high school, which was not at all."

Though Prelutsky, like Spector, has been more successful as an adult than as a teenager, what he'd really like to be is a high school football star. "Absolutely," Burt says of this dream. "You can never have the heroics that a high school hero has."

As we finished lunch, our waiter overheard all the talk about high school. Young, with long blond hair over a short red jacket and black pants, the waiter's face lit up as he told us about playing varsity football in Chicago. He was a defensive safety and, at fifteen, the youngest guy on the team. "I beat out an all-conference defensive from the year before for the job," said the waiter. "The coach called me 'Hands' because I could catch anything around.

"If you can believe this — you gotta see the films — the first game I covered a guy 6'3", the second 6'4", third 6'6", fourth 6'4"."

The waiter said he'd graduated high school in 1968 and had been in Los Angeles just five weeks after working restaurants back in Illinois.

Did he miss high school, I wondered? The sports success and all?

"You miss it," he replied, "but you always go on to something else. I'm into Scientology now. That's why I'm out here. To do my higher levels.

"And I'm gonna get a band together."

Burt and I paid and left, shaking our heads, thinking our own thoughts. Later I asked the columnist if he still would trade places with a high school football star. "You bet your A," he replied. "It's a position that has all the privileges of royalty with none of the responsibilities."

Here is the paradox of our war against innies. Outies don't want to win the war. Were we to wipe out the other side, we'd lose our opportunity to join them. And this is what the war is really all about. The outies' struggle against innies could be ended tomorrow by an invitation to become one.

I know my price: a tryout for the basketball team and special postgraduate award of a letter. At the ceremony marking this occasion, I'd want every innie from my class to stand around muttering, "Geez, I never realized what a guy that Keyes really was."

Doug Kenney has a similar dream, the one he had drawn for the *National Lampoon*'s "Gratuitous Wish Fulfillment Department." (See following illustration.)

The greatest frustration of our quest for revenge is that, by high school standards, we can never achieve it. Not even U.S. President can compare with student body president. Yet these are the standards we fight by. Having lost the opportunity for high school glory, we settle for the next best thing: glory as an adult — always with the desperate hope that our classmates will take note.

This is the *real* Myth of Sisyphus, all the outies pushing boulders uphill, muttering "I'll show 'em. They'll see." And hoping as they push that some innie will notice and say, "Hey — why don't you stop pushing that boulder and come sit with us?"

In *Buried Alive*, her perceptive biography of Janis Joplin, Myra Friedman concluded that the rock 'n' roll singer's real reason for going back to her reunion was in the forlorn hope that there might still be time, time to be included. Joplin's single

Doug Kenny's Gratuitous Wish Fulfillment

press conference during the event, Friedman points out, "was full of forgiveness for what, in Janis' adolescence, had surely been unforgivable, and of her emphasis on a willingness to find some grounds for communication with almost anyone, would they have the heart to try the same."

What "started as a mission of revenge," the biographer concludes, "turned to a mission of atonement. . . . The hope for acceptance was burning within her."

Ambivalence, unrequited love, is at the very heart of the outies' struggle against innies. In none of our artful putdowns of ex-jocks are they beyond redemption. Neither Rabbit Angstrom, nor Brick, nor Biff Loman is in any sense a hopeless character. Jim O'Connor is nearly lovable. Even Stradlater, *Catcher in the Rye*'s boorish athlete, is described by Holden Caulfield as "the kind of handsome guy that if your parents saw his picture in your yearbook they'd right away say, 'Who's this boy?'

"He was a very strong guy," Holden tells us. "I'm a very weak guy."

This is the worst of it, the self-doubt that permeates our cause. We write books, and we put down innies in our books, but we also put down ourselves. Between the lines. By implication. A recurring form of American novel focuses on two boyhood friends. One is a flashy athlete. The other is a klutz. The klutz is the narrator. And in such books — *A Separate Peace, The Folded Leaf, Going All the Way* — the narrators are in many ways less lovable, and certainly less self-loving, characters than the jock who befriends them.

Self-doubt is the essence of our struggle. We fight because we must — for pride, for dignity — and for our very survival. But what we really want is to be more like the enemy. We don't hope to vanquish the other side; all we want is a negotiated truce, after which our armies can merge.

But the opportunity for this to happen is eliminated with the turn of a tassel. We can't go back. However long it lives on in our minds, high school technically ends at graduation.

Yet there is one reprieve, a single occasion after high school when it is possible to reunite so innies can forget for a few hours their encore problem and bask in old triumphs while outies can show off new wares. This reprieve is called the high school class reunion.

Re-uning: What Will They Think of Me Now?

You all know how I feel about school reunions. I only attended mine because the alumni secretary promised me all the girls would be obese and it would be a real ego trip for me.

Well she was wrong . . . five people came up to me and said "What are you doing now? I thought you were dead."

— ERMA BOMBECK

Class reunions are commonly thought of as harmless little exercises in nostalgia. They are not. Seeing the old bodies from high school and displaying your own can be among the more traumatic experiences of an adult life. Wilkinson Blades gets closer to the truth in calling class reunions one of the four worst times in life to get a shaving nick.

High school class reunions are a fascinating, widespread, and virtually unstudied American phenomenom. In preparing for this chapter I subscribed to a national clipping service for a month, thinking perhaps to get one or two hundred reunion reports. I got a thousand. Most were for tenth reunions, though there were also a lot of fifths, about the same number of twentieths, a trickle of fiftieths, and one sixtieth gathering.

Society columnists in Tennessee, Oregon, and California commented on the growing volume of reunions in their region. One Californian streaked his tenth reunion, and several older gatherings hired mock streakers. Other items of interest:

— all twenty-two members of the Kingsley, Iowa, Class of '34 showed up at their fortieth reunion wearing glasses.

— at the twentieth reunion of her Alpena High School graduating class in Michigan, a woman won the award for both most children and best-kept figure.

— the chairperson of the 1963-64-65 reunion of Polytechnic High near Fort Worth, Texas, reported: "Our reunion was great — not at all like the class reunions that Erma Bombeck writes about."

Lest I make reunions out to be lighthearted gatherings, let me repeat, they are not. They try to be. Reunions are very grinny affairs, rather like Christmas newsletters: a place to report good news. People without good news to report — the recently divorced, the ill and bereaved, or those tipping scales more than fifty pounds over their weight at graduation — don't usually come to reunions.

Even for those who don't attend, simply receiving a reunion announcement in the mail can be unnerving. As Lois Gould's heroine tells her analyst in *Final Analysis:* "Yesterday I got a reunion announcement. . . . I tore up this notice the instant it arrived. I pretended I never saw it. Someone has made a horrible mistake, I said aloud, as if that rendered it undelivered. I am considering buying a stamp that says ADDRESSEE UNKNOWN, in case it ever happens again."

Those who don't make it can have fantasies nonetheless of how they would *like* to attend their class reunion: landing in a private plane nearby, then casually strolling to the door; driving up in a rented Rolls-Royce; undulating in as the most devastating sex object present; coming in drag.

One friend tells me he will go to a reunion only when he is so famous that nobody will have to ask, "What are you doing now?"

Five

The evening before Billie Thompson's fifth reunion, she and her husband met me for a drink. An effervescent, full-busted brunette, Billie assured me she wasn't very popular at Delmonico High School. Although a cheerleader, Billie said she first got elected on a "weirdo" platform. Then it helped that her boyfriend was captain of the football team.

I asked Billie's husband Frank, a journalist and former singer, if he were worried about the old boyfriend showing up tomorrow. "Naw," Frank responded with a quick grin. "I'm just along for the ride.

"Besides, I'm her only love."

As his wife and I resumed our conversation, Frank played with her yearbook on the table. Finally, he interrupted to say, "Let me see his picture."

"Okay," said Billie, flipping the book's pages. Since cheerleaders' pictures came before those of the football team, she first pointed to herself on the squad. No separate picture was included of her. Billie blamed this on Donna Darnell, her cheerleader enemy who was also on the yearbook staff.

"I wanna see the football captain," Frank reminded her.

"Oh yeah, okay," Billie said, thumbing the pages once more. "I'll find my football captain for you." Reaching the football section she folded these pages flat, then pointed.

Frank squinted at this picture in the bar's dim light. "Yep," he said finally. "Just like I figured. His neck's as wide as his head."

Billie Thompson was nervous about her upcoming reunion. She hadn't received an invitation for some reason, and heard about it only through a friend. The former cheerleader doubted anyone would even remember her name.

"Donna will remember my name though. She'll say 'Billie. How nice.'" Billie folded her hands like an angel praying and affected an insipid grin. "'So glad you could make it. I was on the committee.'"

Then Billie unfolded her hands, and cocked her head belligerently. "And I'll say, 'Oh. Is that why I didn't get an invitation?'"

Though she'd planned to study it that evening, Billie lent me her yearbook where Donna Darnell, well built, blond, and with a big smile, showed up often as Best Personality, Most Popular, Junior Prom Queen, and Most Likely to Succeed.

Donna was on a lot of tongues at the next mornings' reunion

as early-arrivers sucked cans of Coor's and tried to guess who newcomers were beneath beards and maternity dresses. Hardly anyone had seen Donna since graduation but word was around that she'd become an actress and had done some commercials. "She did Glama Gams," one guy was certain. "When they first came out I recognized the legs instantly."

The sky was hazy over a large public park where Delmonico's Class of '70 was reuniting. An early trickle soon became a stream — women in halters and men wearing tank tops. Many carried lawn chairs and Colonel Sanders' buckets. Some brought babies.

Besides Donna they discussed the classmate who'd become a Playmate under an assumed name, one who was thought to be making porno movies, and another who'd hiked the entire Appalachian trail.

Some comments overheard:

"My husband didn't want to come back. He said it would make him feel old."

"I been going with Emily almost two years next month. Shit, I'm getting old."

"I guess I could have got a bail bondsman, but it was too much hassle."

"I'm not gonna lie for Don. She's a dog."

Billie arrived late and was quickly absorbed by a crowd buzzing around the middle picnic table. A quieter ring of people sat off to one side, in small clumps under the shade of trees. Billie looked around when I asked why people sorted them-selves out this way, then replied, "Well, there's a group and a fringe. People who were like your second-string friends. Some-one, when you didn't have anyone else, to have lunch with that day."

Billie stood by her friend Roberta, who had been head cheer-leader. Roberta added her opinion that some people sat off to the side "because they were that way in high school." Then she giggled into her hand saying, "Oh, that's so catty."

I joined a guy eating bologna sandwiches at a side table, kept company only by his wife. Why wasn't he part of any crowd at the reunion? I asked. "I guess because I wasn't part of any crowd in high school" was the reply. After looking around the guy observed, "Seems like the people who were together then are together now."

Do you wish you were mingling more?

"No," he replied. "No, not really. It's comfortable to say the normal 'Hi' that existed five years ago."

Then why come at all? (He'd driven two hours.)

The guy held his sandwich, pondered a moment, then grinned. "That really is an interesting question based on what I've just said. I haven't really thought about it.

"When the thing came in the mail I just knew I wanted to come is all."

A buzz erupted over by the inner table. Donna Darnell had arrived. I went over and peered through the hive of people surrounding her like reporters at a press conference. Where are you living now, Donna? they asked. We heard you were acting. Are you married, Donna?

"Well, that's my husband there," she replied pointing to a slight guy with thinning hair. "Right now he's in sales, in the fire extinguisher business. We've moved four times — Seattle, Denver, Boise, Cincinnati. Cincinnati's probably where we'll end up. Either that or Cleveland."

Fuller than in her yearbook picture, Donna Darnell wore shorts and a brief halter. Under long straight hair her eyes were laced with jagged red lines. Donna seemed on edge, but looked right at me when I asked how it felt to be back. "It's really weird," she said. "I can't stand it." Donna glanced around, then back at me, and touching my arm lightly whispered, "We had lunch down at that burger stand. I was so worried about coming up here."

She'd gone to college for a time, then left to act and do commercials, which she still did, but less often. Donna planned to give up acting entirely if they moved to Cincinnati. She was thinking about getting into retailing.

She didn't feel that changed from high school, Donna said, "just channeled differently."

Before she could explain what this meant, Donna was whisked off by three guys who wanted a word with her in private.

As Frisbees flew overhead and babies cried, while giggling women poked men in the ribs, Frank Thompson left his wife's reunion with me. Walking to town for hamburgers, we talked about Frank's tenth reunion, which by coincidence was that night. Though he had things to strut (having sung professionally, and now being a featured writer for his newspaper), Frank really didn't feel like attending. "My feeling is that my life's been so much better since high school," he explained while we walked, "that I don't want to go back and relive that bad stuff."

On the other hand, Frank thought maybe he ought to be present to defend himself. He didn't want to be remembered as he was then, skinny and with bad teeth. Maybe he should return to show off the thirty new pounds and dental work, let people know he'd changed. But as his cheeseburger sizzled on the grill Frank wasn't so sure. "You know, there's always the possibility that if you go back people might find you exactly the way you were then."

Ten

Though Frank Thompson didn't attend his tenth reunion, I did — promising to defend him against slurs. (I heard none.)

A few days before this reunion, of Los Ricos High School's Class of '65, the planning committee met to go over last-minute details.

"Is anyone having their hair done?" asked one of the four women present.

"No!" all said in unison.

124

They laughed. "God," said one. "We've really gone down-hill."

The table at which they sat was strewn with red booklets titled Los Ricos — '65–'75. In front of the chairperson, who had been yearbook editor, were several neatly typed pages of names. Using old phone books and city directories, the committee had spent hundreds of hours tracing classmates, most successfully through their parents. They were least successful in attracting class leaders. No cheerleader was coming to the reunion and only one of two student body presidents. His wife was producing him under protest.

One class officer still in town hadn't even responded to the initial questionnaire.

"People see her," a committee member explained, "but she just doesn't want to see people from high school."

On the other hand a WAVE captain who hadn't been that active in high school was flying in from Spain, and the shortest guy in the class was coming from Alaska where he was now a tall psychologist.

"Lois wrote from Israel that she wanted to come," the leader told the group. "But her husband's in antiaircraft and can't leave."

"I saw Julie Garvin at the bank," said a member. "She wanted to bring her kids."

"To a reunion?"

"Well, that's her big thing in life."

The group wrapped favors in silence for a time — a packet of peanuts, a ballpoint pen, a box of matches, and an Air California olive pick. Then one said, "Hey, you know, unless you guys have definite people you want to sit with, it might be nice to sit together at a table."

This suggestion was met with silence. Finally the silence was broken by a discussion of who was likely to sit with whom at the reunion.

"Well, I think it'd be nice if we sat with each other," the first woman persisted. "After working so hard together on this thing."

There was another pause before the chairwoman finally said, "Yeah. Yeah."

"Let's just play it by ear," one of the others suggested.

"Well, if a table started," said the original woman, "we could reserve it while we're out running around."

The committee sat together at the registration table the night of the reunion. Before them a long line of tense faces signed in.

One couple registered, then surveyed the hotel banquet room uncertainly, not seeming to know whether they should enter. "Would it help to see this?" asked a committee member, holding out the reunion list. "You could see who's here and who you'd like to sit with."

Ignoring this suggestion, the couple continued to look inside uncertainly. Then the guy's face lit up. "There's Roland," he said, pointing. "We'll go sit with him!"

The couple walked off, leaving the committee member holding her list.

People greeted each other by asking what they were doing. "Computers," they answered, or "banking" or "law." "Very good," they replied, "That's very good." Most women wore floor-length gowns, and the men tended to suit and tie. One guy at the bar wore a lime green leisure suit, pinched at the waist, with a white Panama hat topping it off.

What's he do? I whispered to the committee.

"He's a chiropractor," one whispered back.

Any good?

"I don't think I'd want to go to him."

Maybe he's good with his hands.

"Well, he used to be."

After a nondescript meal of smothered steak, and an unsuccessful attempt to get people's attention for awards, a country rock band began to play. Reuners stretched to their feet. Men brushed off their pants. Women adjusted the tops of their gowns. Then "Angel Baby" was played and the floor filled with cheek-to-cheek couples. Women not dancing paced the perimeter, clutching their handbags. A balding man in white shoes asked two women sitting alone if either would like to dance. Each said no in turn. After their suitor walked off the two brought their heads together with whispers and a giggle.

In one corner a man sat alone studiously examining the red reunion directory.

As the band swung into "Whole Lotta Shakin' Goin' On," and the floor bounced with rock 'n' rollers, one of the nondancers seemed happy to escape with me to a fire landing. This was Craig Halverson, formerly fall student body president of the Class of '65. Now bearded under rimless glasses, Halverson told me his wife was more eager than he to come to their reunion. She had been the exchange student from Ecuador his senior year. Five years later they remet and married while he was traveling in Central America after a Peace Corps tour in Honduras. Halverson said this experience, and four years of college in the East, had changed him fundamentally from the person he'd been in high school.

"I was the all-American boy image," he explained. "Active, athletic. I guess I remember that favorably. But you get categorized in high school. Later you carve out a new image."

In college Halverson did not run for office. He'd had his fill. "I guess I sort of enjoyed being a student leader in high school," he said, "making decisions such as we made. Maybe it was sort of an ego thing and I don't need that now."

How does it feel being back?

"I guess a lot of people knew and liked me," Halverson speculated. "A lot more people know me tonight than I know."

But it all seemed a world ago, and the reunion was not an occasion he'd have come to without his wife's arm-twisting. Now studying environmental science in graduate school, Halverson felt estranged from classmates who are "more into the

127

straight "American thing." The one guy Craig thought he might like to have seen was his counterpart, the spring student body president. When last heard from, this guy was in college being revolutionary. But that was years ago.

As Halverson told me this, a couple walked onto the fire landing and started making out unself-consciously, then grinding their bodies together against the brick wall. Strains of "Johnny B. Goode" could be heard inside the banquet hall. Halverson went back and I went home.

Twenty

When her twentieth reunion announcement arrived, Sandy Flax was not at all sure she wanted to go. "I'm getting in moods about it," Sandy explained as we sat in her backyard one summer afternoon five days before the reunion was to convene. "I'm depressed thinking about going back — kind of nervous and teary."

Sandy normally has a big, winning smile that she displays often. Her grin is the kind that makes you feel you must be doing something right. With dark hair beginning to be brushed by gray, she retains the enthusiasm of a head cheerleader, football queen, and class president. In 1955, at Rocky Mountain High School, Sandy had been all three.

But in her afternoon's mood, two decades later, Sandy realized that she really didn't value that high school girl. Though giving herself credit for a nice smile, Sandy felt she overused this in her eagerness to be liked.

Then there was "The Set," the top girls' crowd, where Sandy felt plainest of the eighteen members and uncertain if she should belong at all. "I think about how cliquish everything was in that school," she explained, "and I don't want to be reminded of being in that big clique."

But even as she was put off, the former cheerleader was tempted by some memories of high school. Sandy loved making up cheers and planning pep rallies. Some friendships she's kept up till the present. Being selected Most Outstanding Senior Girl was a thrill, as was having the most activities listed under her yearbook picture. Sandy's life at home was painful, and in many ways high school doubled as a family.

When I asked how classmates would probably describe her, Sandy replied without hesitating, "Oh, she's the friendliest girl in the school. The only really friendly girl in the clique, the only one who'll talk to you in the hall, won't snub you. She's really popular.

"At the same time if you were talking to one of the guys, he'd say 'She's a prude. A professional virgin. But one of us'll get her yet.'" Sandy flashed her grin.

"You see," she continued, folding hands around her knees, "when I was in high school I was Miss Priss. I wouldn't go out and pet. A professional virgin." Sandy smiled, and ran her tongue around her lips. "A French kiss was really big business for me my senior year."

Then the smile faded. "But if I go back, when people say, 'Are you married?' how do I explain? Part of me wants to say, 'I was married ten years. I didn't stay a professional virgin. I'm not an old maid.'"

Sandy looked at me imploringly. Then she laughed. "Hal says tell 'em you're sleeping with your psychotherapist.

"Hal says now maybe I can get some of the action I didn't get then."

Hal is Hal Shields, a psychologist and the man Sandy has been living with for over three years. After teaching high school for most of the decade she was married, within three years Sandy got a divorce, left her job, moved in with Hal and entered a Ph.D. program. Explaining all these changes in the two-minute conversations of a reunion didn't seem possible. Especially since Hal couldn't go and the man at her side would be neither husband nor lover but some young guy writing a book about high school memories. Very perplexing.

Then there was the whole problem of how to dress, and how to present herself.

"Part of me," she explained, "wants to be sexy as hell — go in a low-cut dress and have people say 'Little Sandy! Look at that!'

"Part of me wants to go back as a graduate student, thoughtful and intellectual.

"But why do I have to contrive?"

Sandy played with her foot and looked off past the sun, then back at me with a restrained smile. "You know, I don't really want to go back, now that I think about all this."

But Sandy had already made plane reservations. And Gail, her best friend from high school, was expecting us. So by now it seemed less trouble to go than cancel.

The morning we left, Sandy seemed light, restored to her usual bouyancy. She carried only a clipboard, saying Gail would lend her an outfit. This struck me as remarkable daring.

In the airport we killed time by looking over magazines on the rack. Sandy flipped the pages of *MS* and started to take it to the cashier. Then she returned and put *MS* back on the shelf. "I don't wanna walk in with that, like I'm expected to," she explained, "and have people say, 'Ten years ago you would have been reading *Psychology Today*.'"

As we headed for the plane gate, Sandy took out a pack of Trident and, putting a stick in her mouth, told me how her mother used to say only cheap girls chewed gum. So Sandy would go alone to her bedroom to chew and pop and crack gum all she wanted. "Also, when I'd go out with my girlfriends, the first thing we'd do would be to take out our gum and start cracking." As she said this, Sandy popped her Trident and swung her hips freely during our long traverse of the airport's concourse.

Seated on the plane Sandy put a thumb beneath the collar of her blouse and showed me a round silver pin she was wearing. "When I was going through this box of pins from high school there was this pin in it, Brad — hey, see, I called you Brad — Gail's husband — there was this round pin like we used to wear in high school, so I thought I'd wear it.

"Gail looked like Deborah Paget. Rita Pillsbury, who was head cheerleader before me, was also really gorgeous. She looked like Elizabeth Taylor."

As the skyline of her home city grew visible out the window, Sandy's talk grew nonstop, a torrent of names, dates, and events from high school told partly to me, partly to the window. She kept calling me Brad.

"I'm intimidated by Brad. He was the basketball captain a year ahead of us, and only went out with the most gorgeous girls. Tonight there'll probably be a lot of talk about the three girls he went out with — Gail (who won), Ellen Heming (a Catholic, she married a Catholic pharmacist and has eight kids or so), and Betty Turetsky (who was prom queen when I was prom princess). Gail was a football princess when I was football queen. When I got to be football queen I felt, 'Well, Gail should have gotten it because Gail is really beautiful. I'm just friendly.' "

Gail Burton remains a darkly attractive woman. Lounging by their home's pool in a bikini and dark glasses when we arrived, she fell immediately to chattering with her old friend about a prereunion cocktail party the night before where everyone had been asking about Sandy. Gail's eyes have gone faster than her body, and she told us about panicking whenever an old classmate approached — before the letters of a name tag came into focus.

As the two friends talked, scanning the reunion roster, classmates' names reeled off their tongues like a teacher taking attendance.

"Here's Ike Purcell. He's now about 6′4″ with a neck about a foot long. He used to be such a bookworm, and a little mouse.

"There's Rita Pillsbury. Is she gonna be there?"

"Yeah."

"Oh."

"Warren Daniels was there, the creep. He threw up all over me once at the Pines Drive-In. I saw him last night and that was all I could think of." The two women giggled.

Then Sandy's head jerked up from the booklet. "I wonder if people are reading our descriptions and laughing at us?"

Brad Burton joined us, tall and movie-star handsome with a full head of dark hair and the easy smile of someone used to being liked.

"Pete Dubois was there last night," he told Sandy. "They had him cut the cake."

For my benefit the story of Pete Dubois was reviewed, Rocky Mountain's star quarterback who later was blinded in an auto accident. Brad then described the near-fight at last night's cocktail party. A woman had tried to walk out on her husband. He grabbed her arm and created a scene. The reunion chairman tried to be nice, but the husband was belligerent. He was a florist. Twenty minutes later, when the couple starting arguing again, the chairman sent them packing. "Go tiptoe through your tulips!" he yelled as they left.

"You know, you should make a speech tonight, Sandy," said Brad. Sandy looked uneasy at the thought.

"Why?" she asked.

"Well, you were president," Brad replied. "You gotta do your duty." He grinned. "You could turn the reunion into an encounter session. Get people to talk about what they're really feeling."

Sandy giggled. She looked mortified at the thought.

The two women went off to try on outfits, and Brad to get dressed, leaving me alone with the Burtons' daughter Terry. Terry said the whole reunion weekend had been weird for her because she just could not picture her mother in high school, especially as a Peppette. I asked if she'd seen her mother's yearbook picture as a Peppette. "Yeah," Terry replied, "but it's not even her to me."

Terry showed me her own annual, which included lots of color pictures and a section called "Energy Crisis Alters Life-Style." Double-page spreads were devoted both to the Afro Queen and King and the Junior Prom Court, which included Terry in a low-cut white gown. Terry had just finished passing the yearbook around for signatures. Her mom read some and found them insipid. Then Gail dug out her own yearbook to compare inscriptions. There was little difference.

Terry was quite interested in the book I was writing, and wanted to know if Raquel Welch had been a cheerleader. I said she had been.

"Figures," said Terry.

Are you a cheerleader?

"No."

Is making cheerleader still a big deal?

"Oh sure," Terry replied. "If you're not a cheerleader, you're nobody."

Sandy rejoined us, carrying a Fresca, explaining that on doctor's orders she can't drink alcohol.

"But I told Ralph if I don't drink people will say [Brad chimed in] 'Same old Sandy! Hasn't changed in twenty years.' "

"Same old Sandy," added Gail, who just walked in wearing white hair rollers. "Won't drink and keeps her legs crossed."

Sitting in a chair, sucking on her Fresca, Sandy kicked her legs up and whooped, "Won't drink and keeps her legs crossed!"

At the reunion that night, people seemed delighted to see Sandy, and she moved among them easily. When her classmates asked, as they always did, Sandy said no, she wasn't married now, but yes, she had been married for ten years. No, she sometimes added, the man she'd mentioned in the reunion book-let wasn't there, but yes, she did have a friend here, Ralph Keyes. And flashing her hundred-watt smile, Sandy left it at that. No, she wasn't working now, but yes, she had worked — for a decade teaching high school. Now, she added if there was time, she was studying for a Ph.D. in psychology.

The groups Sandy joined usually swelled with her presence and deflated when she left. Pete Dubois's face brightened when he heard Sandy's voice next to him. Groping for her waist with his arm, Dubois said to those around, "Ah, 'Fiery Flax, adds flame to your game.' " Grinning, he explained, "That's the slogan we used when Sandy ran for cheerleader."

The reunion split up by crowd for supper, a center table comprising Dubois, the football team captain, and assorted other members of the leading crowd. The basketball coach sat with them. Sandy and I sat one table over, wondering where Brad and Gail were. They said they'd be late and told us to save them seats. The Burtons' absence worried me. I didn't want to get stuck sitting with some creeps we didn't know. The only other person at our table was a bald-headed guy in an olive jumpsuit who sat smoking a cigarette and looking uncomfortable. Finally Brad and Gail arrived and to my relief the jumpsuited guy moved. As we ate supper and gossiped about people nearby, it dawned on me that for once in my life I felt like an innie. Other people in the center were sharply visible, but I had only a vague notion of who was on the periphery. The worst thing was that it felt comfortable. Not good, but comfortable, as if that's the way things were meant to be.

After supper, as the band struck up "String of Pearls" and couples rose to dance, a classmate named Duke joined our table. Putting his arm around Sandy, he muttered in her ear: "Sure wish I were here alone.

"Some of these broads here by themselves need taking care of."

Sandy was depressed when she stumbled into the kitchen for coffee the next morning. She'd laid in bed the night before feeling middle-aged for the first time. Seeing so many people last seen as teenagers. Most seemed like caricatures of the high school kids they once had been. But if this were true about them to her, it must be true of her to them. The thought was most disturbing, and Sandy's voice grew husky as she told me about it.

But after breakfast, and some huddled giggling with Gail about the previous evening's affairs, Sandy's voice crept back out of her throat. She whispered to Gail about Duke with both aghast and pleasure.

While taking me to the airport (I had to leave early), the two women discussed one of the reunion's organizers, a girl frozen out by The Set. She still lived in town, and Gail felt uncomfortable when they ran into each other. The woman seemed to have something to prove. "It seems like she still carries a lot of bad memories around from high school," Gail observed. "Things I forgot about years ago."

After I left, there was a postreunion party that Sandy told me about when she got home. Duke was there and still flirting with her, saying that even though he was married, he sure believed in variety.

"And people kept saying, 'What's she do? Does Sandy work?'

"So Duke would answer [here she giggled], 'Listen, with the setup she's got, Sandy doesn't have to work.'"

Thirty

At a restaurant in the Delaware Valley, small sheets of colored paper lay at each table setting inside the banquet hall. On these sheets was typed:

(Sung to the tune of "Bye, Bye, Blackbird")

> *Who are you — and who am I?*
> *We're the gang from Poly High!*
> *Hello, Classmates.*
>
> *Talk it up, and move about,*
> *Relax, and let it all hang out!*
> *Hello, Classmates.*

Time was when we lived and loved with vigor;
Now we've lost our hair, our youth, and figure!

Reminisce your cares away,
Shake a hand, smile and say
Classmate, Hello.

At a sparsely populated table near the restrooms, one last, late arrival sat down next to me. The newcomer had no name tag but said her name was Kitty. Wearing a floor-length black gown with a pearl choker, Kitty batted her eyelashes and laughed a lot while telling me she'd originally decided not to come, but changed her mind at the last minute when other plans fell through. "It's very difficult for a person alone to walk into a mixed gathering like this," Kitty explained between glances at the crowd. "It's like going to a cocktail party where husbands or fiancés are supposed to get your drink for you. I'm of the era where a woman didn't do these things for herself. I like to be fussed over. It's one of the nice things about being a woman." Kitty fluttered her lashes once more and smiled at me full force, then looked out over the clumps of people milling among the tables. "You know," she finally said, "I should have worn the peasant blouse that I got in Peru. I didn't even think."

Kitty told me her recent trip to Peru was one of the many she'd taken since her husband died several years ago. An executive secretary, she also plays the harp at churches on the weekend. This was how Kitty remembers being perceived most clearly in high school: as a harpist.

A heavy-set woman lumbering out of the ladies' room stopped by our table. "Hi," she said to my dinner partner. "You're Kitty, the other harpist."

Kitty nodded, with a smile, saying "And your name is . . ." She peered at the woman's name tag. "Gwen."

After the woman left I asked Kitty if it weren't unfair of her not to wear a name tag. "Oh, but it's so much more interesting not to wear a tag," she replied, "more . . . adventurous."

A man passed on his way to the men's room and Kitty leaned over to whisper "I know that guy. He used to be so handsome." She primped her hair and smiled. "I've picked the right spot to sit — by the men's room." Kitty pushed my arm and laughed. Then she pointed to a man at the next table. "Bob Patterson there was always nice to me and I remember. I guess I was sort of aloof. A couple of guys like him went out of their way to be nice to me, and I remember."

After supper there was respectful silence while a tall clergyman who was once president of this class led a prayer. But buzzing began as the emcee took over, announcing that Geritol was available from Sol Weiss at a half-dollar a glass. Hardly anyone sang along to the typed song on our sheets. Finally the band struck up "Over the Rainbow," and with visible relief one tide of people rose to dance while another, including my dinner partner, made for the restrooms.

Wandering across the hall, I overheard a man whisper to the woman beside him, "Two people have become pregnant tonight."

"No," she replied. "Two people have been offered the opportunity to become pregnant."

At a lively table near the band, one of the men explained that this group was mostly Jewish and had stayed close since high school. "Though with very little intramural hanky-panky," he whispered, "which is surprising."

The man's wife, Norma, pointed to a bald-headed man across the table. "I used to date Sol," she said.

"She was good, too," said Sol.

A guy named Rudy then walked up and joined the conversation. Short, well groomed, and nervously gregarious, Rudy told the table that the only reason he was still single was because Norma had jilted him in high school. Norma's husband looked uncomfortable. "That's some wife you got there," Rudy said grabbing his shoulder. "The only reason I didn't go out with Norma was because she's Jewish and I'm Catholic."

I asked Rudy how it felt to be single at a thirtieth reunion. "Listen," he replied, moving his face close to mine, "I'm not unhappy.

"Hey, I'm not lonesome or anything. I did a half-million dollars' worth of sales in the last six months. I just got a commission check for twenty-three thousand dollars. I doubled my salary in the last year. I'm two and a half years ahead of myself on draws.

"I don't look so bad." Rudy held out the lapel of his gray plaid suit. "A hundred-and-ninety-five-dollar suit." Then he patted his trimmed dark hair and whispered. "I use a little Clairol. But at least I've got a head of hair to use it on. If the women do it, why can't the men?

"Listen," Rudy said, turning to Norma and her husband. "How many times you been to Europe?"

"I've been to Las Vegas three times," Norma replied weakly.

Rudy held up fingers on both hands.

"Seven. I've been to Europe seven times."

As the band played "I've Got You Under My Skin," I returned to our table. Kitty was sitting there by herself, tapping the time and singing along. "It's lovely!" she exclaimed, grinning and clapping to the music. "You know you're so deprived not to have grown up with Cole Porter. Best music ever." Kitty touched my arm.

"You know really, I came to listen to the music."

A curly-haired man in a tan leisure suit danced by with a good-looking brunette. "There's Vic Leone," Kitty whispered. "He used to be a state something-or-other."

"We double-dated to the senior prom."

Then the band struck up "Alley Cat," and a group dance started. Kitty led me into this, but I didn't do too well. After it was over she said, "Come circulate with me. It gives me more courage." As we toured the room Kitty was greeted enthusiastically by groups of people and was enthusiastic back. Before lingering with some people who had been in an operetta with her, she whispered in my ear, "Don't go away now."

But I did, working my way over to where Victor Leone sat. On the table before him lay a heavy ceramic plate. This read: POLYTECHNIC HIGH SCHOOL 30-YEAR REUNION CLASS OF 1945.

"I told my wife she'd better feed me off this plate every day," Leone said, tapping the plate. "I'm proud of this."

A cheerful Ed Muskie in miniature, Vic Leone says the primary appeal of a class reunion is to see how people have turned out. And how you've done in comparison. "I think I'm in pretty good shape," he said, surveying the room, "though no better than ninety-nine percent of the others." Leone brushed his temples. "I have gray hair, but I don't use anything for it."

Now head of a private firm, Vic Leone was prominent for several years in his state's legislature before serving a term as state treasurer. When he comes back to reunions, Leone is always amazed at how many people seem to remember him. He recalls being memorable for nothing in high school, a 111-pound nonentity who worked after school and came only to class. Ticking off on his fingers, Leone told me "I was not the class president; I was not on the football or basketball team; I was not a leader in high school at all. No fond memories of ninety-yard runbacks, or debating points or anything. None of that. Just no heavy memories of high school at all."

Then why come back?

Leone looked at me for a few moments, his smiling mouth held open. Finally he said, "It's an ego trip, I guess. Over the years I've maintained myself. I'm in fairly good shape. I like to see how I compare."

Leone obviously compares well, and he has a theory about why. His theory is that you needn't be in later life who you once were in high school. "In fact," the ex-legislator feels, "you're better off not being that." Leone explains that his political colleagues rarely were people who showed promise in high school. He could think of only one member of the legislature in all his time there who seemed like a jock. More were like Nixon, Leone told me, hustlers and pushers to whom things didn't come easily, compared with someone like Ford.

"Ford," Leone thinks, "was propelled not because he has charisma or anything, but because he was in the right place at the right time. But I don't think Ford's too smart. I think that's characteristic of a jock. The only thing he can demonstrate is that he's sincere. It's a typical case of a jock propelled into politics.

"I have to be honest. I resent guys like that."

Did you envy such people at the time?

Leone chewed on the question, then replied, "Well, I'd be less than honest if I said I wasn't envious. Everybody wants the approval and adulation of his peers. But I see the heroes of my class and they're telephone linemen. Guys who heard the roars in high school are now carrying telephone poles, carrying those heavy wires and things." He arched his arm as if carrying a big spool. "It doesn't come easy anymore. They don't know how to hustle. They become cops and firemen and things. A couple of our football players are cops, a couple firemen. Nothing wrong with being a cop or fireman, but it's limited. And they don't have nearly the income I do now.

"But I didn't get the adulation at the time."

Do you enjoy getting it now?

Leone grinned. "I love it. Sure. I like to be known. I like not to be just another person, to get a better table at a restaurant." As he told me this, Leone's hands waved the air, his eyes sparkled, and his mouth smiled in a debonaire way.

"Sure. I love it."

Kitty walked by, looking around the room, and when she saw me came over to ask where I'd been. Her feelings were hurt that I'd been ignoring her. Going to the floor, we danced the last three numbers. It felt like people were paying us an inordinate amount of attention, particularly a group of women who sat unescorted at a table near the dance floor. But Kitty seemed to enjoy the notoriety.

As the band packed up its instruments, a group in one corner kept singing and doing old cheers. On the dais two of the star football players were talking loudly. "Remember when we used to line up in the huddle and say . . ."

"Hey, Tom!"

"And then we wouldn't tell him the play!" They roared with laughter.

As I held one last conversation with a surgeon who said she'd been on the honor roll but would rather have been at the prom, Kitty hovered nearby, waiting for me to walk her to her car as I'd promised. But the room almost emptied and I was still talking. Finally, with her coat on and buttoned, Kitty brought me some notepads I'd left at our table, and walked off by herself.

Forty

As I stood at the bar, watching and listening, the woman before me said to another, "I told my beauty operator today, 'You've got a problem. You've gotta take forty-four years off my life.'

"She said, 'I don't think I can.' "

To the side a white-haired man clutched a white-haired woman after she shrieked with delight upon seeing him. Then he pulled out his glasses and put them on to read her name tag.

"You're my girl when she ain't around," said a balding man clutching a petite gray-haired woman, and gesturing at the woman to his side.

"You had your chance," said the woman in his embrace. "You had your chance and you blew it. You did too. Ask him. You blew it."

All three laughed, rather a little too heartily.

This reunion had begun as a fortieth for the Haywood High

School Class of '35. But others asked to come and the gathering was now all-class. Wigs seemed more common, or at least more apparent, at this reunion than at any I'd yet attended. Most natural hair was gray and held tightly in severe permanents.

Beside me at the bar, one such woman, with friendly lines covering her face, said she could tell I didn't belong there. I was just too damned young. Conceding the point, I asked how she could tell who did belong.

"Well, after you look at the tag," replied the woman, "you recognize some facial features and then maybe you remember something you did with that person." Nudging my arm, she took a last swallow from her drink, winked and added before walking off, "Maybe you'd better not put that in your book."

Sitting next to me at supper was Rae from the Class of '40. Delicately boned under frosted brown hair, Rae was a former cheerleader. Tonight she was alone because her husband didn't feel well. Rae said the most interesting thing to happen to her in the evening so far was meeting her date to the senior prom. The boy she'd dated just before getting married was also at the re-union. Telling me about seeing him, Rae's face lit up. "It was thrilling," she said. "It really was."

Her date to the prom was a little fuzzier in Rae's memory. "I remember him," she explained, "but I didn't remember I went to the prom with him. Obviously I wasn't in love with him, or I would have remembered."

And the other guy?

Rae's face brightened once again. "The other one, yeah! I haven't got over it yet."

After supper people stood as their class year was called. Representatives were there from the classes of '25 to '58.

I asked Rae if her old beau stood up with his class.

She nodded with a smile. "Yeah. He stood up." Her smile broadened. "I happened to notice."

Do you think he'll ask you to dance?

"I doubt it. He just had an operation for phlebitis."

Rae looked off around the room, where couples had begun dancing to swing music from a small band, then took my arm and pointed discreetly. "This is the fella," she whispered. A slim, distinguished-looking gentleman with wavy graying hair and a trimmed moustache walked beyond her finger. He limped and walked slowly with the aid of a wooden cane.

As Rae got up to join him, a crew-cut man wearing an American Airlines tieclip danced by with his wife and asked what I was doing. When I explained, the man said, "Well, I just saw the first little gal I went out with in high school. I shoulda married her." His wife yelped, and the guy slapped her behind. "She's gone home. She's married to a drunk."

Rae returned in the company of both her old beau and her prom date. A heavy-set red-faced man, her prom date stood by mopping his face with a handkerchief as Rae clutched the old beau's hand and smiled into his moustache. Then she joined her ex-date on the dance floor. As they whirled off, the old beau sat and watched, hands resting on his cane.

After a few dances, some fast, some slow, Rae left the floor and walked over to join her old beau at the distant table to which he'd moved. There they sat for the rest of the evening, with heads bent close together.

Well past midnight, Rae returned to collect her things from our table before leaving. She said that for her the reunion had been great. "I've had so much fun."

Was it good seeing your old beau?

Rae looked me over cautiously, then replied, "Yes. Both of them. The one I went to the prom with, and the one I almost married."

Doesn't it feel a bit dangerous?

"No. Not when they're married and everything.

"You see we grew up together, and knew each other since we were little." She put her hand down almost to the floor. "We knew each other's brothers and sisters. We went to the same church.

"It's nice to catch up."

Rae gave me a pleasant smile and walked off.

Fifty

A small patch of grass has replaced the old Brigham Township High School building, which burned to the ground nearly ten years ago. In this park one sunny day before Easter, heads of white hair milled slowly about, peppered by dark wigs, polished by a few bald heads, and dignified with a felt hat or two.

One group gathered around a picnic table that was cluttered with large glossy photos. The photos were of plays and operettas put on by the Class of '25. Hands from the crowd reached out to run gnarled fingers over young faces in the blown-up pictures.

The voice behind one finger moving from face to face murmured, "Percy's gone. Willet's gone. Tucker's gone."

"Charlie Tucker was such a handsome guy," one woman whispered to another.

"Larrabee was stabbed in Mexico," mumbled one of the picture pointers.

Then a finger darted from the crowd to stab a photograph as a voice cried, "Hey! That's me right there!"

Seated to one side, wearing glasses under a brown hat, was Roger Aiken. Fifty years before Aiken was president of this class. Sitting down beside him, I asked what he'd been doing for the past half-century.

"Oh," Aiken replied slowly. "I taught school. I taught school forty years to get this pen." He showed me his pen — a gold Cross ballpoint with black trim.

I asked how it felt to be among high school classmates after all this time. Aiken looked around for a time before responding, "Oh, it's kind of strange to see how people change. Now with me, I feel about the same because I live with myself every day. But I see big changes in many, especially the ones who moved away. The ones here change gradually."

Roger Aiken has lived all his life on the plot of ground his father homesteaded. For the past four decades, his wife has lived there with him. Aiken told me that although she had gone to another school, one or two couples in his class did marry. But looking around he couldn't see any. Aiken thought, "Maybe they died or something."

After their picnic and time to rest up, this group toured the new Brigham Township High School — a sprawling concrete plant outside of town that accommodates 3,000 students and several hundred cars.

Led by Brigham's principal, the tour wound slowly along the tunnels of hallways, in and out of a cavernous library, and through laboratories shiny with chrome. Their last stop was at the gym — as big as a small airport — and with room for three full-court basketball games at once. The old high school had a crackerbox of a gym, where the walls were out of bounds and a shot arched too high would bounce off the ceiling. Shuffling about just inside this cathedral of a room, the reuners muttered in hushed tones.

As we left, a woman accosted the superintendent to tell him she'd been born fifty years too soon.

"Well, I think it's beautiful," said another woman walking beside her, "But I liked our eighteen-room place better."

"It was smaller," the first woman agreed. "But we knew everyone."

"This new high school," a bald-headed guy named Harold was saying afterward, "let's see, three thousand students divided by four — seven hundred and fifty in a class. I bet they won't have a fifty-year reunion. They won't have the togetherness."

While others got ready for the banquet that night, Harold Van Zant and Stu Thornton, the reunion's organizers, made last-minute preparations in Thornton's insurance office.

"I was particularly happy that the gals looked so nice today," observed Thornton, who has a salt-and-pepper moustache.

"Some of these gals were kind of quiet and shy in high school. But now their appearance is very good. They look right good."

"They were also very friendly," added Harold.

"We'd give each other a kiss to break the ice. Now Olivia, I used to think, was my girlfriend, but it turns out she wasn't."

The two chuckled.

Olivia was at my table that night, an extra table put out in the hallway because so many more people than expected attended their fiftieth reunion's banquet. Tightly-corseted, Olivia had dark hair pulled back behind a full face.

"Don't you remember me?" she asked a lawyer sitting across the table.

"Sure I do," the lawyer replied. "But you were way out of my class."

A latecomer was put out in the hallway with us, Nellie Riley, whose red hair was piled high in a bun over granny glasses. Nellie explained that her bus from Kansas City broke down on the way and she'd just now arrived. Wearing a long colonial skirt and simple white blouse over her ample bosom, Mrs. Riley was surprisingly seductive for a grandmother pushing seventy. She had a way of peering over her glasses with an elusive smile.

As Nellie darted glances around the motel banquet room, I asked if this were a group of people among whom she'd felt popular. Her eyes examined mine for a moment before she replied without flinching, "No, I was a wallflower." Nellie then gave me a saucy look, and took a beat before adding, "In other words, I didn't always have my program filled for all the dances."

But then at least it was partly filled.

Mrs. Riley giggled. "Well I was partly a wallflower at least."

Is it uncomfortable being back?

"Not yet," said Nellie with her sweet and pungent smile. "I haven't been snubbed yet."

Since Brigham is a Mormon community, there was no drinking or dancing after supper; only talk of the past. Roger Aiken ("He always had a touch of greatness about him," Nellie told me) began the program by talking about fallen members of the Class of '25, choosing to focus symbolically on their first casualty: a popular girl who died of pneumonia during her senior year. "That was a lesson to us then," Aiken told his hushed listeners. "Now we're all used to that problem, and must look forward to it."

Each of the forty class members present then stood to tell briefly what they'd been up to for the last fifty years — work, spouse, children, grandchildren, hernias, arthritis, deaths in the family, and how good it was to be back. "You know, they say you go back to a reunion and see a lot of old folks," one man concluded after telling of his forty-three years with Du Pont. Then he set his jaw and made a fist. "Well, I wanna say all you women are charming and all you men have still got it."

As speakers got on and off the mike, contrasts between them were still painfully apparent. Some sparkled like Mae West doing a last encore, others trembled as if making a maiden speech in first grade. Nellie, so charming at our table, could only stammer a couple of sentences about being a retired librarian and widow, while Olivia, who'd been rather dull up close, seemed to lose all the pounds and years as she radiated before the crowd. "I've got some advice for young people," Olivia said. "Never be afraid to get old. It's much more fun to be old than to be young."

Many spoke of hoping to get together before too long. One woman suggested a seventy-fifth reunion. Her classmate felt that wasn't soon enough. "Now that most of us are retired," said this second woman, "I hope we get together more often because, as Roger said, we may not be around too much longer."

The banquet ended abruptly, but people filed out slowly. Lingering in the motel lobby, they whispered a few last words and seemed reluctant to drop each other's hands. But finally hands had to part as members of the Class of '25 walked separately to the parking lot and drove off into the still summer night.

Now Can We?
(Go All the Way)

My reason for writing this is the hope that a certain person
will see it. I haven't seen him in ten years, nor do I have the
slightest idea where he is. But I will always remember him.

When he was living in Niagara Falls, New York, I was one
of the hundreds of girls who panted over him. He had the
sleek sorority chicks, and the "bad girls" who "did it." He
also owned the secret hearts of many shy and unattractive
nobodies like me.

One night at a record hop, when I was fifteen and he was
about seventeen, he invited me to go for a walk with him.
We went to a vacant lot and laid down on the grass and
necked until I was in a state of excitement I had never known
before.

. . .

On the way back, I asked him why he didn't take advantage
of the situation by trying to "go all the way." He said he had
enough sex to keep him happy, and, therefore, never did it
with virgins. He told me my body was so nice I should be in
one of the men's magazines.

. . .

His gentle, tender, considerate actions are among the most
beautiful memories of my life.

In those ten years I have progressed pretty far in the love-
making department. My dream is that someday we'll run into
each other again and I will be able to express the feelings his
memory inspires. . . .

— *Penthouse* Forum

One appeal of reunions is the hope of seeing an early sexual fantasy. Or perhaps not just seeing. Maybe, the hope goes, perhaps now, at long last, we'll be able to . . .

I was struck at reunions by their muted sexuality, which sometimes wasn't so muted. If anything, the raunchiness got stronger over time. Perhaps with the passing of years one's sexual fantasies grow more desperate. Or one is freer to be open with them when less can be done about it. I don't know. I do know that those at their fiftieth remembered no less vividly than fifth reuners who it was they really wanted to see.

Folk wisdom says there's no love like first love. Our romantic and erotic fantasies confirm that wisdom. From personal reverie I know that no fantasy is quite so titillating as one of consummating a relationship kept chaste during high school. To this day I can't figure out why when Carla invited me over because her parents were out of town I didn't go. Sometimes I wonder if the invitation's still open.

Other people have described for me similar frustrations living on after high school. "Yeah," one man replied when I wondered if he had adolescent memories I hadn't asked about. "Feeling this attractive girl lean up against me in science class each week — and remembering I never did anything about it."

A psychiatrist says he finds regret about not pursuing teenage sexual opportunities to be the rule rather than the exception among patients. "Similar episodes are always reported in the course of the analysis of any adult," writes Dr. Gerald Pearson. "There is always poignant regret for nonconsummation of some adolescent love affair and for the eventual loss of the partner."

A sexually active bachelor in his mid-thirties winced while telling me about dating in high school a girl with a reputation, one rumored to have gone all the way. During a month of heavy petting, mutual fondling, and everything but actual intercourse, my friend kept himself in control out of principle. Also, he realizes today, out of fear. And today he knows how frustrated this integrity born of fear made his partner. "The last night in my car," this man recalls, putting a hand to his face, "I had a heavy hard-on. But she stopped me from touching her, saying, 'Now let's see how *you* like it.' It wasn't till years later that I understood what she meant. Finally we got to her house, and as I walked her to the door she said, 'Good-bye.' Then she patted my erection and said, 'Be good to junior.'"

Head held to ground, my friend grimaced, saying, "I sure would like to live that over."

Obviously this must be a common desire — to combine adult wherewithal with the passion of adolescence and act out a sexual memory. The problem is that most such memories can't be acted out. Because most high school sex took place largely in the safety of one's imagination. And there it was portrayed in rich, vivid hues. A girlfriend or boyfriend might have starred in such productions. Perhaps they featured the unattainable cheerleader, maybe a football star.

Or our dreams may just have starred Debbie Brooks rubbing up against us in the hall that afternoon. Was it an accident? Or a message?

Maybe, we'd lie there thinking, tomorrow after school Debbie's mom might be gone and she'll invite me down to their den, and . . .

Or why wait till after school? Why not take Debbie by the hand after fifth period Biology and lead her silently but firmly over to that janitor's closet by the gym? She might dig it. We'd shut the door behind us and start groping in the dark. Probably she'd like doing it standing up, first getting a little height on an overturned bucket, then pulling down those nylon panties and bending just a little so that . . .

Nah. That sounds kind of sloppy. Maybe she'd rather be lying down anyway.

I know. When Mr. Kelly leaves his office. He's got this long desk, and . . .

Adult sexual fantasies just can't match those we made up in high school. Something about all the new juices flowing and dammed by a wall of frustration stimulated glorious sexual dramas starring us and our friends which can never be matched in the adult mind. Even worse is that adult reality generally can't top our high school fantasies. Or match them. Or even come close.

In fact, compared with high school's aspirations, sexual reality can really be a drag. Gore Vidal once pointed out that a man whose first sex occurs after adolescence will have spent his most aroused years masturbating. In order to give that act meaning, his mind becomes a pornographic set, the canopied beds of a harem, "a Dionysian festival." This being the case, asks Vidal, what adult reality could compare? And "should he be a resourceful dramatist he may find actual love-making disappointing when he finally gets to it. . . ."

It's not really startling to note that sexual memories can eclipse adult reality. Nor is it headline news when high school classmates show up in grown-up erotic daydreams. One poor man I know has his frustration televised every time the largest-breasted girl in his high school shows up singing Country & Western.

Such frustration can be a cultural resource. Unconsummated young love results in our *Summer of '42*s, and *Portnoy's Complaint*s. Consuming youthful fantasies are what help us write *Lolita*s. Or seek Lolitas. Or seek the actual one.

153

But what flesh-and-blood actor could possibly be cast in the part assigned them by our fantasies?

A popular alternative is not to try casting the fantasy at all, but simply to fall back on high school reruns for the prime time of adult daydreaming. A preference for the fantasies of our most sexually alive years is what sells *Playboy* by the million every month, and ensures that there will always be erotica with "teenage" in the title (e.g., *Teenage Lust, Wanton Teenagers, Teenage Cheerleader*).

In one recent year alone, three erotic movies had cheerleader themes: not just *Teenage Cheerleader*, but *The Swinging Cheerleaders*, and *The Cheerleaders*. Defending his disdainful review of the latter, *New Times* film critic Frank Rich explained that "the mere mention of the word 'cheerleader' sets my telltale heart aflutter...."

One reason cheerleaders are so prominent on the American landscape is leftover male yearning. Pleated skirts slipping down thighs are a staple of men's magazines, and when Hugh Hefner's girlfriend Barbi Benton takes it all off for *Playboy*, note is taken that she was once a Sacramento cheerleader.

The *Evergreen Review* once ran a classic fantasy, a "candid" spread of high school cheerleaders undressing in the locker room. A miniature camera, we were told, had been smuggled inside. To compensate for this admitted invasion of privacy, *Evergreen* said they were donating $500 to the student council of the girl's midwestern high school.*

Michael O'Donoghue, the free-lance writer, conceived and produced this *Evergreen* spread. When I called to ask how he got the idea, O'Donoghue explained that naked cheerleaders seemed a surefire sale for *Evergreen*'s series on erotica. Cheerleaders un-

* The last picture of the cheerleader collage on page 88 is from *Evergreen*'s layout. Years later this spread was adapted as the illustration for the *National Lampoon*'s fantasy about being invisible in a girl's locker room; *Lampoon* editor P. J. O'Rourke says he had the *Evergreen* pictures taped to his wall in college.

dressing he figured would turn an editor on. Cheerleaders undressing he figured would turn any man on. Cheerleaders undressing he knew turned *him* on.

"I sure would like to get me ahold of a cheerleader," said O'Donoghue.

When Michael O'Donoghue graduated from a New York high school in the late 50s he remembers having been "a weirdness" — a person who read books. He also remembers going to games and salivating high up in the stands while watching girls cheer others on the floor below.

"It was something I was always denied," O'Donoghue complains. "The idea of having girls cheer you on is terrific. But why limit it to high school? Why not cheerleaders for other things? Like writers. 'Hey, Mike! Mike's my man!'

"Great! Terrific!

"I sure would like to get me a cheerleader. I've never gotten a hand on anyone who was a cheerleader. I had a drink with one once. But one of the things in life denied me is to stuff a cheerleader.

"Boy, I'd like to get my hands on a cheerleader. That fabulous acrylic nylon underwear. Really exciting."

It's not that cheerleaders, or even cheerleader-types, are so sexy. They're not, ordinarily, any more sexy than Den Mothers. What is sexy about cheerleaders is the wild hopes pinned on them at the time, hopes that live on in the adult imagination. For those guys who weren't getting any in high school, which was most guys, sitting in the stands week after week watching female classmates — get this — shake their rears! bounce their breasts! lift high their legs! and then — flash their crotch!! — this was exciting stuff, as close to striptease as most of us ever got. That cheerleaders looked so well washed only added to the fantasy. Their very cleanliness made us want to soil them. *Makes* us want to soil them. Remembering this closest approximation of sex at a time when our bodies had such need, we go to see the movies, examine closely the picture spreads, and keep our eyes open for cheerleader-types today who may call us down from the stands and into their beds.

"My hand went up her pleated, cheerleader-type skirt," John Bowers wrote of an ex-cheerleader in his memoir *The Colony*, "and I felt her underwear. . . ."

But his mission isn't accomplished. Under the pleated skirt is a block of ice. "Imagine that!" writes Bowers. "And she had been a cheerleader, the symbol of all we ever lusted for. Those innumerable fantasies of pleated skirts going up and crimson panties coming down, all in a halo of white teeth and locomotive energy. What irony! She just couldn't."

In Joe McGinnis's novel *The Dream Team*, an energetic young gadabout tells the main character her game is sex fantasies. She proposes to the book's young writer-hero that they try this together:

For instance: I'm the high school cheerleader. I'm a senior and I'm the most beautiful and the sexiest girl in the school. Not only have I dated five or six guys from the football team all at once, but I even go away some weekends to date guys who are big names in college. Now, suddenly, I'm at a party. And you're at the party, too. Only you're just a skinny sophomore with acne on his face. You've only just started to masturbate and you've never, never even made out with a girl. You're shy, but you're the scholarly type, and I get into a conversation with you because I like intelligent conversation. Only the whole thing is too much for you. You don't know whether you're going to shoot a load in your pants or run away. And then I start getting friendly. I say, very demurely, 'I wouldn't mind if you asked me to dance.' The lights are low. *And* it's an unchaperoned party. With empty bedrooms upstairs. Okay, we can pick it up from there.

But fantasizing isn't always enough. Sometimes we want to put an actual, remembered head on the young bodies of our dreams. Occasionally we even want to do more.

A divorced mother of seven described for me her long, lonely night when she could barely beat down an urge to write the American Medical Association for the address of a boy she once knew in high school, a boy who later became a doctor, the only boy she had let touch her breasts.

Though she stifled the urge, others have told me of succumbing to it, of actually seeking out old classmates to discuss doing now what didn't seem possible then. For one woman in her late twenties, the problem was that her prospective partner was also the only friend she had left from high school. After discussing at great length whether to risk a good friendship with sex, they finally decided against it. I've heard similar stories often: the temptation to renew a high school affair, the approach, and the pulling back.

When I raised this topic with a couple married sixteen years, the husband chuckled and said he knew of "one strong attempt along that line."

This seemed to cause a flurry between the two, and I looked over at his wife, whose face had turned the color of a king's robe. "Was it you, Lisa?" I asked.

She nodded. "I went back to visit my mother and called my boyfriend from high school just to wish him a happy birthday. He's now a wealthy executive with seven kids and a huge house."

And then?

"Well, he took me out to lunch, and then we went to a museum. It was a romantic occasion. It felt very good. Then we had supper together."

Before she could continue, Lisa's daughter cried in the other room and she left her husband and me alone. I asked how he reacted to the whole affair. Tom smiled benevolently. "It was cute. She'd been back a few days and I knew there was something bothering her. After a while she broke down and told me there was something she wanted to tell me. I was kind of nervous. I thought she'd met some guy and wanted to leave me. It turned out they'd just sat and necked in the car. I thought it was really romantic and a nice thing." His smile tightened. "I haven't always reacted that well."

Lisa returned with their five-year-old daughter, placed the girl in her lap, and helped her put on skates. I asked how she remembered telling Tom.

Again Lisa blushed. "I just remember sitting in his lap and crying."

Her old sweetheart had followed their afternoon and evening together with letters and calls, wanting her to "go to the shore" with him. Though a tryst was never mentioned, it was implicit. "He didn't say it," Lisa explained. "There was no invitation — but it was pretty obvious."

"Didn't he invite you to a motel?" asked Tom.

Lisa looked irritated. "Oh, he might have.

"But I haven't called him up the last few times I've been home, though I'd still like to see him without that other stuff."

Hearing such stories didn't especially surprise me. I figured other grown-ups must dwell on old lusts from high school, because I do, and speculate about what it would be like to do more than speculate.

Nor was it surprising to hear about old classmates even broaching the possibility with each other.

What has raised my eyebrows is the number of people who tell me they not only wished to bed a high school fantasy, but tried — and did.

"It blew my mind," said one woman at a supper party. "I met this guy in a restaurant in San Francisco. We hadn't seen each other since high school nine years ago in Montana."

On the plump side, thought not unappealing, the woman assured me she was most unattractive in high school and rarely was asked to dance by anyone, let alone by this old classmate. "When we were in high school he was way above me socially," she explained. "We never had much contact.

"So, at any rate, we ended up spending the night together.

And you know what? He was awful!" My friend whooped, and clapped her hands together. "He was terrible in bed!

"It felt so good to find that out.

"I felt terrific all the way home. It felt like I'd somehow settled that part of my life."

Repeatedly such stories have been volunteered during interviews, sometimes when I asked for them, often when I didn't.

While describing her tenth reunion, a woman casually let it drop that among the more interesting events was ending up in bed with her old boyfriend. "I'd been too prudish at the time," she explained, "and it just felt right to do now what we couldn't do then. It seemed very natural."

Was he married?

She nodded, then shrugged.

How was it?

She smiled enigmatically. "I liked it."

Then she walked away.

After hearing more than one such unsolicited testimonial, I began to add a standard question to my inquiries: Have you ever, in fantasy or in fact, consummated a high school love affair that was left chaste at the time?

"Sure," replied P. J. O'Rourke. "Absolutely. Barb Sanders. And I felt that way about Patsy Rosen until I heard she'd gained fifty pounds and lives in a tract house with her kid. I still think a lot about Denise Sinclair. I bet she wouldn't be so snobby now. Her and her fuckin' junior executive husband."

P. J. then proceeded to tell me that four years after graduating, he did have an affair with a classmate last lusted after during his first year of high school. They were both home the summer after college ended, bored, with not much to do. So they did what could only be dreamed about before.

How was it? Good?

"I suppose," O'Rourke said unconvincingly. "It wasn't everything you dream of. Not a real fantasy wish-fulfillment. Not the sort of thing you'd cut your hand off for.

"Now we're friends again."

O'Rourke's report is the most common I've heard from those who try to act out a teenage sexual fantasy: high hopes, low reward.

A writer just past thirty told me of looking up his high school sweetheart several years after he had married and she hadn't. First they kept things platonic. Then they didn't. Finally, after two years, they went all the way.

But the experience was not what he'd imagined. "It was tense," he explained, "and never very much fun. We were just playing out a thing from the past."

They slept together a couple of more times, then called it an affair.

"She ended up saying, 'You weren't really interested in me. You were just interested in a vagina from the past.'"

A twenty-two-year-old divorcee told me of a somewhat more satisfying experience. Four years out of high school, as her marriage foundered, this woman called the first guy she'd ever gone out with. "I wasn't really ready for an affair," she explained, "but I just wanted to see the first person who really cared for me.

"So I called him up and he said he was married, and I said I am too, but let's get together and see what happens. We met in a parking lot, and things just happened.

"The relationship now is pure sex. It wasn't sex at all in high school. We went out when we were only sophomores, which was just touching the sweater. I never really knew him except for touching the sweater.

"We've been seeing each other about a year now. But it's been a very shallow thing. He looks at the clock a lot when we're together. Which really doesn't bother me because he's only out for sex, and I'm only out for sex.

"He's really not my type."

Repeatedly I've been told such stories — how the cold water of reality dashes hot fires of imagination when it comes to renewing high school affairs. In fact, it's exceptional to hear a report of any other kind. Perhaps the added trauma of having known each other in another form by itself precludes sexual satisfaction. One man told me of picking up a classmate at their twenty-fifth reunion much as he might have picked someone up at a bar. The woman wasn't an old fantasy, not even a person he'd known very well at the time. But their experience back at the motel wasn't very good, he told me: a combination of too much drink and too little relaxation.

It's not fantastic hopes alone that make sexual reunions frustrating. Part of the problem is the simple passage of time. Even those bedded during high school may in later years meet this old lover only to find that as their memory has been enhanced, their power has declined.

A twenty-four-year-old man told me of renewing his first love a decade later with mixed results.

He talked to me a few days after this had happened, calling his partner "my first and last lover — with ten years in between."

"She's been married five years. Just long enough to be getting bored with her old man. I saw her when I was back home on a visit, just a few hours before leaving town. I had my stuff all packed, and we met in a coffee shop. I asked how it was with her old man. She said not so good. We got flirting. She was about to go back to him, so I — just kidding — told her, 'If you really liked me you'd kick out your old man for the weekend.'

"Well, at that she pulled out a key and said, 'Here's the key to my friend's apartment.' We both smiled. I said, 'Is this for real?'

"She said, 'Why not?'

"So I stood up my taxi, missed the bus, and met her at her friend's apartment. We spent about an hour and a half together, then she had to get back to her old man."

How was it?

He frowned. "Not so good. Not so good. It was kind of nervous and strained. There was some novelty to it; something

161

I had daydreamed about for a long time. It turned out she had too. It was hard to believe this was really happening.

"But in high school it was fresher somehow. Less jaded."

Did you discuss the experience afterward?

"Not much. It was pretty fast.

"But she told me something which surprised me — that none of the relationships she'd had since lived up to ours. Ours was kind of a standard. She told me that ever since she's had a thing for small, dark-haired men like me."

There is nothing remarkable about seeking our first love in other people's eyes. Nor that disappointment is so likely if we seek our first love in fact. At some level I think we know this, and remain content to stick with memories, or fantasies, or literature. "Remember first love?" asks a writer of women's fiction, "when you held his hand, wore his ring, and trembled from a single kiss? . . .

"If you can capture that memory without becoming maudlin and update it for today's young readers, you have the makings of a light romance writer."

Of course, even as one feels a lot excited, it's easy to feel silly poring back over such feelings after so many years have passed. But embarrassment is no more the point here than in any other dimension of intensely remembered high school. One can no more be "reasonable" or "mature" about the memory of early yearning than about hunger after fasting: the urge is there and must be fed.

Medical psychologist John Money goes so far as to argue that early love is more in the realm of biology than romance, a natural drive whose "acute phase" lasts for a maximum of two years during adolescence. Dr. Money feels that "the phenomenon of falling in love can be analyzed as an imprinting phenomenon," and that those heavily focused on an early lover may be capable in later years of loving only someone with similar characteristics.

"Nature's obvious purpose in designing the falling in love

syndrome," he concludes, "was to draw the human male and female together as soon as their sex organs matured for reproduction, and keep them together long enough to ensure the next generation."

If Money is right — if a couple of years during adolescence is the time when we love as never again — America's way of handling the associated lust guarantees frustration. As a blending of cultures, this country has never given its teenagers clear sexual guidelines. Some societies take a more permissive approach sexually and others are clearly restrictive, but we've always been a little of both. American girls especially, trying to decide how far to go, have historically gotten a mixed message: go as far as you must, but not too far — and good luck!

In *The Cheerleader*, Snowy parks with Dudley, a frequent date but not a steady one. She is confused. "Without the going-steady guide, she had had to invent her own code of morals: French kissing was the limit, except with Victor and Dudley; Victor she allowed only to Get Fresh, but Dudley wasn't so easy to stop and each parking session became a contest, but because she didn't really want to stop Dudley, he kept winning, and tonight he won a blow job. . . ."

Such confusion! What frustration! With clearer standards as adults we may retrace our steps and clear up some of the confusion. But frustration is harder to eliminate — especially when we dare to try resolving a frustration of the past.

Perhaps the luckiest adult fantasizers are those whose dreams remain intact for lack of an opportunity to shatter them.

The focus of this chapter has been on the difficulty of rekindling early love and lust. But I want to conclude with some exceptions to quench the romantic thirst in both my readers and myself. Because the search for an early lover doesn't always end in frustration. Not only have some high school sweethearts found they still care about each other after an interval, a few even court and marry.

One such couple, in Morgantown, Kentucky, reunited after an interval of sixty-eight years, two wives, and one husband. They'd first courted in her fourteenth year and his twentieth. The two were married in his eighty-eighth year and her eighty-second. They report an initial spat over what to name their first son.

More recently Tommy Smothers married Rochelle Rolley, his classmate at Verdugo Hills High near Los Angeles. She'd come backstage when he played Harrah's in Reno and the comedian was smitten. Within months they were wed. He's now stepfather to her seven children by two prior husbands.

Though most publicized in his case, this "Smothers Syndrome" isn't all that extraordinary. As I talked around about this book, people would remark regularly, "Well I know a couple who got back together and married years after they were high school sweethearts."

Finally I spent an afternoon visiting with such a couple, Bob and Janet Lawrence, at their home in Irvine, California.

The Lawrences were sweethearts at Beverly Hills High School in 1942. He was a senior, she, a sophomore.

"How many times did we go out?" Bob asked Janet when I inquired. He turned to his wife. "Two? Three?"

"I know once we saw *Love Letters*," Janet replied, "with Jennifer Jones and Joseph Cotten. And then we went to an Italian restaurant."

As her husband shook his head in amazement at such recall, Janet laughed and added, "I know you think I'm crazy."

"I do," he replied. "You sure it was me?"

"It was you. An Italian restaurant in Hollywood. You just had too many gals. You don't remember."

Janet Lawrence has the trim figure and lively manner of a former cheerleader. Under frosted brunette hair, her almond eyes shone brightly over a constantly laughing mouth while she relived this earlier time. Sitting next to her on their back patio, Bob Lawrence smiled less often but was attentive. The former

actor, now a college dean, has black wavy hair graying at the temples and the girth of an ex-fullback. Throughout their dialogue Bob Lawrence looked at his hands while shaking his head in amazement at the trivia his wife seemed to have stored away.

"I remember how I used to walk down Wilshire Boulevard," Janet continued, "and you'd be working at the Warner's in your uniform." She turned to me. "He was the doorman — and I would try to catch his eye, and he never did look at me, *never*."

Janet's voice grew pouty.

"You just wouldn't give me a tumble.

"He stood me up once," Janet said turning back to me.

"I didn't really stand you up," Bob quickly interjected. "It was a mistake."

Now he turned to me. "It was very difficult, you see, because Janet had these three sisters and you couldn't do anything in Beverly Hills without being seen by one of them."

"Bob and I supposedly had a date," Janet continued. "We were going to a movie or something. Anyway, my sister worked at the Fox Beverly Theater and she came home that night and said, 'I thought you had a date with Bob.'

" 'Well, I did,' I said, 'but he never showed up.'

" 'Well he was there at the theater with another girl,' my sister said." Janet tittered. "So that was, you know . . ."

"That was the end of that," Bob said.

"It wasn't really though," his wife added, turning back to him, "because then I saw you after that, when I was graduating from high school. You came back from the service . . ." She returned to me. "You see he came back two years later and I asked him to sign my yearbook and he wrote me a *beautiful* long note.

"I still have it."

Bob was sitting quietly now, hands clasped over his mouth, a little smile visible through folded fingers.

"Why are you smiling?" asked Janet with a laugh.

"Because I don't know how you can remember back that far."

"Oh, gosh, Bob, you know — you were *important.*"

When Bob Lawrence returned from the war, he married someone else. So did Janet. Each had three children. Though Janet recalls getting very excited once when she heard that Bob was back in Hollywood teaching, they didn't see each other for more than two decades — until his twenty-fifth reunion in 1967. Bob was master of ceremonies. By then divorced, Janet decided at the last minute to go see her sister, who was Bob's classmate, in the reunion program. It occurred to Janet that Bob Lawrence would be there, though she doubted he'd even notice her. Probably, Janet figured, Bob would be more interested in her sister.

But the master of ceremonies did notice his old girlfriend. "She looked scrumptious," he recalls. "Just *scrumptious.*"

After the reunion Bob found out where Janet was working and invited her to lunch. "So we had lunch," he remembers.

Janet (to herself, softly): "And we had dinner."

Bob: "And then we saw each other again."

Janet: "And again."

Bob: "And again."

Janet: "And again."

The two burst out laughing. "And now here you are," said Janet.

Bob exhaled. "Yeahhhh."

Three years after their personal reunion and twenty-eight years after their first date, Bob and Janet Lawrence were married.

They being among the elite who actually do what many dream about, I wondered what the two could tell the rest of us about their storybook marriage.

"Well," began Janet. "You know, in retrospect, I don't think Bob and I would have done very well married young and having a family. Mainly because I would have been too immature and I wouldn't have been able to cope with a lot of things, and he wouldn't have with me either.

"Though in some ways I think that if Bob and I had raised a family together it would have been good, because he's very family-oriented. I think from that standpoint we would have made a good team. But . . ."

Her tone grew wistful. "Okay. That's all."

Bob pondered a long time before adding, "Another dimension is that I think that our relationship, which is really, you know, what — nine years old — tends to take a perspective of being thirty-some years old. Because even though what we did in high school was relatively superficial and casual, as we discuss things we have a thirty-some-year history we can play with. That tends to give some stability to the relationship which in a sense isn't real. But it has that sort of structure."

As the darkness muted our faces and kids' yelling around the neighborhood died down, the former Janet Stevenson went into the house and returned with her yearbook.

Bob took the annual and turned to its back pages, which were covered with one long inscription. "Here's my backward writing," he said handing us the book. Then he grabbed it back, saying, "I think I'd better read this first."

Janet walked over to join Bob at his chair, adding, "Yeah, I want to censor it first."

As Bob mumbled his comments aloud in a mocking voice, Janet read over his shoulder and giggled.

"God," Bob said, "this is terrible."

"I loved it," said Janet. "I *loved* it. I've read it so many times over the years."

"This is nauseatingly terrible," said Bob.

But he let me read the inscription — lines of blue ink covering three red pages at the end, dated June 19th, 1943.

Dear Janet:
This is '43, just about this time last year we were going out together and having a good time. In fact I don't think I have ever enjoyed myself as much as I enjoyed myself with you — then all of a

sudden Bang and we were no longer going out together. Well, that couldn't be helped, I guess it did not make much difference to you anyway....

Then, one day I went to Beverly to visit. I don't know why, but I stopped and talked to you, and the more I talked, the more I started thinking about the old days, the more I wanted to go out with you again. So I didn't say anything. Then I saw you at the theater, decided that it wouldn't hurt to ask you, and we went out.

With a big rush, all those old feelings came back, and I wanted to be with you more and more. So things go along.

Where I go from here is a mystery. I don't know how you feel, I don't know whether I will ever find out. The military has a cute way of changing its mind every so often and I may have to leave one day. I can't count on tomorrow, so I live only for today. Tomorrow I will worry about when it gets here. That's the only way I can live —

Remember that whereas I may not see you for a long time, wherever I may be, I will always be thinking about you, and looking forward to the day when I can be with you again.

BOB LAWRENCE

The High School
Imprint

What years of confusion!
And when will they be over?
Can you give me a tentative date please?
    — ALEXANDER PORTNOY

Listening to people recall high school, you'd think they spent three years under fire at Anzio. Or scrambling for the last plane out of Saigon.

Because if people feel embarrassed later talking about high school, what they remember feeling at the time was fear, danger and fear.

Some things feared in high school:
— not being asked to dance
— being turned down after asking someone to dance
— going crazy
— forgetting one's locker combination
— getting busted
— getting beat up
— menstruating in class
— being called on by the teacher
— sex
— PE showers
— cheerleader tryouts
— walking the hallways

High school is just scary. Even your body knows, and tightens its sphincter muscles as you walk the halls. The tragedy of the situation is that while everyone is more or less afraid at this time of life, the greatest fear is of anyone finding out. Our own terror hid us from each other's. "I was so frightened," Dory

Previn recalls. "I was so terrified about the other person that I never knew they were going through the same gamut of fears and joys and opinions and judgments."

Both in fantasy and fact, adolescence is a time when we feel danger from all sides. Some of the danger is internal: the changes our body is going through. Is that swelling on my chest breasts or cancer? The blood flow menstruation or hemorrhaging?

Will my penis grow long enough to do the job?

Does masturbation drive you insane?

These are frightening questions, and we remember vividly the time of life when they're posed. All feels new during adolescence, everything a first: our moods, the changes in our bodies, and sex. As Anna Freud points out, although specific changes occur at any age, adolescence is the time when change takes place across the board. Such wholesale transformation has to feel dangerous.

Then there's the range of social dangers, the ones presented by our peers. Such anxiety is associated with dances, which reek with the danger of rejection. This is the fear that led us to hide in the rest room, or made us try to stay in motion and a little out of breath so all would believe we had just jitterbugged off the floor.

As one girl wrote on a note to herself before leaving for her first high school dance:

1. Get purse and sweater.
2. Leave the house.
3. Don't be scared.

(Her mother saved the note, then returned it when the woman turned twenty-five.)

The real danger, and actual fear, felt by American adolescents is not normally a topic taken too seriously. We nibble around the issue a lot, talk about adolescent trauma or storm and stress, but what no one has come flat out and said is that the high school years *are* dangerous. They're dangerous physically: the leading cause of death from ages fifteen through nineteen is accidents (automobile, drowning, with guns, etc.). They're dangerous legally: over half the serious crime in this country is committed by those under twenty-one. And they're dangerous emotionally: many counselors feel postpuberty is a time when floating in and out of psychotic states is commonplace. "Normal healthy adolescents," writes one psychologist who works with them, "are, by adult standards, notably psychopathic, manic, and schizoid in their psychological makeup and behavior."

For such reasons, adolescence is a time when we not only *feel* in danger, we *are* in danger. And a time of such trauma must be memorable.

It isn't the events themselves that are so memorable in high school as the feelings with which they're associated. It's the same phenomenon as remembering exactly what we were doing the instant we heard of John Kennedy's death. Our activity itself may not have been of any consequence, but the news of our President's assassination acted like a flashbulb in the memory — illuminating all else within range and capturing it by association in a snapshot of recall.

In the same sense it's not the details themselves that are so memorable during high school — the names of classmates or their exact words in rejecting us — but the association of fear that fixes such "trivia" in our mind.

This helps explain why our most vivid memories from high school are the worst ones. Things hurt more during high school and we remember longest that which cut most deeply. Just as survivors recall vividly a flood or earthquake, we can remember for a lifetime Mary Jenks snubbing us in Home Ec. But who remembers the day in 1954 when everything went all right? San Francisco's earthquake was commemorated by survivors' 1906 clubs, two of which are still alive nearly seven decades later, but there are no 1905 clubs to celebrate a year when the earth stayed firm beneath our feet.

Psychologist Scot Morris emphasizes that it's the intensity of feeling that records such memories so indelibly. A clinical psychologist interested in the origins of human behavior, Dr. Morris says that the vivid recall of dangerous moments was at one time a matter of survival. "When the human ape was being chased by the other kind across a savannah," he points out, "it was very helpful to be able to recall exactly how he got away so he could later repeat the maneuver."

Such vivid recall may not have the same survival value today, Morris adds, but we still don't forget the few seconds before an auto accident, or minute details of the ocean floor while scuba diving beneath fifty feet of water. Being so close to death makes us intensely alive in a way we recall with precision, if not pleasure.

High school memories as well are ones we treasure not because we love them — few of us do — but because we like to remember having once felt so alive — in danger, threatened, aroused, our feelings bubbling over freely, our senses at the alert.

Dr. Gerald Pearson, whose lifework has been counseling adolescents, says he never fails to be impressed by the teenager's enhanced ability to see, hear, taste, and smell. Dr. Pearson isn't sure why high school kids should have such acute senses, but he suggests accelerated sexuality as one factor and perhaps some physiological causes we don't understand.

I would add to this the danger factor. The fact that feeling so constantly threatened makes all sensations a little more vivid: every meal like the last of a condemned man, all smells like the flowers beside a patient's deathbed, and each sound heard with the ear of a soldier patrolling the jungle.

War is the analogy I keep thinking of to describe how we remember high school. Veterans often tell me they remember their wartime experiences with intense ambivalence: hating the memory and hoping never again to go through combat, while feeling that the constant danger made them alive in a way they sometimes miss.

I don't think it's any coincidence that both high school classes and wartime combat units constantly hold reunions. Each group is bonded by a sense of shared danger. In war as in high school, friendships are forged that have special depth; love affairs become particularly poignant. We're thrown together with people from all walks of life, and the sense of shared danger sticks indelibly to our mind. There will always be a market for books about war, and there will always be a market for books about high school.

Adolescence in this country in many ways has become a state of war — with one's parents, society in general, and each other. The American way is to escape from your family during adolescence and turn to classmates instead for solace. But will they give it? Can they? Will we be liked? Can we win popularity to substitute for our family's love?

Such questions lie at the heart of the terror felt by American teenagers and their obsession with status. Having rejected our parents as part of becoming adult, we still need the love and comfort a family once provided. So we turn to our classmates instead, and seek their good opinion. But there's a difference between the generous love of a family and the niggardly approval dispensed by peers. In the American high school tribe, there's only so much good opinion to go around in the form of status. And over this scarce resource we war savagely.

One reason foreigners have such trouble understanding the impact of high school on Americans is that in cultures where family matters more, peer groups matter less. A research study once compared Chinese-American high school students in Hawaii with Caucasian-American counterparts in Chicago. The primary distinction was that because the Oriental students belonged to tightly knit families, they were less involved with each other — "like loose sands which do not stick together." The Hawaiian students had fewer clubs and activities than the Chicagoans, who had turned from their families and clung to each other as a substitute. Yet this peer-group family did not offer emotional security because, as the researchers point out, "peers nowhere have any great love for each other. In fact peers . . . always compete with each other, and therefore one must be continuously on the lookout for trouble with them, trouble which might lead to rejection."

During high school we don't just *want* the company and good opinion of our peers, we crave it, we need it — we're desperate for their regard as a source of emotional survival. And in one of life's crueler ironies, at this time, when we need acceptance most, we also become nearly paranoid in our sensitivity to rejection. During adolescence one's skin feels turned inside out. Every nerve is exposed. No move is made that isn't on stage, and all in the audience are watching with X-ray eyes. Nothing escapes the merciless scrutiny of those from whom you most need mercy.

Therefore, at a time when your need for approval is at its peak, your chances of winning it have never been lower. Your family might have cared about you automatically, but you must earn the esteem of high school classmates, and often on very bizarre and elusive terms. Most of us can't, and spend our adolescent years feeling cared about neither by family nor friends.

Yet we don't give up; we keep hoping forlornly — hoping even as adults — to win the love of our classmates in the form of status. The fear that we won't makes high school very memorable indeed.

But there's a curious paradox about the memorability of this time of life. While adolescent memories get fixed in our mind by association with painful feelings, the pain itself may long have been laid to rest. Like a dinosaur's remains, a skeleton of facts left over from high school lives on long after the flesh of feeling has decayed.

While interviewing the parents of high school students, psychiatrist Daniel Offer found them most cooperative in talking about their children. Then he inquired about their own adolescence, with curious results. Writes Offer: "When we asked, 'What do you recall about your own teen years?' we got descriptions of the town, the family, the social pattern, but very little of the *feelings* of those years. One mother said, 'Oh, what a terrible question!' Another said, 'Oh, that's not fair!' Many said, 'I don't remember much about it.' "

This reluctance to revive the feelings of adolescence is what can make it so difficult for grown-ups to be around teenagers — such as their children. It's commonly accepted among counselors that one reason adults have such trouble raising teenagers, or teaching them — or counseling them, for that matter — is because of the feelings their children set off inside themselves.

The adolescent, write psychologists Elizabeth Douvan and Joseph Adelson,

may make us remember the emotional tempests we want to forget, or may force us to re-imagine the fiction of our adolescent origins. . . . Even the psychotherapist, devoted to an ethos of self-knowledge, may find himself emotionally invested (as he ruefully recognizes later) in his adolescent patients — stirred, irritated, indulgent, and overprotective; wanting to take sides, to console, to argue; or finding himself strangely distant, unmoved, or bored. It is an age hard to know truly.

For such reasons, adolescence has always been difficult for this culture to handle. The anxiety is self-perpetuating. High school kids must not only confront their own stirred-up feelings but those of their parents as well. As one psychologist puts it, a family with teenagers witnesses two crises: that of the adolescents, and that of the parents' "reactivated adolescence." This is not pleasant to deal with, for either child or parent. To the relief of both, the child is therefore pushed even further from his family, more deeply into the pain of adolescence. Eventually this process will make it harder for him to deal with his own teenage children. Thus is the cycle repeated, in the American muddling-through approach to growing up.

In other cultures, elaborate rites of transition initiate the young into adulthood. Among ceremonies employed for this purpose are ritual dancing, a change of name, extended isolation, public circumcision, and the running of gauntlets. Such rituals don't necessarily reduce the danger felt during adolescence. They may even enhance it. But what puberty rites can do is serve as a map for those setting out on scary roads. Others have gone that route, and those left alone in a distant shelter, or being clubbed through a gauntlet, know they will probably make it through. The reward for participation is inclusion.

In this culture we feel no such assurance. All we feel is scared. Societies more "primitive" than our own may subject their young to rites. We subject ours to high school.

Jean Shepherd once began a story about adolescence:

"Puberty rites in the more primitive tribal societies are almost invariably painful and traumatic experiences."

I half dozed in front of my TV set as the speaker droned on in his high, nasal voice. . . .

"A classic example is the Ugga Buggah tribe of lower Micronesia," the speaker continued, tapping a pointer on the map behind him.

A shot of an Ugga Buggah teenager appeared on the screen, eyes rolling in misery, face bathed in sweat. I leaned forward. His expression was strangely familiar.

"When an Ugga Buggah reaches puberty, the rites are rigorous and unvarying for both sexes. Difficult dances are performed and the candidate for adulthood must eat a sickening ritual meal during the post-dance banquet. You will also notice that his costume is as uncomfortable as it is decorative."

Again the Ugga Buggah appeared, clothed in a garment that seemed to be made of feathers and chain mail, the top grasping his Adam's apple like an iron clamp, his tongue lolling out in pain.

"The adults attend these tribal rituals only as chaperones and observers, and look upon the ceremony with indulgence. Here we see the ritual dance in progress."

A heavy rumble of drums; then a moiling herd of sweating feather-clad dancers of both sexes appeared on screen amid a great cloud of dust.

"Of course, we in the more sophisticated societies no longer observe these rites."

Somehow the scene was too painful for me to continue watching. Something dark and lurking had been awakened in my breast.

"What the hell you mean we don't observe puberty rites?" I mumbled rhetorically as I got up and switched off the set. Reaching up to the top bookshelf, I took down a leatherette covered volume. It was my high school class yearbook. I leafed through the pages of photographs: beaming biology teachers, pimply-faced students, lantern-jawed football coaches. Suddenly, there it was — a sharp etched photographic record of a true puberty rite among the primitive tribes of northern Indiana.

The caption read: "The Junior Prom was heartily enjoyed by one and all. The annual event was held this year at the Cherrywood Country Club. Mickey Eisley and his Magic Music Makers provided the romantic rhythms. All agreed that it was an unforgettable evening, the memory of which we will all cherish in the years to come."

Presumably our culture has advanced beyond the need for puberty rites. But as Shepherd and any high school graduate know, all we've dispensed with are "official" rites. Without adult guidance, American adolescents just make up their own rituals of transition. And high school is the setting because high school is where they are. Whoever says gauntlets went out with primitive tribes has not recently walked a high school hallway.

But there's a fundamental difference between the American adolescents' tribe, and ones more deserving of the name. In high school, all members are about the same age. This tribal gathering is limited to those between fourteen and eighteen. A few grown-ups are present, of course, teachers and janitors and so forth, but such people can generally be ignored except when they act up.

Isolated together in high schools for thirty or more hours a week, America's adolescents quickly get down to the serious business of initiating each other with proms and sock hops, pep rallies and homecoming parades, daily hallway inspection and club initiations of all kinds.

One anthropologist has gone so far as to call the entire high school experience "an extended puberty rite."

Except that this rite does not reduce the anxiety of adolescence, it enhances it. Acceptance is less often the reward for participation than rejection. And high school's rituals don't make you feel more sure of becoming an adult, they make you feel less sure. High school does not prepare you to grow up. It prepares you only for high school.

As a result, when we do grow up — chronologically — we fall back on what we know best to get along: the high school in our minds. It's often argued that high school is heavily influenced by adult values. My argument is just the opposite: that adult values grow directly out of high school.

Erik Erikson believes that the way we resolve our adolescent identity crisis determines fundamentally what kind of adults we become both singly and in aggregate. Because following puberty, not only are individuals confirmed in their identity, but societies as well. "This process," says Erikson, "also implies a fateful survival of adolescent modes of thinking in man's historical and ideological perspectives."

In America such perspectives are those learned in high school. And since these perspectives bear so little relation to what comes later, what we do after graduation is simply try to force adult society into the one already seared on our brains, a world consisting of crowds and status, jocks and cheerleaders, schlepps and leftouts. A boss may always be the principal to us, a civil service test our midterm.

Kurt Vonnegut has called high school "closer to the core of the American experience than anything else I can think of." What interests me as much as his insight is the frequency with which it is cited by others. It's as if we know instinctively that

Vonnegut said something important, though we're not sure exactly why.

There's a reason, I believe, a natural, understandable explanation for the durability of adolescent outlooks. This reason I call "secondary imprinting" — the shaping of adult consciousness by adolescent experience.

Behavioral scientists talk already about the primary imprinting, which takes place just after birth.

In the classic example, ethologist Konrad Lorenz exchanged himself for a mother goose just as her eggs hatched. When the goslings stepped from their shells, Lorenz was the first being they saw, and the baby birds followed him about in a brood. Lorenz had been "imprinted" as their mother.

In a similar sense, what happens to human babies just after they are born may fundamentally shape the adults they become. Being separated from one's mother, to take an extreme example, can make it difficult for a person ever to trust the commitment of another human being.

The theory is that earliest childhood constitutes a "critical period," one in which any event may shape forever our outlook as adults. Newborn babies, it is assumed, are uniquely open — vulnerable, changing daily, in constant flux — and, if we believe Sigmund Freud, quite sexy little critters. But no matter how basic, early childhood is not the only critical period of human development. According to one definition, "any period of life when rapid organization is taking place is a critical period."

By such a definition, adolescence is an especially impressionable stage of life, one comparable to that after birth. Psychoanalysis has historically drawn parallels between the two stages, describing adolescence as a time when infantile traumas are reawakened. In order to cope with this revived turmoil, writes analyst Peter Blos, it is necessary to return to the emotional state of infancy. This is why he says "adolescence has been called a second edition of childhood. . . ."

Therefore, if earliest childhood is an imprinting time of life, adolescence may also be — as a revival of this critical period.

But there is a fundamental difference between primary and secondary imprinting. The primary imprinting after birth is largely unconscious. The skilled hand of a psychiatrist can be necessary to loosen such unconscious memories and float them to the surface. Most of us never have such an experience.

But the secondary imprinting of high school is highly conscious. Painfully conscious. We may not remember how mother held us in her arms, but we do remember how Debbie Brooks held us at the prom. Even if early childhood is more shaping of the adult we become, we think more often about our adolescent imprint because it's the one that is conscious in memory.

"Everyone has a moment in history," writes John Knowles in *A Separate Peace*,

which belongs particularly to him. It is the moment when his emotions achieve their most powerful sway over him, and afterward when you say to this person "the world today" or "life" or "reality" he will assume that you meant this moment, even if it is fifty years past. The world, through his unleashed emotions, imprinted itself upon him, and he carries the stamp of that passing moment forever.

For Knowles, as for so many of us, that shaping "moment" took place during high school, the time when we're imprinted with a concept of the world hard to shake as adults. This is secondary imprinting.

Secondary imprinting can mean if we were fat in high school, we'll carry that weight in our minds for the rest of our lives. If rejected then, we can feel unpopular today, no matter how many elections we've won. Or if popular — attractive and well liked — we may not accept a single wrinkle, or hear the loudest snub.

A poll of sixty thousand *Psychology Today* readers found that those who liked the way they looked as adolescents continued to like it until middle age, whether their appearance had changed or not. The reverse was also true. "Adults who thought they were unattractive teenagers currently have lower self-esteem," this survey found, "than those who felt beautiful, even adults who blossomed in maturity. Perhaps such people never fully accept the fact that they have changed; the 'ugly duckling' feeling lasts long after the swan has emerged."

This grip on our adult mind of what happened in high school may be close to the surface, allowing us to actively review adolescence for a lifetime. Or the imprint may be barely conscious, making us uncomfortable around a "cheerleader-type," say, without knowing quite where this feeling began. Or we may have powerful memories from high school that need but a trigger to set them off, what behavioral scientists call a "releaser stimulus." The smell of chalk dust could be such a releaser of memory, the taste of pizza, or perhaps a reunion announcement.

This is why many tastes are set during adolescence — tastes in dancing, in sex, or music. Our later preference for what we remember from high school has less to do with discrimination than association. Johnny Mathis may not be the best singer ever, but if "The Twelfth of Never" was playing the night Carla Rollins let us touch her breast, Mathis will be an eternal taste. No songs we ever hear in succeeding years can match the old songs, the ones we heard during high school. It's not that the music itself is so great, but the memories certainly are.

The high school imprint shapes American adults in such diverse ways — shapes our tastes, our feelings about ourselves in a crowd, and feelings about our bodies. Knowing this makes us realize intuitively that hearing what a person was like in their teens will tell us something basic about who they are today.

This is why "What were you like in high school?" is not a trivial inquiry. Hearing from another person how they saw themselves as teenagers gives us basic data about how they see themselves today. I think we know this, if not always consciously. And this is why we wonder so much about what people were like in high school — and sometimes have the temerity to ask.

Some psychotherapists say that to grow at all as an adult it is first necessary to revive the trauma of our teenage years. The very art of psychoanalysis, a practitioner has written, "may well be regarded as a second chance at adolescence . . . and by reducing the need for repression it provides a second chance for a better solution."

Most of us can't afford this solution, or choose not to undertake it. Yet we do think a lot about high school and continue to act out our adolescence in conscious and unconscious ways.

We may realize this, may know if only in the privacy of our thoughts, how strong is the imprint of high school. Sometimes we wonder if it ever ended. This is not a reassuring feeling. More commonly it is a source of embarrassment and shame. Being too open with high school memories leaves one subject to the charge of being "immature." Such stigmas help us to be ashamed and guarded about leftover feelings from adolescence. When Ann Landers chides an advice-seeker by saying, "Emotionally you are *still* back in high school," she's being less than helpful. To some degree we're all still in high school emotionally. Repressing those feelings, feeling guilty about them, and worrying about what Ann Landers might think only makes the memories harder to deal with.

High school memories must be dealt with for the same reason Hillary climbed Everest: because they're there. They can't be wished away.

Also, they can be fun. I enjoy my memories from high school, painful as many of them are. Even all that vengefulness is a terrific source of energy. And by reviving the memories, by getting high school out on the table and off my back, I've found it's become a much more pleasant companion.

Exorcising High School

The adolescent viewpoint is and should be precious to us.
— ARTHUR MILLER

101 Ways to Get High School off Your Back

1. Go back to high school. Walk down the Up staircase. Tread on the plaque. If anyone asks for your hallway pass, tell them to stuff it.
2. Read over your old yearbook inscriptions. (Take a stiff drink first.)
3. Sue the yearbook for defamation.
4. Write your high school principal. Demand a recount of the election you lost.
5. Return to your high school braless. Walk briskly down the halls.
6. Become a high school treasurer. Embezzle.
7. Work in a high school cafeteria. Give smaller portions to students who resemble classmates you didn't like.
8. Get elected to the school board. Tell high school principals what to do. Don't take any guff.
9. Become a state governor. Impound funds for secondary education.
10. Return to your high school as an outside agitator.
11. Give a speech at your high school. Speak your mind.
12. Make the commencement address at any high school.

Announce your topic as "A Freshman in Life." Speak on "Capitalism, Football, High School, and Other Aspects of American Decadence."

13. Arrange to be in the news at the time of your reunion. Don't attend.
14. Send fake reunion announcements to classmates who did you wrong.
15. Become corresponding secretary of your class. Sell its mailing list to the Young Socialist Alliance.
16. Write to the lead of your class play. Ask for an autographed, 8 x 10 glossy.
17. Donate your classmates' pictures to an antique dealer.
18. Send a copy of your Ph.D. thesis to the counselor who said you weren't college material.
19. Retrieve the bubble gum you left under Seat 3, Row 29, Section M of the gym.
20. Leave old notebooks inscribed BORED OF EDUCATION on your coffee table.
21. Wear pleated white miniskirts. Don't wear underwear.
22. Bronze your old car. Make it into a planter.
23. Dye your saddle shoes one color. Use them for bowling.
24. Wait a decade or two, then look up the people you envied most in high school.
25. Read the obituary column. Watch high school disappear before your eyes.
26. Throw a "come as you would have been" party.
27. Arrange to be given a nickname.
28. Drive a '57 Chevy (or a '49 Ford woody).
29. Buy a 'vette.
30. Chaperone a prom.
31. Read high school papers.
32. Eat in a high school cafeteria. Sit at any table you choose.
33. Teach high school. Marry a pupil.
34. Pass as a high school student. Seduce the principal.
35. Become a principal.

36. Disrupt a homecoming parade.
37. Look up a teacher you didn't like. Tell him or her why.
38. Look up a teacher you did like. Tell him or her why.
39. Discuss with a classmate what you couldn't talk about then.
40. Look up your high school sweetheart.
41. Wait forty years, then look up your spouse's high school sweetheart.
42. Join an encounter group. Behave as you would like to have behaved in high school.
43. Ask how you're coming across.
44. Learn how to dance.
45. Write down everything you remember from high school. Don't show this to anyone.
46. Read your kid's yearbook inscriptions. Reread your own. Compare the two.
47. Frame a blown-up picture of your teenage self. Hang it by your mirror.
48. Have your portrait taken as it *should* have appeared in the yearbook.
49. Tell your kids how high school felt for you.
50. Become a high school counselor. Listen carefully.

Special List for Outies
51. Tell people you lettered in football, or led cheers. Act dumb.
52. Wear a letter sweater.
53. Make up Gerald Ford jokes. Start a fad.
54. Check the welfare rolls regularly for ex-cheerleaders and football stars from your class.
55. Make a study proving outies do better after high school.
56. Become a football coach.
57. Become a marine sergeant. Be tough on guys who look like jocks.

58. Become an author. Write caricatures of ex-jocks.
59. Play Biff Loman in *Death of a Salesman* (or Brick in *Cat on a Hot Tin Roof*) (or anyone in *That Championship Season*).
60. See a George S. McDonald movie.
61. See a Marilyn Chambers movie.
62. Become a movie director. Cast ex-jocks and cheerleaders. Tell them what to do. Don't take any shit.
63. Become a sportswriter. Ask embarrassing questions.
64. Play NFL football.
65. Become an NFL cheerleader.
66. Buy a team. Cut lots of players.

Special List for Innies
67. Read Sartre.
68. Get a Ph.D.
69. Vote for liberals. Talk about it.
70. Don't hold chains at games.
71. Melt down your gold megaphone or football. Make it into a peace pendant.
72. Put ecology bumper stickers on your Volvo.
73. Tell people you find Howard Cosell "penetrating."
74. Teach Latin.
75. Grow a beard.
76. Marry a geek.

77. Invent an alternative to combination locks for lockers.
78. Produce low-cost private shower stalls.
79. Design high school rings. Design them weird.
80. Mass produce small gold megaphones and little gold footballs for gumball machines.
81. Combine pictures from your yearbook into a work of art. Call it *American Primitives*.
82. Make a 3-D collage from your prom corsage, Slam Books, virgin pin, etc.

83. Conduct a study of adolescent sexual customs.
84. Write erotic books with *Teenage* in the title.
85. See *Teenage Fantasies*.
86. See *High School Fantasies*.
87. Make an obscene movie with your high school as the setting.
88. Use that wallet-stained Trojan.
89. Do it in the back seat.
90. Or on a principal's desk.
91. Make an obscene call to the person in your class to whom you would most like to make an obscene call.
92. Write a blistering attack on secondary education in American society.
93. Write an article about your classmates called "How Did They Turn Out?"
94. Call up the mother of your high school friend. Tell her you're en route to Paris for *Vogue* and just wanted to say hello.
95. Write songs about high school.
96. Sing songs about high school.
97. Become a regular on talk shows. Talk about classmates. Say what you really thought of them.
98. Make a disaster movie about crumbling high school buildings.
99. Start a restaurant called The Class Reunion.
100. Publish *Playboy*.
101. Write a book called *Is There Life After High School?*

Somewhere, in each of us, lurks a high school kid. For a grown-up with any pretensions to maturity this isn't pleasant to admit. But he's there. That kid can't be wished away. At best he can be repressed, but the teenager within will still find ways to get out and embarrass us.

An alternative is simply to let him loose. Get high school leftovers off your back by putting them out in front. Release the beast, tame him, and make friends. Better yet, make him earn his keep.

Among our more interesting adults are those who exorcise lingering high school demons by putting them to work. Hugh Hefner, for example, calls *Playboy* "a projection of my own adolescent dreams and aspirations." While student council president at Chicago's Steinmetz High, Hefner recalls being too shy even to put his arm around a girl. A Steinmetz classmate told me she remembers Hefner as "nothing outstanding. Serious. Very businesslike. Not one bit wild, but really nice."

Ten years out of high school Hefner started *Playboy*, and with the fortune that ensued eventually built himself a Disneyland of an estate in Los Angeles. A recent visitor described this estate to me as an environment only a sixteen-year-old could have dreamed up.

Like Hugh Hefner, Betty Friedan is an adult enjoying herself in a way not possible during adolescence. While growing up Betty Goldstein in Peoria, Friedan had too big a nose and wasn't asked to join a sorority. Valedictorian of her high school class, she founded a literary magazine and dated infrequently, "mostly misfits like myself." Of the future feminist, her classmates predicted: "I guess that book she wrote is pretty popular — *How to be Popular and Why Bother*." Ms. Friedan has commented on how painful those years were for her, and how at the time she'd vowed that if they didn't like her, classmates would some day learn to respect her.

After graduating from Smith College, Betty Friedan enjoyed a successful writing career, then founded the National Organization for Women. Recently she was made a member of the Girl Scout board. While controversial among colleagues, Ms. Friedan is respected.

Since her divorce in 1969, Betty Friedan has dated, thrown parties, been in encounter groups, and lived in a commune. About her fourth decade of life Ms. Friedan once said: "The second adolescence of my forties is so much more interesting and fun than my first adolescence."

Then there is Kurt Vonnegut. Vonnegut includes high school frequently in his writing, sprinkles his speech with terms such as "stuck-up," and in interviews refers fondly to Shortridge High in Indianapolis, from which he was graduated in 1940. But not all of his memories are fond. Vonnegut also remembers vividly the senior dance at which gag prizes were given to students. A football coach gave the skinny aspiring writer a Charles Atlas body-building course.

Vonnegut felt sick. He considered slashing the coach's tires. Instead he left the dance, went home, and brooded. He continued brooding for the next three decades. One night the adult Vonnegut called Indianapolis and got the coach's phone number. Then he called the coach.

"I got on the phone and told him who I was," the author said in a *Playboy* interview. "And then I reminded him about the present and said, 'I want you to know that my body turned out all right.' It was a *neat* unburdening. It certainly beats psychiatry."

The Hefner-Friedan-Vonnegut approach to exorcising high school by reviving it is not an easy one. Nor is it socially safe. In fact, many people find such an approach downright juvenile. Disgusting. Immature.

And they're right. But then "maturity" could be overrated as a virtue. Perhaps one way to stay alive and creative is to keep high school memories close to the surface. Wade in the memories of high school. Grovel in them. Get sick of the memories, and have fun with them. Let the kid out to play anytime you feel like it. If anyone accuses you of having a high school mentality, threaten to jam their locker.

But this approach is easier to recommend than practice. For one thing, it's not always easy to revive adolescent feelings. For another, there are strong social taboos against doing so. Finally, and most inhibiting of all, is our own fear about what might crawl out if we open the lid too widely on the high school kid within.

Psychiatrists say adolescence can be among the most difficult periods of life for an adult to reflect on accurately. Anna Freud says she is impressed by how seldom in the treatment of adults she succeeds in reviving their adolescent experiences full force. "The memories of the events of the adolescent period are, normally, retained in consciousness and told to the analyst without apparent difficulty," she explains. "What we fail to recover, as a rule, is the atmosphere in which the adolescent lives, his anxieties, the height of elation or depth of despair, the quickly rising enthusiasm, the utter hopelessness, the burning. . . . These are elusive mood swings, difficult to revive. . . ."

In the course of research for this book, I developed a set of questions that seemed best to revive such feelings. They are:

1. What were you like in high school?
2. Did you have a nickname?
3. If I were to grab a classmate of yours while you were in high school, point to you walking by in the halls, and ask, "What's he/she like?" what would they be likely to say?
4. Do you ever dream about high school?
5. Does any part of your high school building stand out particularly in your memory? If so, do you know why?
6. Is there a most triumphant moment you felt during high school that you'd like to live over? A worst moment?
7. Was there a position in high school to which you unsuccessfully aspired?
8. Do you know what's happened to your high school sweetheart?
9. What was written under your senior picture in the yearbook? How many times did your picture appear within?
10. If your class held a reunion nearby this weekend, would you attend?

Often those who answered these questions in writing (sometimes for pages) would tell me that the process revived old memories that they assumed were long forgotten. One man shared the questionnaire with his lover; he said it opened whole new areas of their relationship to explore.

When I would raise my questions in person, the results could at times be startling.

At one point I interviewed the head of a research project on high school counseling, a white-haired man, slow of movement and given to nervous chuckles. While describing his research the man kept using phrases such as "measures of social adjustment" and "leadership correlates" with a voice that barely left his throat as his hands rested firmly on the desk.

Then I asked what high school had been like for him. Flushing a bit at the question, the researcher said he'd graduated midyear 1925 because of staying out half his junior year to pick apples. This was partly to make money, he told me, but, more important, to grow bigger so he could play football.

"You see," he explained, raising one hand off his desk, "I was small in high school and the school had twelve hundred students or so, too big for someone my size to get noticed. So I wanted to play football. At my size, how else was I going to get people to pay attention to me? But I never got past one hundred and thirty-five pounds and the coach wouldn't even let me scrimmage, which annoyed the hell out of me."

As the man told me this story, his whole demeanor changed — but especially his voice. What had been a barely audible monotone describing research had now raised part of an octave, remembering grievances fifty years old. The voice was alternately petulant, pleading, angry, and triumphant — that of someone much younger, the voice even of a boy.

The guy stayed out another year and a half picking apples before college, grew big enough to play ball there, and made the team over two classmates who'd played for his high school — "which pleased me, I must admit." Pressing his palms against the desk, the man leaned back and laughed — a deep laugh, not a nervous one — a laugh of triumph and frustration conquered.

Commonly at the end of such a session, the person I was talking with would seem a different human being altogether — lighter, more animated and alive.

Why, then, do we tend to keep the high school kid so tightly locked inside? For one thing, he's risky to let loose in public. There are strong social stigmas against being too free with adolescent enthusiasms.

A journalist once visited Hugh Hefner's estate and was asked by the publisher if he wanted anything. "Anything?" thought the reporter. "I was suddenly overwhelmed by the adolescent and utterly reprehensible notion that for this one and only moment in my life, *any* request would be granted."

Utterly reprehensible.

We have names for those adults who seem to be enjoying themselves with teenage exuberance: charges such as "perpetual teenager," "high school mentality," and "arrested adolescence." Such labels are commonly hung on adults who do interesting work. Winston Churchill, for example, was once accused of being a "petrified adolescent" by his political opponent Aneurin Bevan (remember him?).

In creative fields, especially, successful adults are commonly described as being adolescent in temperament. Once a painter himself, Erik Erikson says that in his experience artists experience not just one but many adolescences in the course of a lifetime.

Any number of authors make a living off their teenage memories. Philip Roth has called his early work an attempt to fictionalize the first eighteen years of his life. John Updike, who puts himself in the Twain-Joyce-Hemingway tradition by mining his adolescence so thoroughly, says that a writer's basic problem is learning how to convey experiences worth reading about, experiences "usually accumulated by the age of twenty. . . ."

This could be the most creative approach of all to exorcising adolescent demons: recycling them into an art form. However this takes courage. Once the lid is loosened on high school memories, they're liable to crawl out and make the lid-lifter look ridiculous.

But any creative act carries this risk. To try something original, you must always risk looking absurd.

One reason outies become more creative adults than innies is that they already look absurd. They've had egg on their face for years. Outies have little to lose by looking ridiculous. Dredging up high school memories and recycling them into art is less risky for them than for innies. The worst thing that can happen is that they'll be made fun of. And that's already happened.

"The popular kid is out having a good time," film director Francis Ford Coppola has said. "He doesn't sit around thinking about who he is or how he feels. But the kid who is ugly, sick, miserable or schlumpy sits around heartbroken and thinks. He's like an oyster growing this pearl of feelings which becomes the basis of an art."

The artist who can recycle adolescent memories imaginatively is guaranteed an audience. This is not because those memories are unique, but because they're universal. Director George Lucas calls *American Graffiti* "a ten-year reunion with myself, or rather with my teenage fantasies." But when we went to see his fantasies, what we really saw were our own. The only thing unique about the artist's experience in such a case is his nerve in reviving those experiences and his courage in sharing them.

Jules Feiffer says that while writing the screenplay for *Carnal Knowledge,* in conjunction with psychoanalysis, he kept having to confront himself as he was at sixteen, seventeen, and eighteen. In the process he realized that what most distinguished his adult from his teenage self was merely a change of setting. If some miracle were to put him back in high school, Feiffer says, "I don't think I'd do a hell of a lot better now than I did then. If I were single again tomorrow and taking out a girl on the first date, it wouldn't be worldly, sophisticated, forty-two-year-old Jules Feiffer. It would be some seventeen-year-old schmuck wearing

AT SIXTEEN:

I WAS STUPID, CONFUSED, INSECURE AND IN-DECISIVE.

AT TWENTY-FIVE:

I WAS WISE, SELF-CON-FIDENT, PREPOS-SESSING AND ASSERT-IVE.

AT FORTY-FIVE:

I AM STUPID, CONFUSED, INSECURE AND IN-DECISIVE.

1-13

Dist. Publishers-Hall Syndicate

WHO WOULD HAVE GUESSED THAT MATUR-ITY—

IS ONLY A SHORT BREAK IN ADOL-ESCENCE.

that as a disguise and still worried about whether or not he was going to get laid. Or a cheap feel. Or even a French kiss."

Feiffer's conviction touches on a fundamental fear holding at bay our adolescent demons: the fear that if we let them out and took too close a look, we might find they resemble very clearly the person we are today.

This fear lies at the heart of our difficulty in coping with high school memories. Most of us don't want to be who we were in high school, and we assure ourselves we're not.

But all alone, in the middle of the night, we sometimes wonder. What would it be like if I went back to high school today? Would anything have changed? Would I?

In her thirty-third year, after a decade of marriage, Lyn Tornabene let down her hair, bought some knee socks, made herself up artfully, and enrolled in high school. A confessed youth cultist, Tornabene later explained in *I Passed as a Teenager* that she thought it would be fun to go back, and perhaps revert to a more innocent time of life. She did.

Within days as a high school student the writer found herself frightened in the hallways, worried about making friends, shy with boys, intimidated by grown-ups, petrified about PE, scared she'd give the wrong answer in class, and cheating on tests so as not to get a bad grade.

"I could never have guessed that I would have moments of complete regression," reported Tornabene, "and that on some days I would feel about school that I had never left it at all.

"I didn't think about anything but girlfriends, teachers, classes, and, well, boys — or my lack of appeal to them. I was worrying about whether or not I was homely, and I was spending more hours than I care to enumerate staring in mirrors."

Tornabene, in other words, confirmed our worst fear about how much change we might find by going back to high school: none whatsoever.

But listen to her conclusion. After ten weeks of reversion, Tornabene called her most valuable souvenir "the marked change in my attitude toward life. It's the pleasure I take in being myself — in being this adult. . . . Since my bizarre excursion into their world I have an acute sense of pleasure in being my own age. Not in looking it and not in feeling it, but in being it. I don't mind the gray in my hair anymore. . . .

"Be young again? Not on your life."

This is the hidden side of the coin, the reward for unleashing an adolescent within. In order to break, high school fever must first be heightened.

Like Lyn Tornabene's, my own experience in writing this book is that while I've never felt closer to my high school self, nor have I ever felt more grown-up. Confronting the demons directly — eyeball to eyeball, pimple to pimple — somehow has made them less ominous. Almost friendly. The process has been like a modified exorcism that instead of driving off a haunting spirit, simply makes him less of a nuisance.

The biggest reward has been to grow more conscious of when I'm striking a posture left over from high school. There's not usually anything to be done about it: I'll always be nervous at dances and around men who look like they played football. But just knowing this, and knowing why, often is enough. At best I can choose consciously when to be a grown-up, and when to unleash my high school kid, rather than let him take me over unconsciously.

And all of this has come from discovering both how much things have changed since high school and how little.

One way of discovering this was by finally mustering the courage to discuss with a couple of old classmates what until recently seemed impossible. Like: do I seem any different?

Mike Mulligan says no. He says I haven't changed a bit since high school, and am doing today about what he figured I'd be doing.

Friends can be cruel that way.

But Mike also disputes my recollection that he used to hate me. The way he remembers it, I was stand-offish when we met.

(Actually I was scared out of my mind.) And Mike remembers our first meeting. It was up in the gym bleachers, and I was wearing a rust-brown suede jacket.

Mulligan was surprised at how out of things I remember feeling in high school. He thought I was considered pretty statusy by most classmates.

When I asked how a random classmate might describe me, Mike struggled for some time before replying, "Smart. Real active. Dates some neat chicks, though I don't know how."

This visit was a good one. And not as scary as I'd expected. It even made me feel courageous enough to call Paula Gottschalk, a classmate who was not a close friend. Paula had been one cut above me socially — at the bottom of the top, even as I felt top of the bottom. This disparity created a Berlin Wall between us.

When I called her twelve years later, Paula was quite willing to get together. She wanted to know what I was up to. I told her. "Well, you always were kind of heady," she observed. What did Paula mean by that?

We made a date for lunch, and I then spent the next half-hour reviewing every word of our phone conversation. Particularly that last remark. What did she mean by "heady"?

"Heady" turns out to be a positive part of Paula Gottschalk's vocabulary. "You always were way ahead of the rest of us," she explained when we got together. "I remember envying you because you were your own person and wanting to be friends with you. But I was scared because of the group."

Paula shook her head and banged the table. "Stupid! Stupid! Stupid!

"What a hateful experience!"

Paula said her biggest regret from high school was not having the strength to get to know people she really would like to have known, but couldn't because of "the group."

This group comprised the top ten girls in our class, among whom Paula felt eighth or ninth. She said the real elite numbered seven, who then called her and one or two others in if they needed extras for a party. "But they really didn't like me," she added. "Nobody liked each other in that group. There was horrible infighting.

"I was so miserable in high school," Paula concluded. "I don't remember anything good about it."

Needless to say, hearing how much fun life wasn't in the crowd above me, or at least in its women's auxiliary, made me feel better about not having been part of it. Also hearing Paula repeat over and over how jealous she was of people like myself who seemed not to be so worried about losing status. (It's easy when you feel you've got little to lose.)

The acid test was to discover if I could make it through a day back in my high school.

On a crisp fall day, after months of talking with other people about high school and wondering how it would feel to actually go back — I did.

The tips of my ears picked up a chill in Illinois's air as I retraced the familiar path between my parents' home and Central High School. In the distance rakes scraped against concrete.

Before I expected it, the fortress of a school building stood before me — a huge vault of tan brick covering an entire block with an air of deceptive calm.

My hands were cold.

After a moment's hesitation I stepped into the sauna-like warmth inside, both comforting and threatening at once. A familiar smell raced through my nose, one I couldn't define but knew instantly as the odor of Central High.

Seconds after my feet touched scarred linoleum, a rude shrieking bell released a flood of human bodies that dashed out of rooms and raced up and down hallways, clutching books and shouting to the beat of locker doors slamming. Many of the bodies wore wool and leather jackets with big white C's sewn to the breast. I glanced instinctively at each letter to see what it was for — a little oval ball for football, a round one for basketball, W for wrestling, or T for track.

Two of these lettermen passed a lone girl, and one made an oinking noise. "Lotta pigs around here today," said the other.

From the waist down, Levi's on many female bodies contrasted with my memory. But from the waist up chests still pushed at sweaters and blouses with varying degrees of authority. And their eyes rolled each other over in a familiar way as mouths whispered and fingers arched in waves.

In the outer hallway, my feet remembered to avoid the brass CHS plaque. Two males voices behind me laughed. My body stiffened. Were they laughing at me?

Turning sharply to the right, I walked out the back doors into the circular drive where Auto Shop kids worked on jacked-up cars as they'd done perhaps since there were Model T's to be worked on. Bike racks by the drive were new, as well as the fifty or so bikes filling them.

A fresh-faced blond, filling nicely her yellow sweater, passed in front of the bikes. My glance went from her hair to her face, lingered over the chest, then examined the book clutched against it. *Accounting.* Commercial course. Not my type.

Across the street, just steps from where Carl Malone and I had it out over Roz Rosenberg, a large group of white kids and a smaller black group now stood smoking cigarettes and sucking soda through straws.

Malone had met me by my locker one day after school — him on one side, Howie Dubin on the other — and as I twirled my combination and tried to look cool, Malone muttered, "I want you to stay away from my woman, Keyes."

We started in the hallway and ended up out back, right where the kids stood now. Malone had me by nearly a hundred pounds. But to this day I'm convinced if I only hadn't let him get hold of me, if I had just jabbed and backpedaled till Malone got tired, I could have taken him. As it was he left a mark under my eye that still turns red when I'm tired. Malone won the fight, but I won Roz — for a couple of weeks at least. She ended up with Howie Dubin.

Today's smokers across the street began to make me uncomfortable with their sullen stares, and I turned to reenter the school building. Before pushing through the glass doors, I checked the reflection, then pulled my body erect.

The gym felt like it might be safe territory, and I made my way there to a steadily rising crescendo of balls thumping wood. Here nothing had changed — the boxlike room, the gray shorts under white T-shirts, and the pervasive smell of sweat.

One of the PE teachers and I began shooting baskets together. His brother had been my classmate. I was hitting pretty well and glanced around to see if the basketball coach was paying attention. This was the same coach who had cut me on the first round of tryouts for the sophomore team fifteen years before. I hoped he saw some improvement. But the coach didn't seem to notice either me or improvement.

Finally I went over to where he sat by the stage and introduced myself.

"Keyes," he said. "Yeah. I remember you. How's it goin'? What'd you say your first name was again?"

Before I could tell him, a tall guy about my age walked in and was greeted effusively by the basketball coach. The two quickly fell to reminiscing about games of the past, and how they beat Springfield that year. As the two talked, the coach glanced in my direction occasionally, as if wanting to include me in the conversation without quite knowing how.

My stomach rumbled. I wondered if I'd missed the lunch bell. Then it occurred to me that it didn't matter. I could go to the caf when I wanted, and did, hurrying along the deserted hallways, worried I'd get stuck back in line.

Cafeteria smells were a relief from the school's general mustiness — gravy mixed with steam and the air's competing perfumes.

Behind me in line stood a small and attractive girl with shyly downcast eyes. The plaid jumper she wore and her bobbed curly hair reminded me of other girls who once stood by me in the cafeteria line. Before reaching the trays I introduced myself and we chatted for a minute. Her name was Sue. She was a junior.

I thought about asking Sue if she'd eat with me, but decided against it. Probably she'd say no. Just as I started to walk off alone, trying to look like I knew where I was going, Sue's little voice said as if in a dream, "If you're not eating with anyone, you could eat with me and Martha."

Sue and I joined her friend Martha, who was sitting by herself at a table in back. The table next to ours was crowded with a group of girls who seemed especially animated. I asked if this was the popular crowd. Sue glanced cautiously over her shoulder, then looked back with a tight smile and nodded. Fingering the box of suckers she was selling for Future Homemakers, Martha added that the girls at that table acted real high and mighty sometimes.

After school Sue found me in the hallway and asked if I'd walk her home. Heading south on Newberry Street, we kicked leaves and told jokes just as I'd done on countless walks home with Lynn Blanchard before I stopped talking to her.

Lynn had been about my best friend in high school, a good-looking brunette who had the misfortune (in my eyes, which about reached her nose) of being rather tall. Lynn and I went to a dance together once and after an evening of cheek-to-chest dancing became best friends. She walked me home after that fight with Malone.

But Lynn was rude to a friend of mine, I thought, then didn't ask me to double-date with her to some dance — so I stopped talking with her and haven't to this day. And to this day I regret doing that. Lynn was a friend. I wish I'd got mad at her and taken it from there. But it felt easier at the time just to stop talking. Sometimes it feels easier still.

The sun was hot on my face as Sue and I scattered leaves with our feet. Sue was telling me about a guy she used to date but didn't anymore. "Guys like girls that put out," she said, "and I don't put out a thing."

Finally Sue had to turn west on Fairfax, leaving me alone to continue home. On my right was a football field where a broad-shouldered army in white was running in place ("Quick! Quick! Quick!"), falling on their stomachs ("Down!"), rising and high-stepping ("Get 'em up! Get 'em up!"), then falling to the ground once more.

I stood watching for a few minutes, enjoying the players' energy and their pageantry. It occurred to me that in all the years of living nearby I'd never stopped to watch football practice.

Only two blocks on Thomas Street now lay before home. As I started in that direction, the sun hit my body full force, so I unbuttoned my jacket and let it flap open in the breeze.

Notes

These notes are intended primarily to cite my sources of information, because studying History in college imprinted me with the feeling that it's somehow immoral not to. But they are also an opportunity to throw in asides, engage in speculation, share bits of gossip, and supply supplementary information of all kinds that for some reason or another (usually stylistic) failed to make its way into the text.

As background and source material for this book I've tried to read widely if not exhaustively in the literature of adolescence and secondary education. Though my intent is not to produce the definitive work on high school, I do want to know and share what's gone before me.

An early research problem was this: I began looking under the heading "High School." But most indexes and card catalogues include little under that heading. Then I realized that "Education, Secondary" was what this topic is called officially, and under this heading more turned up. But still not what I was looking for. Most of what's written about Education, Secondary, has little to do with anything I and others remember most vividly from high school. What does "curriculum design" have to do with the looks Debbie Brooks used to give us in Biology? How does one relate the issue of open classrooms to the hallways where *important* things took place? And does "Extracurricular Activities" have enough scope to cover the evening we read over for the hundredth time what classmates wrote in our yearbook?

Material closer to what I was looking for finally turned up under "Adolescence." Which illustrates in part what this book is about: the degree to which "high school" and "adolescence" have become synonymous in our vocabulary and culture. When Americans say "I remember high school," what they mean is "I remember my adolescence." But when I tried to find out what students of American adolescence have to say about popularity, the topic we're obsessed with at the time and remember most insistently as adults, I discovered "popularity" turns up not even in the index of most studies. The closest topic most list is usually "Peer Relations."

A glaring exception is sociologist James Coleman, who has studied high school as a social system with particular attention to its distribution of status. Coleman's major work on this topic, *The Adolescent Society* (New York: The Free Press of Glencoe, 1961), is controversial for a number of reasons. My hunch is that he committed heresy by studying seriously, and in its own context, a social system that inflicted so much misery on those of us who later make studies.

In an interesting footnote to his research, Coleman once said of himself that he'd always been sensitive to what was expected of him, and that "this sensitivity probably accounts for a kind of bias found in *The Adolescent Society* towards the demands of the adolescent system" (in Phillip E. Hammond, ed., *Sociologists at Work*, New York: Basic Books, 1964, p. 209).

In our interview Coleman speculated that one reason high school isn't studied as well as it might be is because of the negative experience many of his colleagues had there. "An awful lot of sociologists were outside the system," he explained, "because the system had a set of values which didn't value the things they could do well — and consequently they want to kind of blind themselves to this whole period because it was an unpleasant experience. For me, it wasn't an unpleasant experience in the same way, though it was an enormous waste of time. But I didn't have the sort of blocks to looking at it that way."

Because his research is so exceptional in this regard, I've relied perhaps overmuch on the findings of James Coleman that are reported in *The Adolescent Society*, and on his shorter work *Adolescents and the Schools* (New York: Basic Books, 1965).

Additional sociological perspectives have been given me by Edgar Z. Friedenberg's work, especially *The Vanishing Adolescent* (Boston: Beacon Press, 1959) and *Coming of Age in America* (New York: Random House, 1965). Friedenberg writes with such elegance that it is hard to read him without regular nods of agreement. Nor can one easily quibble with his argument that American secondary education has blurred legitimate distinctions and rewarded mediocrity. What I find difficult to accept is Friedenberg's assumption that we wanted it any other way, and that high school students have a frustrated hunger for competence. I recall no such hunger. Nor do I remember seeing any. Mostly I recall being starved for status. And this famine is the one others tell me they remember as well.

One classmate said she was never so humiliated as when the yearbook predicted success for her. She didn't want to be successful, the woman told me. She wanted only to be liked.

For psychoanalytic perspectives on adolescence, I've depended on the Group for the Advancement of Psychiatry's *Normal Adolescence* (New York: Charles Scribner's Sons, 1968); *Adolescence and the Conflict of Generations* by Gerald H. J. Pearson, M.D. (New York: Norton, 1958); Peter Blos's *On Adolescence* (New York: The Free Press of Glencoe, 1962); and essays by Anna Freud.

Psychiatrist Daniel Offer's written efforts to pay better attention to "normal" adolescence broadened my perspective, as did our conversation. Dr. Offer does not attribute to the quest for status nearly the importance that I do, finding it only one among many important influences in a group of 73 midwestern high school students he studied in the 1960s. But by being chosen for its "normality," this sample was weighted toward those who *have* status, athletes and school leaders who can afford to be casual about their social standing. The fact that Offer himself at seventeen was fighting Arabs in his native Israel might add to his circumspection about status in American adolescence.

While our perspectives differ, I found Dr. Offer's work a thoughtful and necessary antidote to a lot of romantic nonsense that has been written about adolescent rebellion and "today's youth." His first findings are reported in *The Psychological World of the Teenager* (New York: Basic Books, 1969), his follow-up research in *From Teenage to Young Adulthood* (with Judith Offer, New York: Basic Books, 1975).

In addition, the writings of Erik Erikson, and Elizabeth Douvan and Joseph Adelson's *The Adolescent Experience* (New York: John Wiley, 1968) have been helpful.

Finally, I've tried to read widely among essays and reports of research from varying points of view that bear on this topic.

Foreword

ix Ann Landers's correspondent wondered if these were the happiest years of his life in the *San Diego Evening Tribune*, October 1, 1974.

High School Fever

1 John A. Rice, the founder of Black Mountain College, wrote about wincing at adolescent memories in *I Came out of the Eighteenth Century* (New York: Harper & Brothers, 1942), p. 186. Rice's quotation is cited in Norman Kiell's *The Universal Experience of Adolescence* (New York: International University Press, 1964), p. 25 of the Beacon Press edition, an awesome compilation of material on this period of life.

3 Ford's speech was televised on August 12, 1974. The Associated Press transcript (*Los Angeles Times, San Diego Union*, August 13, 1974) contained only Ford's reference to running for class president as a Progressive. Losing to a Republican must have been ad-libbed or scribbled in at the last minute.

3-5   William J. Schuiling, who is president of Financial General Bank-shares in Washington, talked with me in his office on the twelfth floor of that city's First National Bank Building on October 24, 1974. He is a long-time friend and supporter of Gerald R. Ford.

7   Mia Farrow recalled not being asked to dance in *Seventeen*, October 1965, reprinted in Edwin Miller, *Seventeen Interviews Film Stars and Super-stars* (New York: Macmillan, 1970), p. 220; and again in her *Life* cover story, May 5, 1967.

Charles Schulz has mentioned the yearbook without his cartoons in *The Saturday Evening Post*, January 12, 1957, and April 25, 1964, as well as in *Time*, April 9, 1965; *National Enquirer*, September 16, 1973; and in *Charlie Brown and Charlie Schulz* by Lee Mendelson, in association with Charles Schulz (New York: Signet, 1971), p. 19.

Warren Beatty refers to the football scholarships he turned down in profiles in: *Seventeen*, May 1961; *Time*, September 1, 1961; *Horizon*, January 1962; *Vogue*, January 1, 1962; and *Redbook*, May 1974.

Dory Previn talked about not getting the play lead during our interview for my profile of her in *Human Behavior*, January 1974.

7-8   According to the *Digest of Educational Statistics* (U.S. Department of Health, Education and Welfare, 1972), p. 33, 93.7 percent of Americans aged fourteen through seventeen were enrolled in high school in the spring of 1970.

In 1890, only 6.7 percent of the eligible fourteen-through-seventeen-year-olds were enrolled. This figure rose to 51.4 percent by 1930, 86.1 percent in 1960. Ibid.

8   Rhoda talked of her cheerleader-tryout hands on CBS television (January 27, 1974) to describe the nervousness of wondering why her husband had gone to see a psychiatrist. She added, "I was the only one whose pom-poms ran."

Ali MacGraw has talked of her wallflowerish adolescence in *Look*, August 11, 1970; *Time*, January 11, 1971; and in *National Enquirer*, April 25, 1971, where she referred to never having had a date.

Kissinger's classmate called him a fatso in *Newsweek*, October 1, 1973. His colleague told Nora Ephron that Kissinger was the kid nobody ate lunch with (*McCall's*, November 1972, p. 128).

In the Hallways of Your Mind

11   Zappa called high school a state of mind in our interview on October 27, 1974.

13   The Los Angeles radio program was "The Ken Minyard Show," KABC-Radio, September 7, 1973.

14   Harry P. Bahrick, Phyllis O. Bahrick, and Roy P. Wittlinger of Ohio Wesleyan University reported their research on recall of classmates in *Psychology Today*, December 1974. (The artist who did *Psychology Today*'s layout for this article tried to fuzz up the yearbook pictures he used, but still heard from readers who recognized classmates.)

15   People also tell me of classmates not seen in years popping up incongruously in their dreams, and one woman says her caught-in-public-without-any-clothes-on dream is usually set in her high school's hallways.

15n   The *Harvard Magazine* letters were reported in *Time*, January 28, 1974.

19–20   After several years as an Academy Award-winning lyricist, Dory Previn has in recent years recorded six albums of her songs, published a book of lyrics, and written the screenplay for ABC-TV's movie *Third Girl from the Left*. Her comments were made in an interview with me at a restaurant near her home in the Hollywood hills on August 30, 1974.

20   Dyan Cannon was reported by Noonie Knight in *Movie Life*, February 1972, p. 18 as saying: "You should have seen me when I was in high school. My breasts used to be absolutely *huge*. Really vim vam voom. I used to go around the house with oranges in my bra to make them flatter. I was so ashamed of them. I wished they wouldn't stick out so much. I walked slouched over all the time so they wouldn't look so big."

21   Edgar Z. Friedenberg writes of telling time by period in *Coming of Age in America* (New York: Random House, 1965), p. 33 of the Vintage Books edition.

Earlier versions of high school were often located simply within the community. After secondary education became compulsory, huge schools had to be built for this exploded population. Only slowly have we realized what a separate tribe this physical isolation has helped create.

22   Eric Berne writes about names and nicknames as a source of feedback, then part of your "sweatshirt," in *What Do You Say After You Say Hello?* (New York: Grove Press, 1972), pp. 77–79, 167, 176 of the Bantam edition.

Burt Reynolds says his family nickname of "Buddy" got changed to "Greaseball" or "Mullett" by classmates in recognition of his Italian-Indian origins, then reverted to "Buddy" after he began to win foot races. As told to Claire Safran in *Redbook*, January 1974, p. 73.

22–23   Coleman's quotation is excerpted from *The Adolescent Society*, p. 314. His comments were made in an interview inside his maroon Eldorado as we drove to Chicago from O'Hare Field on October 22, 1974.

24–26   Barbara Howar was described by Nora Ephron in *Esquire*, August 1973, p. 52; Barbra Streisand by Burt Korall in *Saturday Review*, January 11, 1969, p. 108; Karen Carpenter by Tom Nolan in *Rolling Stone*, July 4, 1974, p. 66; Ingrid Superstar by Paul Carroll in *Playboy*, September 1969, p. 278; Cybill Shepherd by Julia Cameron in *Rolling Stone*, April 10, 1975; p. 54; Erica Jong by Burt Prelutsky in *Calendar, Los Angeles Times*, May 25, 1975 (in response a letter writer accused Prelutsky of "writing like a smarty-pants sophomore"); Richard Nixon by Larry King in *New Times*, September 9, 1974, p. 16; Warren Beatty by Rex Reed in *Do You Sleep in the Nude?* (New York: Signet, 1968), p. 32; Fran Tarkenton by New England Patriot defensive back Ron Bolton, to Dave Brady in the *New York Post*, October 28, 1974; Lyndon Johnson by Barbara Howar in *Laughing All the Way* (New York: Stein & Day, 1973), p. 160 of the Fawcett edition; Hugh Scott by John Chervokas in *Esquire*, December 1974, p. 204; Steve Allen by Dick Adler in the *Los Angeles Times*, February 14, 1974.

27 Sally Kempton refers to Dustin Hoffman's characterization of Katherine Ross in *Esquire*, July 1970, p. 80.

Lauren Hutton's opinion of fellow models was quoted in *Newsweek*, October 1, 1973, p. 68.

27–29 Zappa made his comments in an interview with me on October 27, 1974, in Waterbury, Connecticut's Holiday Inn.

28 The rock 'n' roll star thinks the book he read in college was Wayne Gordon's *The Social System of the High School* (Glencoe, Ill.: The Free Press, 1957).

28–29 "Status Back Baby" is on his *Absolutely Free* album, Verve Records.

33 My local historical society recently put out a call for old yearbooks, calling them one of their most valuable research tools (*San Diego Evening Tribune*, February 3, 1975).

An American invention, the high school annual followed those of colleges, which had been publishing yearbooks since *Profiles of Part of the Class Graduated at Yale College, September, 1806*. See Edgar G. Johnston and Roland C. Faunce, *Student Activities in Secondary Schools* (New York: Ronald Press, 1952), pp. 185–188.

I know a guy in New Jersey who collects yearbooks. "Some people get out a good record to play in the evening," he says of this hobby. "I get out a good yearbook."

Martha Mitchell's yearbook caption has been quoted by *Time*, December 5, 1969, p. 39; *New York Times*, May 1, 1970; *Newsday*, May 23, 1970; and *Newsweek*, November 30, 1970, p. 20.

Marilyn Monroe was shot in a yearbook pose by photographer Milton Greene. This picture was reprinted in *Life*, September 8, 1972, and *People*, April 29, 1974.

Ann Landers suggested looking for a woman's picture in her yearbook on October 10, 1974, *San Diego Evening Tribune*.

34 In Pete Gent's *North Dallas Forty*, his football-playing hero, in bed with a woman, reaches for the dope in her bedside table drawer where "a small plastic baggie lay atop the Fightin' Bobcats Yearbook. I had thumbed through the book before. Joanne had gone through and neatly snipped out every picture of herself" (New York: William Morrow, 1973, quoted from p. 74 of the Signet edition).

I've read on a variety of occasions about yearbooks being withdrawn from circulation, especially for sexual or racial innuendo.

Reference was made in the *Salt Lake Tribune* (July 13, 1973) to a student who sued his yearbook and all concerned for $38,000 for libel. A yearbook salesman told me he knew of several such cases.

Eydie Gormé appears in the 1946 annual of William Howard Taft High School in New York, lent me by a classmate. Dwight Eisenhower's yearbook is referred to in *Ike* by Stephen F. Ambrose (New York: Harper & Row, 1973), p. 20, and *National Geographic*, July 1969, pp. 9, 11; Ed Muskie's in *New York*, February 7, 1972, p. 30, and Mel Brooks's in a classmate's letter to *The New York Times Magazine*, April 20, 1975, p. 21.

As the Tables Turn

37 The letter to *Project Talent News*, Palo Alto, California, appeared in May 1974.

39–46 Robert Logue talked with me on April 3, 1974. Though reticent about the details of his race against Nixon, Logue does say the account of Earl Mazo is substantially correct. Mazo writes in *Richard Nixon: A Personal and Political Portrait*, "It was the first and last time he ever underestimated the opposition. At stake was the student body presidency of Whittier High School. For years the contest for the position had been between the political machines of the junior and senior class, controlled by their respective faculty advisers. Though he had just transferred from Fullerton High School, the senior class organization nominated Nixon; the junior class group nominated a friend, Roy Newsome. The campaign was progressing according to form when a venturesome boy named Robert Logue defied tradition by entering the race as an independent. On top of that, while Nixon and Newsome stuck by the practice of relying on their respective 'machines,' Logue made a vigorous personal campaign. He electioneered at recess, shook all the student hands he could reach, and produced banners and literature urging one and all to 'Stop, Think and Vote for Bob Logue'" (New York: Harper & Brothers, 1959, p. 21 of the revised, 1960 Avon edition).

47 The exact words of Vonnegut's classmate were: "When you get to be our age, you all of a sudden realize that you are being ruled by people you went to high school with.

"You all of a sudden catch on that life is nothing but high school. You make a fool of yourself in high school, then you go to college and learn how you should have acted in high school, and then you get out into real life, and that turns out to be high school all over again — class officers, cheerleaders, and all" (*New York Times*, September 13, 1969).

Requoting his friend in a later essay, Vonnegut endorsed this position and added, "Richard Nixon is a familiar type from high school. So is Melvin Laird. So is J. Edgar Hoover. So is General Lewis Hershey. So is everybody." From the Introduction to *Our Time Is Now*, John Birmingham, ed. (New York: Praeger, 1970), p. x, reprinted in *Esquire*, February 1970.

This conviction, actually this fear, is so widespread that Vonnegut's observation is cited regularly by others. Lois Gould, for example, writes in *Final Analysis:* "Of course it was a man — Vonnegut — who wrote about the day you wake up and discover that your high school class is running the country. But I have that feeling too" (New York: Random House, 1974, p. 86 of the Avon edition).

47–48 Dan Wakefield's novel is among the most pure of literary tributes to enduring high school memories and the wish to change.

After being challenged to fight years later by a lesser athlete who hasn't gotten over his feelings about Big Rods, Gunner exclaims, "High school. Fuckin' high school. Doesn't it ever get over with?" (*Going All the Way*, p. 198.)

48 *Maude*, CBS-TV, April 10, 1973; *Rhoda*, CBS-TV, April 28, 1975; *All in the Family*, CBS-TV, February 10, 1973.

Even television advertising draws on the wish to transform. In one soap ad a beautiful woman shows us her picture as an ugly teenager before explaining how she blossomed with the help of Camay (ABC-TV, February 1, 1975). An ad for Cheer has a greasy hood roller-skating as a woman's voice asks, "Remember creepy Jimmy Carlson?

"Today he owns a Taco stand. . . .

"And a supermarket, and a bank . . ." (NBC-TV, February 3, 1975).

Offer told me about his research in an interview on October 21, 1974, at Michael Reese Hospital in Chicago, where he is associate director of the Institute for Psychosomatic and Psychiatric Research and Training.

It should be pointed out that Dr. Offer sees persistence as more fundamental than change among the adolescents he's studied, and that the comments he noted about change came from no more than 25 percent of the sixty-one students he's following after graduation.

49 McGovern's yearbook caption is referred to in Robert Sam Anson's *McGovern: A Biography* (New York: Holt, Rinehart & Winston, 1972), p. 30. The senator recalled his gym teacher's taunt and its effect for Richard Meryman in *Life*, July 7, 1972, p. 36.

50 John Gunther writes of "Grotties" in *Roosevelt in Retrospect* (New York: Harper & Brothers, 1950), pp. 172–173. Merle Miller referred to this part of Gunther's book in his profile of another Grottie outie, Joseph Alsop (*Harper's*, June 1968, p. 49).

In a delightful episode in Merle Miller's *Plain Speaking* (New York: Berkeley Publishing Co., 1974, pp. 34–35), former President Truman is asked by a child, "Mr. President, was you popular when you was a boy?

Truman's reply: "Why no. I was never popular. The popular boys were the ones who were good at games and had big, tight fists. I was never like that. Without my glasses I was blind as a bat, and to tell the truth I was kind of a sissy. If there was any danger of getting into a fight, I always ran. I guess that's why I'm here today."

Miller's comment: "The little boy started to applaud, and then everybody else did, too. It was an eminently satisfactory answer for all of us who ever ran from a fight, which is all of us."

The story of Truman and Ross is told by his daughter Margaret Truman in *Harry S Truman* (New York: William Morrow, 1973), pp. 3, 46–47, 52–53, 227–228.

Sandy Duncan talked about not making cheerleader in *TV Guide*, September 18, 1971, pp. 38, 40. This also is referred to in *The Sandy Duncan Story* by Rochelle Reed (New York: Pyramid Books, 1973), who writes, "She envied those blonde, winsome girls who performed before deliriously happy crowds on the Tyler High School football field, kicking high into the air as confetti and streamers buried them knee deep on the green grass — while Sandy sat home alone" (p. 15).

Tom Bradley referred to his high school loss in a testimonial dinner speech reprinted by the *Los Angeles Times* (June 3, 1973), and excerpted in *The American Way* (November 1973, p. 14). His point had to do with the racial snub involved in this largely white high school.

51 Isaac Hayes has recalled his high school years for *Ebony*, March 1970, and *Penthouse*, September 1973, p. 59, from which his quotation is excerpted.

Lauren Hutton talks, obsessively, of her unhappy adolescent experience in interviews, such as those reported by *Newsweek*, April 29 and August 26, 1974; *Time*, September 17, 1973; and *Vogue*, June 1973, p. 86, from which her quotation is excerpted. Differing versions of the falsies incident are reported by *Vogue* and *Newsweek*.

Dustin Hoffman is among the most high school-minded of public personalities. In a *Rolling Stone* profile he told Tim Cahill, "I've been a star for about six years. But my feelings about myself and my work are based on the first thirty years."

Hoffman has detailed his high school traumas in *Newsweek*, January 22, 1968; *Redbook*, September 1968; *Time*, February 7, 1969; *Seventeen*, May 1971; *Movie Stars*, May 1971; *People*, December 23, 1974; and *McCall's*, September 1968, p. 143, in which he made the excerpted comment to Mel Gussow.

To Earl Wilson, Dustin Hoffman observed, "Some of the guys and gals, who were such great lookers when young, don't look so good now. Us homelies age better. We got no place to go but up" (*San Diego Evening Tribune*, June 14, 1971).

52-53   Jack Block wondered about post–high school turnarounds in *Lives Through Time* (Berkeley: Bancroft Books, 1971), p. 1.

53   The thirteen-year follow-up was by Percival Symonds with Arthur B. Jensen in *From Adolescent to Adult* (New York: Columbia University Press, 1961), p. 195; the fifteen-year follow-up by H. S. Lief and J. Thompson, "The Prediction of Behavior from Adolescence to Adulthood," *Psychiatry*, XXIV, 1961, pp. 32–38; Block's quotation is from p. 268 of *Lives Through Time*.

The comparison of early- and late-maturing boys is by Mary C. Jones and Nancy Bayley, "Physical Maturing Among Boys as Related to Behavior in Adolescence and Adult Years," in *Psychological Studies of Human Development*, Raymond G. Kuhlen and George C. Thompson, eds. (New York: Appleton-Century-Crofts, 1963). See also Jones's later study with Paul H. Mussen, "Self-Conceptions, Motivation, and Interpersonal Attitudes of Late and Early Maturing Boys," ibid., which confirmed the earlier findings.

54   The study of 351 graduates and a select group of 20 was reported by Robert Hess, "High School Antecedents of Young Adult Achievement," in *Studies in Adolescence*, Robert E. Grinder, ed. (New York: Macmillan, 1963), in which the excerpted quotations appear on pages 411 and 408.

The follow-up at age thirty was reported by Jean Walker MacFarlane in *Vita Humana* 7 (2), 1964, p. 124. Her findings are discussed at greater length in Chapter 4.

55   Lloyd Temme wrote about adolescent social systems in "Old and New Addresses: Finding the Sample and Gathering the Data," mimeographed, Center for Study of Social Organization of Schools, Johns Hopkins University. Temme's finding 85 percent of the 9,000 graduates studied more than fifteen years before is a remarkable achievement. He feels sure that with more time and funds he'd have found them all.

In the space available I've not done justice to the breadth and depth of

Lloyd Temme's study, which could be the most exhaustively documented correlation ever attempted between high school and vocational records.

57 About the Friedman twins, see 1960's *Current Biography* on Abigail Van Buren and 1957's on Ann Landers (New York: H. W. Wilson Co.) as well as *McCall's*, August 1973. Though not all observers would accept Bowie Kuhn's record as a vindication of his classmates' prediction, it is reported in 1970's *Current Biography*, and 1973's *Celebrity Register* (New York: Simon & Schuster).

Donald Rumsfeld appears as vice-president of his junior class in New Trier (Illinois) High School's 1949 annual.

High school success stories who have learned new routines include the following ex-football players: clothing designer Bill Blass, author James Michener, and James Dickey, the poet.

Peter Falk made the first of his comments about college slippage to W. C. Heinz in *The Saturday Evening Post*, February 22, 1966, p. 93, the second to Dick Hobson in *TV Guide*, March 25, 1972, p. 32. Like so many of the ex-statusy, Falk frequently talks about his high school heroics by making fun of them, and plays up the fact that he was breaking windows with a gang after school. Falk recalls acting in high school only as a last-minute fill-in (*Rolling Stone*, April 24, 1975, and *Senior Scholastic*, February 28, 1972). A classmate later told *National Enquirer* how, in *The Importance of Being Earnest*, Falk broke out laughing uncontrollably on stage and later swore to others he'd never be an actor (January 6, 1973). But Falk himself said (*Good Housekeeping*, September 1973) that he'd secretly wanted to be an actor since he was sixteen, though he didn't get started until ten years later.

57 Dr. Lawrence told me of his survey in an interview on September 5, 1974. Though the correlation between early and later success has interested him for years, the educator says he's never been able to formally study it for lack of a suitable definition of "success."

Coppola's college metamorphosis is described in *Newsweek*, November 25, 1974. Eva Marie Saint's experience is covered in *Cosmopolitan*, March 1955, and *Current Biography*, 1955.

Both Coppola and Saint had siblings who were more recognized than they in high school, less thereafter. I've heard often of such a syndrome. Most recently actress Stockard Channing (*The Fortune*) told Walter Clemons in *Newsweek* (June 16, 1975, p. 77), "I had an older sister, Leslie, who was blond and beautiful. I was the original ugly little sister. I used to powder Leslie's back, hook her into her Merry Widow and clean up her bathroom after she went downstairs to meet her date. I thought it would make me beautiful and popular when I was 17. It didn't, but I didn't turn out too badly."

58-60 Art Linkletter's childhood development is well known in his hometown, and was described by him to me in an interview in his Beverly Hills office on September 3, 1974. He wrote of the "obstacle course to success" in the *San Diego Union*, November 4, 1963.

61 Peck's history, too, is well known in San Diego, and was summarized by *Time*'s cover story on the actor, January 12, 1948. Peck spoke of his high school frustrations to Dave McIntyre for the *San Diego Evening*

Tribune, March 15, 1963, from which his quotation about sleepiness is excerpted. The Spreckels Theater meeting of Peck and Lustig is described by *Evening Tribune* columnist Neil Morgan in *Neil Morgan's San Diego* (San Diego: Neil Morgan's San Diego, 1963), pp. 32–33. A footnote to this story is that although Dick Lustig won a role in *Oh, Wilbur*, and is pictured in its cast, he ended up as the play's student director.

61–64 Lustig talked with me at his home on July 31, 1974.

ᴸᵒᵒᵏⁱⁿᵍ *Looking Back on a Great Future*

65 Merle Haggard sings "Sidewalks of Chicago" on his *Hag* album, Capital Records, 1971.

67 The erotic actress who was Most Likely to Succeed at Southwest High School in Kansas City is described by Joe Hyams in *Cosmopolitan*, March 1972, where George McDonald's high school heroics are also referred to, as they are in *Playboy*, July 1971. Marilyn Chambers regularly talks of her cheerleader–beauty queen past in the usual put-down manner. In her *Oui* interview (February 1974, p. 69), Chambers told Al Goldstein, "I was a high-school cheerleader, up for homecoming queen — all that garbage." Her cheerleader past is also referred to in *Playboy* (April 1974) and *Knight* (June 1974, p. 21), where Charles A. Fracchia says Chambers was thrown off the squad for drinking beer.

Mary Rexroth, daughter of poet Kenneth Rexroth, has said the men she performs with in porno movies are "of a type, basically pretty straight guys. Like he was busy being the all-American boy and discovered America didn't want him." In Kenneth Turan and Stephen Zito's *Sinema* (New York: Praeger, 1974), p. 103.

67–68 Art Mitchell's interview with me was held in his San Francisco office on July 16, 1974.

68–70 McDonald's interview began at Sausalito's No-Name Bar and ended in his second-story walkup on July 17, 1974.

71 Rita Mae Brown's *Rubyfruit Jungle* (Plainfield, Vt.: Daughters, Inc., 1973), p. 97, is a lively, well-written account of growing up lesbian.

Memoirs of an Ex–Prom Queen (New York: Knopf, 1972) is another literary tribute to the encore problem. "Barely fifteen," Sasha Davis recalls about being crowned Queen of the Bunny Hop, "that April night I reached such heady heights that the triumphs of the rest of my life were bound to seem anti-climactic" (p. 67 of the Bantam edition).

72–73 Coleman's comment about being able to spot female ex-leading crowd members was made during our interview. He did not claim to be able to do this for women past forty, or for men at all.

73 David Harris's high school success is referred to in *Esquire*, September 1967; that of Ed Sanders in *Avant Garde*, January 1968; and Rennie Davis's in *Playboy*, June 1974, p. 112, where Davis told Robert Scheer, "I was athletic, played varsity basketball, was president of the student body, editor of the school paper, in every organization. . . . I found early an ability to organize — people looked to me in a kind of a leadership way.

. . . I was the best-known person in the school, awarded best all-around in the yearbook personality thing." (The Guru Maharaj Ji himself is now married to a former high school cheerleader and homecoming queen.) Another innie-radical is Weatherman fugitive Bernadine Dohrn, who according to a classmate was "an activities jock," dated the top guys, and was in Prom Court. To Lindsy Von Gelder, *Esquire*, April 1971, p. 164.

73 Michael Wolff wrote of his classmate Angel Atwood in "Cheerleader for a Revolution," *The New York Times Magazine*, July 21, 1974, in which her father is quoted on page 11.

SLA member Joseph Remiro, later convicted of assassinating Oakland's school superintendent, was a male cheerleader in high school. See John Bryan's *This Soldier Still at War* (New York: Harcourt Brace Jovanovich, 1975).

The entire SLA episode was an interesting study in high school–awareness by the media. Nancy Ling Perry, slain along with Angel Atwood, was for a long time referred to in the press as a "high school cheerleader" though she did not actually hold this job after junior high school. And Patricia Soltysik was regularly cited as the girl who wanted to be a cheerleader but didn't make it. Our fascination was as revealing as the information itself.

73–74 Tennessee Williams describes Jim O'Connor in *The Glass Menagerie* (New York: New Directions Books, 1945, 1949), p. 61. Williams's stage directions portray Jim O'Connor as "HIGH SCHOOL HERO BEARING A SILVER CUP" (p. 20).

74 Jean MacFarlane's observation is from her *Vita Humana* report, pp. 121–122.

Erik Erikson writes of identity formation in *Childhood and Society* (New York: Norton, 1950) and focuses on "Adolescence" in *Identity, Youth and Crisis* (New York: Norton, 1968), pp. 128–135.

In a comparison of Erikson's theories with those of others, psychologist Dorothy Rogers asks, "Does the adolescent sell a bit of himself, at too dear a price, to gain acceptance by others . . . ? Perhaps feeling out of step may help motivate the adolescent to become adult. If he settled too comfortably into adolescence he might forever remain just partly grown up." Dorothy Rogers, "Two Related Concepts: Stage Theory and Critical Period Hypothesis," in Dorothy Rogers, ed., *Issues in Adolescent Psychology* (New York: Appleton-Century-Crofts, 1969), p. 161.

75 I attended the Reverend Jackson's service on October 19, 1974.

76 Writes Harvard nutritionst Jean Mayer: "It's been shown over and over that when a group of adolescent boys who do not know each other are put together, they will instinctively tend to choose the tallest boy as their leader" (*San Diego Evening Tribune*, July 24, 1974).

See also the Jones & Bayley and Jones & Mussen studies already referred to, which are only two of several such reports on the enhanced status given boys who are "early maturers."

After conducting a similar study of girls, Margaret Siler Faust found physical maturity only "an important part of a composite of factors in creating a girl's reputation during adolescence." In Dorothy Rogers, *Issues in Adolescent Psychology*, p. 100.

For women, the remembered trauma of having been tall is at least equivalent to having been small for a man looking back on high school. Bea Arthur ("Maude") says her fondest teenage wish was to be a petite blond ingenue. This wish persisted after she became an actress. "All those Hollywood ladies were so pretty and so *short*," she has said. "By the time I was 12, I was 5 feet 9½ inches — in my stocking feet!" To Guy Flatley, *TV Guide*, November 18, 1972, p. 30.

Among freshmen interviewed at four high schools, Coleman found that being out for football, basketball, or both was the one attribute shared by everybody mentioned by classmates as belonging to the leading crowd.

Writes Coleman: "A striking discovery was the similarity of all the schools in the importance attached to athletics. Greater similarity among them was found in this than in any other dimension of the research" (*Adolescents and the Schools*, p. 40, 37).

Willy Loman talks of Biff's unmatched athletic glory in Arthur Miller, *Death of a Salesman*, in *New Voices in the American Theatre* (New York: Random House, 1955), p. 120.

76–77 After spending most of an academic year at a small midwestern high school, anthropologist Jacquetta Hill Burnett was struck by the degree to which the school's schedule revolved around its teams, particularly football and basketball. Noting that the athlete's banquet was held right after basketball season ended, she was at first puzzled. Why didn't it take place before track season? Then she realized that the answer lay in the schedule. As an afternoon event, track made no money, didn't attract cheerleaders, and was attended by few spectators of any kind. "Track meets after school," the anthropologist concluded, "just didn't fit the community time schedule." "Ceremony, Rites and Economy in the Student System of an American High School," *Human Organization*, Spring 1969, p. 7.

In recent years some high schools have begun holding football and basketball games in the afternoon because of violence at night games. It will be interesting to see what effect such a change may have on high schools' social systems, as may cutbacks on athletic budgets, and the increasing sexual integration of high school sports.

Coleman points out that although the prestige of a girl leading cheers can't compare with that of a star ballplayer, the two are comparable in that athletic stars and cheerleaders both get attention from the school as a whole. The sociologist found that the girls interviewed commonly felt their parents would be more proud of their making cheerleader than biology assistant. *The Adolescent Society*, pp. 48, 33.

77–78 Ruth Doan MacDougall's *The Cheerleader* (New York: Putnam's, 1973) captures as well as any book I've read the feeling of being *in* high school. The quotations excerpted are from pages 55–56, 144.

78 In an *Esquire* (October 1974, p. 221) layout on former cheerleaders, Nancy Collins wrote about the advantages of this status, "You can wear your uniform to school on Fridays." Ms. Collins concluded about cheerleader status, "It ultimately comes down to power."

79 C. Wayne Gordon made the observation about powerful students in "The Roles of the Teacher in the Social Structure of the High School," in John Chilcott, Norman Greenberg and Herbert Wilson, eds., *Readings*

in the Socio-Cultural Foundations of Education (Belmont, Calif.: Wadsworth, 1968), p. 453.

This accurate perception of a teacher's complex political relationship with high school students (ask anyone who's taught them) is consistent with my own memory of the constant, quiet war of attrition we waged against high school teachers. Substitutes in particular could be wiped out in a matter of hours. Regular teachers took a little longer. We could be cruel.

I never cease to be amazed by what cows radical critics of high school believe its students to be. I don't recall being "oppressed" by high school. The institution wasn't that powerful. As I recall we went to hang around before and after school, during lunch and in the hallway between classes. If being bored in class and pretending to respect our elders was the price of admission, then this was the price.

81 Edgar Z. Friedenberg writes of an innie's weak ego in *The Vanishing Adolescent* (Boston: Beacon Press, 1959), pp. 167–168 of the Dell edition.

82 Warren Beatty called himself a "cheerful hypocrite" in *Time* (September 1, 1961, p. 53).

Rabbit Angstrom was first sketched as "The Ex-Basketball Player" in Updike's poem of that title in *The Carpentered Hen and Other Creatures* (New York: Harper & Row, 1957), then as "Ace" in "Ace in the Hole" (*The New Yorker*, April 9, 1955), before being painted more fully in *Rabbit Run*, where the ex-athlete describes his dilemma on p. 64 (New York: Knopf, 1960) and in *Rabbit Redux* (New York: Knopf, 1971).

83 Though his subject is an ex-college athlete, Irwin Shaw's "Eighty-Yard Run" in *Mixed Company* (New York: Random House, 1941), pp. 13–28, is the classic portrayal of an ex-jock who returns as a tailor's dummy to his field of glory fifteen years later, to run once more down the field. Tom Buchanan, too, is an ex–college football player described in *The Great Gatsby* as "one of those men who reach such an acute limited excellence at twenty-one that everything afterward savors of anticlimax . . ." (New York: Charles Scribner's Sons, 1925), p. 6 of the paperback edition.

Philip Roth wrote of Whitey Nelson, the alcoholic ex–high school baseball player in *When She Was Good* (New York: Random House, 1967); Larry McMurtry's ex-football players are Duane and Sonny in *The Last Picture Show* (New York: Dell, 1966, 1972); Wakefield's ex-jock of course is Gunner of *Going All the Way;* and Frederick Exley has put sharply into prose the syndrome of a less athletic son trying to shed the weight of his father's football glory in *A Fan's Notes* (New York: Harper & Row, 1968).

Jason Miller once said of his ex-jock characters in *That Championship Season:* "You find men like those in small towns all over America. The great team, still revered, almost a religious symbol. You go into bars — their pictures are all over the place. And, curiously, there is a religious instinct under this adulation so long after the real event. It is a religious instinct that cannot find another expression." To Glenn Loney, *After Dark*, January 1973, p. 52.

In Tennessee Williams's *Cat on a Hot Tin Roof* (New York: Signet Books, 1955), p. 111, Brick's athletic glory was in college. Arthur Miller's ex-high school jock is, of course, Biff Loman.

84 Zappa talked about cheerleaders in our interview. He classifies them with stewardesses and *Playboy* bunnies as "all from the same aura."

84–86 In Marylou and Ron Humphrey's *Cheerleading and Songleading* (Rutland, Vt.: Charles E. Tuttle, 1970), pp. 16, 20, 22, 47, the following criteria are listed for a good cheerleader:

"Every cheerleader must show confidence all the time. . . .

"A popular cheerleader or song leader is expected to be peppy and enthusiastic all the time.

"Assume that you are always in the public eye. . . .

"*Keep smiling* regardless of what happens."

Writing about what it was like to lead cheers in the fifties, Louise Bernikow said in *MS* (October 1973, pp. 67, 98): "Half the time, in real 'civilian' life, I had to keep pulling those gray flannel skirts down, making sure 'nothing showed.' . . . The other half the time, as a cheerleader, I dropped a skimpy red costume over only bra and panties and got out there in the middle of a gym full of screaming spectators to wiggle my hips all over the place.

"What does it do to the mind of a 16-year-old girl to be Marilyn Monroe one moment and Little Goody Two-Shoes the next? I don't know, but it sure wasn't sane."

Ms. Bernikow wrote of hiding for years that she'd been a cheerleader until she discovered that status also included among her acquaintances: a painter-poet, an acid freak, an unwed hippy mother, an actress.

"God knows I tried hard to kill her," Bernikow concludes of the cheerleader within. But: "Every time I say 'sure' when I mean 'no,' every time I smile brightly when I'm exploding with rage, every time I imagine my man's achievement is my own, I know the cheerleader never really died. I feel her shaking her ass inside me and I hear her breathless, girlish voice mutter, 'T-E-A-M, Yea, Team.' "

87 Dan Greenburg writes of his cheerleader in *Scoring* (New York: Dell, 1972), pp. 204, 234; Philip Roth of his two Monkeys in *Portnoy's Complaint* (New York: Random House, 1967) and *When She Was Good*, pp. 60–61.

Don't Get Popular, Get Even

91 Richard Reeves's comment about getting even was made in *New York*, November 25, 1974, p. 42.

93–94 Revenge statements: Bobby Darin to Edward Linn in *The Saturday Evening Post*, May 6, 1961, p. 63; Nora Ephron in *Wallflower at the Orgy* (New York: Viking, 1970), p. 156; Mike Nichols to Nora Ephron, *Wallflower*, p. 156; Rona Barrett in *Miss Rona: An Autobiography* (Los Angeles: Nash Publishing Corp., 1974), p. 25; Betty Friedan to Paul Wilkes, *The New York Times Magazine*, November 29, 1970, p. 27; Bette Midler in *Newsweek*, December 17, 1973, p. 64; Janis Joplin in *Newsweek*, January

15, 1968, p. 77; Dan Greenburg in *Scoring*, p. 16; Robert Blake to Charles Champlin, *Calendar, Los Angeles Times*, August 5, 1973, p. 64; Mel Brooks to Harry Stein, *New Times*, February 22, 1974, p. 57; the Johnnie Walker advertisement appeared in *The New York Times Magazine*, August 25, 1974, p. 23 and elsewhere.

94 Sam Keen's books are: *Gabriel Marcel* (Richmond, Va.: John Knox Press, 1967); *Apology for Wonder* (New York: Harper & Row, 1969); *To a Dancing God* (New York: Harper & Row, 1970); *Telling Your Story*, with Anne Valley Fox (Garden City, N.Y.: Doubleday, 1973); and *Beginnings Without End* (New York: Harper & Row, 1975). His collection is *Voices and Visions* (New York: Harper & Row, 1974).

96 Beverly Katz screams at Sasha Davis in *Memoirs of an Ex-Prom Queen*, p. 16 of the Bantam edition.

"At Seventeen" is on Janis Ian's fine *Between the Lines* album, Columbia Records, 1975.

Zappa said in our interview that innies don't play his kind of music.

About Alice Cooper (real name: Vincent Furnier), see *Time*, May 28, 1973; *Newsweek*, May 28, 1973; and *People*, April 1, 1974, p. 26, where his talent-show victory is mentioned.

John Denver worked over ex-classmates during his ABC-TV special on December 1, 1974. After thumbing his nose at Marcia, Denver grinned to show he wasn't being hostile.

97 Janis Joplin returned obsessively to high school in interviews: *Time*, August 27, 1973; *Newsweek*, October 19, 1970; *Time*, October 19, 1970; *Newsweek*, January 15, 1968; *Time*, August 9, 1968; *Newsweek*, February 24, 1969; *The New York Times Magazine*, February 23, 1969; and *Playboy*, August 1970. In *Rolling Stone*, September 17, 1970, and October 29, 1970, her reunion appearance is breathily covered. Scenes of Janis discussing her upcoming reunion with Dick Cavett, then attending it, are included in the documentary movie *Janis*.

She told Al Aronowitz of the *New York Post* about her plan to jam it up their asses, as quoted by Deborah Landau in *Janis Joplin: Her Life and Times* (New York: Paperback Library, 1971), p. 29, where the singer's fan is quoted on pp. 22–23.

Myra Friedman's biography of Janis Joplin, *Buried Alive* (New York: William Morrow, 1973), is the best. Friedman portrays with detail and sensitivity the singer's reunion homecoming, her last public appearance.

98 Sam Houston Johnson describes his brother Lyndon as weighing less than a cheerleader in *My Brother Lyndon* (New York: Cowles Book Co., 1969–70), p. 17.

I heard the Ultra-Brite cheerleader commercial on KOZN-FM Radio, San Diego, June 18, 1974.

99 Slightly differing versions of Mike Nichols's story about remeeting his tormentor are reported by Nora Ephron in *Wallflower*, p. 155, and by *Newsweek*, November 14, 1966, p. 96. (In Ephron, Nichols is quoted as calling the guy "a shit," in *Newsweek*, "a son-of-a-bitch.")

Larry McMurtry and his hometown were covered by the *Los Angeles Times*, February 17, 1972.

In addition to Whitey Nelson, the alcoholic ex-third baseman, Philip Roth portrayed Ron Patimkin as a classic dumb jock about to teach

PE in *Goodbye, Columbus* (Boston: Houghton Mifflin, 1959). Roth's *My Life as a Man* (New York: Holt, Rinehart & Winston, 1974) is a fictional memoir of interesting construction in which two preliminary autobiographical short stories ("useful fictions") are discussed by the book's narrator, who is the author of these stories.

The comment about schoolyard humiliation is from the second of these useful fictions (p. 37). "God," the author later writes, "how I thought I was suffering in adolescence when fly balls used to fall through my hands in the schoolyard, and the born athletes on my team would smack their foreheads in despair" (p. 86).

Roth himself, according to 1970's *Current Biography*, was assistant editor of his school paper and a student council member at New Jersey's Weequahic High School, from which he graduated in 1950. Weequahic High shows up often in *Portnoy's Complaint*.

Arthur Miller played football, ran track, and did poorly at two New York high schools in the early 1930s. In *Memory of Two Mondays* (New York: Dramatists Play Service, 1956), p. 7, Miller's eighteen-year-old hero works (as did the playwright) in an auto parts warehouse after graduating from high school, where, he says "I just played ball and fooled around, that's all."

Jason Miller played three sports at Saint Patrick's High in Scranton, where he also acted and recalls being an incipient delinquent (*Current Biography*, 1974).

John Updike is vague about his high school background, though *Time*'s cover story (in which his classmate is quoted) says Updike was class president and editor of the paper at Shillington High School in Pennsylvania, where his father taught (*Time*, April 26, 1968, p. 73). More than any other contemporary author, Updike has picked over high school memories in his writing, ignoring college almost completely. "I feel in some obscure way ashamed of the Harvard years," he has said. "They were a betrayal of my high school years, really" (ibid.).

Though today an avid player of different kinds of ball, Updike was not a teenage jock. He failed his army physical due to allergies. In a rare autobiographical essay, the author talked of his childhood clumsiness with girls, especially the one who later became May queen of their senior class. Martin Levin, *Five Boyhoods* (Garden City, N.Y.: Doubleday & Co., 1962).

99–100   The Olinger story quoted is "The Happiest I've Been," *The New Yorker*, January 3, 1959, p. 24.

100   Tennessee Williams is self-described as "delicate and sissified" in Benjamin Nelson, *Tennessee Williams: The Man and His Work* (New York: Ivan Obolensky, 1961), p. 5. Williams wrote of discovering writing as an escape from tormentors in the Foreword to his *Sweet Bird of Youth* (New York: New Directions Books, 1959), pp. vii–viii.

On Dick Cavett's show, the sixty-year-old playwright explained his fear of eating alone by saying: "I feel so unpopular. Of course, I am unpopular" (ABC-TV, August 22, 1974).

101–103   Birds dump on PE teachers in the *National Lampoon*, November 1970, p. 32; sex education uses live models in October 1974, p. 52; and Nancy Reagan advises in July 1971, p. 74.

To put together their *1964 High School Yearbook Parody* (1974), the *Lampoon* staff first took Polaroid pictures of current high school students (with their hair pulled back), then sorted them by stereotype. "One of the odder things that happened," P. J. O'Rourke told me, "is how we typecast these kids before we even knew them: the class clown, Romeo, the class brain. All the categories still exist, though not as intense."

O'Rourke thinks their yearbook parody has done so well precisely because it's the satirizable document Americans have most in common. "High school is the one thing uniting all Americans," he explains. "Most people went to high school, and high school is always the same." These comments and those in the text were made by O'Rourke in our November 14, 1974, conversation.

103   Mopsy Strange said *Lampoon*ers are fighting their adolescence in *The New York Times Magazine*, December 10, 1972, p. 104.

An innie we accidentally let slip into a position of power in the print media is *Human Behavior* editor Marshall Lumsden, who tells me he lettered in sports and held class office.

On television Dan Rather is an ex–football player who carried the innies' talon against Richard Nixon. Rather was removed from the White House beat after Nixon resigned, perhaps due to the difficulty of staying objective with a fellow jock as President.

"Ford," Rather told us after Richard Nixon went back to San Clemente, "moves with the easy grace of an athlete. One gets the feeling with Gerald Ford he's sure of himself. He accomplished as a youth those things many of us just dream about" (CBS-TV, August 9, 1974).

Steinem wrote about Streisand in the *Ladies' Home Journal*, August 1966, pp. 64, 112.

Halberstam characterized reporters as high school outsiders in *Esquire*, April 1974, p. 111.

104–105   Talese's self-description is from *Playboy*, January 1971, p. 127. His subsequent comments were made in an interview with me at his East Side Manhattan townhouse on October 31, 1974.

105   Nora Ephron compared reporting to being a *Wallflower at the Orgy*, p. ix, where she talks with Nichols, pp. 155–159. Ephron reviewed Shulman in *Esquire*, August 1972; her column on breasts was in *Esquire*, May 1972, p. 158.

106-108   Ephron's subsequent comments were made in an interview with me at her East Side Manhattan apartment on November 11, 1974. She wrote about her high school's pom-pom routine in *Esquire*, December 1974.

108   More exruciating than rejection is not feeling noticed enough in high school to even be rejected.

"While some of us were fighting to be most popular in the class, I was fighting to be recognized" is the way one of my Prescott students described this feeling in her essay "Memoirs of an Ex–Prom Waitress."

Charles Schulz recalls no one in his high school caring enough to hate him (*The Saturday Evening Post*, January 12, 1957).

109   Alice Munro talks of vanquishing her hometown in *Lives of Girls and Women* (New York: McGraw-Hill, 1971), p. 206 of the Signet edition. Munro is a Canadian, but what the hell.

Of former Supreme Court Justice William O. Douglas, a boyhood friend once told Milton Viorst: "Bill hated the Yakima [Washington] 'establish-ment' and when he left town to go to law school, he vowed he would cut those people down to size. He's worked ever since — with a widening horizon — to keep that vow" (*The New York Times Magazine*, June 14, 1970, p. 38).

William Loeb, owner of the *Manchester Union Leader*, was taunted by classmates at Hotchkiss. "Later," wrote Robert Sam Anson and Gordon Weil of the publisher, "Loeb told his second wife that the experience had made him decide 'right then and there that I was going to get back at them' " (*New Times*, January 10, 1975, p. 16).

Larry King wrote about rejecting his class's apology in a report on his adult confrontation of the class's Most Likely to Succeed. King's essay is a classic of satisfaction sought but not attained (*New Times*, November 16, 1973).

110   While accepting the Newbery & Caldecott Medal for his book *Island of the Blue Dolphins*, author Scott O'Dell reminisced about Jack Iman, the schoolmate of several decades past who used to beat up on him regularly. "My nemesis," O'Dell called him. "My tormentor. The embodi-ment to me of all evil."

Years later O'Dell read that Iman had become a prizefighter. Repeatedly the author went to see his ex-tormentor fight, just waiting for him to get whipped. Finally it happened, and O'Dell went back to the loser's dressing room to gloat, confident he wouldn't be recognized.

But, as the author told his audience, "though he was just returning from another world, Jack Iman recognized me at once. Unsteadily he came towards me, put his arms around my shoulders and wept." Lee Kingman, ed., *Newbery & Caldecott Medal Books: 1956–1965* (Boston: The Horn Book, Inc., 1965), pp. 101–102. O'Dell's speech was given in 1961.

110–113   Burt Prelutsky's column about his tennis coach appeared in *Calendar, Los Angeles Times*, July 14, 1974. His comments were made during lunch at a Beverly Hills restaurant on September 3, 1974. Burt's review of *Up the Down Staircase* was in *Los Angeles*, July 1967. Spector was covered by Prelutsky in *WEST, Los Angeles Times*, February 18, 1968.

After our conversation, Burt Prelutsky devoted a column to Herb Al-pert's success both in high school and later, *Calendar, Los Angeles Times*, October 6, 1974, a bit of class treason I've chosen to overlook.

113   Doug Kenney's "Gratuitous Wish Fulfillment" appeared in the *National Lampoon*, December 1971.

Myra Friedman's quotes are from the Bantam edition of *Buried Alive*, pp. 357, 359.

115   Holden Caulfield evaluates Stradlater in J. D. Salinger's *The Catcher in the Rye* (Boston: Little, Brown, 1953), pp. 28, 30 of the Signet edition.

In *The Folded Leaf* (New York: Harper & Brothers, 1945), William Maxwell describes how Lymie perceives Spud, his coordinated friend: "Every movement of his body was graceful, easy, and controlled. Lymie, who was continually being surprised by what his own hands and feet were up to, enjoyed watching him. . . . The wish closest to Lymie's heart, if he could have had it for the asking, would have been to have a well-built body, a body as strong and as beautifully proportioned as Spud's. Then all his troubles would have been over" (pp. 90–91 of the Vintage Books edition).

Re-uning: What Will They Think of Me Now?

117   Name tags are the big item at reunions. The size of the tag and letters penned on it are a major topic of conversation since reunion participants spend so much time squinting at each other's chests. Erma Bombeck, who writes often about reunions (the chapter epigraph is from her August 7, 1974, column in the *San Diego Evening Tribune*), has talked of the difficulty of socializing with people who spend "30 minutes or so talking with my left bosom." To Betty Dunn, *Life*, October 1, 1971, p. 67.

The most compassionate reunion I attended was a thirty-fifth, where nametags were nearly a foot square, with letters one inch high, and hung around the neck.

Tips for reunion organizers: nametags can't be too big; outdoor reunions during the day are more fun; the less it costs, the more attend; some classmates don't want to be located; awards needn't be cruel.

Giving awards is a popular activity at reunions, a mild resurrection of the casual cruelty of adolescence. Grown-up slam books, sort of. Reunion awards too often are given for things like Most Gray Hair, Most Weight Gained, Baldest, Most Times Married — flattering things like that. Even the common award for being first to make a reservation may reveal more eagerness to classmates than the recipient might wish to be known.

A friend who emceed his twentieth reunion in Idaho was struck by how many of the awards he was giving had to do with procreation — Most Children, Least Children, Most Recent Child, and — to his horror — Most Grandchildren. To his greater horror, the last one turned out to be a contest.

Reunion miscellany:

I heard several reports of fistfights at reunions, particularly between jealous husbands, but never witnessed any. I did see lots of tense spouses.

Reports are about evenly divided, and stated with great certainty, about whether male classmates have changed more, or female.

More than one veteran of successive reunions has told me that the changes between a twentieth and twenty-fifth can be striking.

The only place I've seen more cleavage, even wrinkled cleavage, than at reunions is at the beach.

One's class reunion is no time to mess around.

119   I could find no research on the subject of high school class reunions. A nonfiction book has been written about one man's twenty-fifth: Robert Douglas Mead, *Reunion* (New York: Saturday Review Press, 1973), and a paperback novel called *A Reunion of Strangers* by Parley Cooper (New York: Berkeley Medallion Books, 1973) is built around characters returning home for their tenth.

Psychoanalyst George Pollock has studied the traumatic effect of anniversaries in general, especially holiday depression. Such trauma, Dr. Pollock writes, extends to commemorations of all kinds since they "serve as a trigger for the release of the repressed conflict, which appears as an anniversary reaction." "Temporal Anniversary Manifestations: Hour, Day, Holiday," *The Psychoanalytic Quarterly* XL (1), 1971, p. 130.

After attending his twentieth college class reunion, psychiatrist Walter Menninger commented about the experience: "As we look at the wrinkles and gray hair on our old friends, we're faced with our own mortality. It reminds us we're not going to live forever" (*The Arizona Republic*, March 17, 1974).

Wilkinson Blades called reunions one of the four worst times to get a shaving nick in a CBS-TV ad, November 17, 1972.

Carol Kelly Vaiden said in the *Memphis Press Scimitar* (July 29, 1974), "Reunions are alive and well and growing more numerous each summer." Jeryme English wrote in the *Oregon Statesman* (Salem) (July 19, 1974), "More high school class reunions have been held this summer than ever before." In the *Camarillo* (California) *Daily News* (August 2, 1974), Robin Newcomer Braun said, "This year . . . it seems that there are more reunions going on than I ever noticed before."

The *Santa Maria Times* reported on July 17, 1974, of Santa Maria High's tenth reunion, "At the height of the festivities a streaker appeared on the stage. He was a friendly streaker, not the peek and run type. Stayed right up there, dancing for the crowd. He was encouraged to get off the stage and he did.

"(Only to appear later in the crowd, happily dancing with his classmates — still in the buff.)"

At a fiftieth reunion of Thomas Jefferson High in Omaha, Nebraska, a streaker was part of their hired Road Show (*Nonpareil*, Council Bluffs, Iowa, July 28, 1974).

A thirtieth at Galena High in Kansas had a Streak Contest and Streaker Award (*Galena Sentinel-Times*, Galena, Kansas, July 18, 1974).

An all-class reunion of Oregon's Hereford Union High School was disrupted by a "streaker" in a red bunny suit (*The Record-Courier*, Baker, Oregon, July 11, 1974).

The beglassed Kingsley High reunion was reported by the *Lemars Daily Sentinel*, July 29, 1974; Alpena High's reunion was reported by the *Alpena News*, August 7, 1974; Polytechnic's in the *Fort Worth Star-Telegram*, August 10, 1974.

120 Though Gould's heroine was concerned primarily that her age not be on record anywhere, the effect is the same. Lois Gould, *Final Analysis*, p. 181 of the Avon Books edition.

Final note: If you ever want to become a missing person, don't let a reunion organizer try to track you down. They are tenacious, cunning, and will stop at nothing to get their person. Reunion organizers look through old phone books. They call relatives. They announce your name over the air.

One organizer spent two years making an estimated thirty-five hundred phone calls and writing hundreds of letters, including forty-eight to everyone with the same name of a classmate listed in the phone book of Indianapolis, his last known location. *Los Angeles Times*, March 11, 1973.

If you are ever thinking about organizing a reunion, think twice. This is an incredibly demanding and thankless job. On the other hand, I would advise personnel managers to hire a successful reunion organizer for any job in the outfit.

How Can We?

149 The *Penthouse* Forum letter ran February 1974, pp. 22, 24.

151 In a description of his twenty-fifth reunion, Otto Friedrich wrote, "My guess is that in the Concord High School of the 1940's, sex remained largely a matter of daydream and potentiality, and that there was very little actual fornication. If this is true, then we all have the same memory, all the classmates of 1945, of possibilities unfulfilled, and this is part of what draws us together" (*Harper's*, May 1971, p. 96).

152 Gerald H. J. Pearson, M.D., writes of leftover adolescent sexual frustration in *Adolescence and the Conflict of Generations* (New York: Norton, 1958), pp. 120–121. Dr. Pearson's book remains a solid, accessible statement of a psychoanalytic approach to adolescence.

153 Gore Vidal wrote of enduring sexual fantasies in *The New York Review of Books*, March 31, 1966, p. 4.

Writer Ralph Schoenstein calls his actual adult sexual conquests "just a bitter-sweet memory of the fore-playing 40's and 50's" (*Penthouse*, January 1973, p. 58).

On television I once heard a movie director call himself a "sexual adolescent," as if this were out of the ordinary. I thought we all were.

"Where cunt is concerned," Alexander Portnoy says of himself, "he lives in a condition that had neither diminished nor in any significant way been refined from what it was when he was fifteen years old . . ." (*Portnoy's Complaint*, p. 101).

154 Frank Rich mentioned cheerleaders in *New Times*, July 12, 1974, p. 56.

Barbi Benton (they always seem to have names ending in "i" — Teri, Suzi, Barbi) is referred to as an ex-cheerleader in *Playboy*, December 1973, p. 145.

Playboy ran locker-room strip pictures of an Oakland Raider cheerleader in their September 1974 issue, and noted that their February 1975 Playmate was once a cheerleader in Tulsa.

Penthouse's May 1974 centerfold was cited as both a cheerleader and prom queen, and their January 1973 issue included a picture spread from *The Cheerleaders*.

In their photo layout on "50's Fantasies," *Gallery* included an undressed cheerleader waving pom-poms in the dream of a high school boy musing, ". . . . Jeez, how do they really, if they do . . . *do* it?" (July 1973, p. 67).

Esquire doesn't stoop to actual cheerleader strips, but did once run a spread on ex-cheerleaders in their outfits today (some showing panty; October 1974), after putting college cheerleaders on its cover and insides, September 1972.

154–155 The *Evergreen Review* spread ran in August 1967. Their undressing cheerleaders looked a bit beyond adolescence.

The *Evergreen* pictures were adapted as art to illustrate one of the *National Lampoon*'s recurring fantasy sequences about what it would be like to slip invisibly into the girls' locker room ("Invisible Robkin in the Girl's Locker Room," by Chris Miller, *National Lampoon*, February 1973).

Woody Allen says he renounced atheism when "once, in the dress department of Bloomingdale's my hand accidentally brushed against the thigh of an eighteen-year-old cheerleader with long hair and an overbite and at that moment I could swear I heard a choir of angels" (*Esquire*, July 1975, p. 80).

156 John Bowers is an especially cheerleader-conscious author. In his novel *No More Reunions* (New York: E. P. Dutton, 1973), Bowers's main character Boney masturbates to experience "relief at last from blondes and big tits and the locomotives of cheerleaders" (p. 13 of the Pocket Books edition). After scoring two points in a basketball game Boney first looks up to see them register on the scoreboard, then back "to see Meredith's satin-covered behind on a cheerleader leap" (p. 106). Later he daydreams of a school where letters are awarded for sexual prowess, "and at the end of the year, we all have our pictures in the yearbook, the cheerleaders lying back with heads out of sight, maroon skirts raised, identified only by their quims" (p. 119).

Bowers's comment about the frigid ex-cheerleader is on pages 105–106 of the Pocket Book edition of *The Colony* (New York: Dutton, 1973).

McGinnis's fantasizing woman holds forth on page 109 of *The Dream Team* (New York: Random House, 1972). I suspect this fantasy could only have been written by a male writer.

159 P. J. O'Rourke's story is from our interview.

160 Singer Paul Simon has talked of later trying to get something going with a teacher he'd had a crush on at eighteen. They dated once or twice, but nothing sparked and he finally concluded that it was no use, "you can't go back and reconstruct a relationship. Once it's gone, that's it." As told to Edwin Miller, *Seventeen*, May 1968, p. 207.

162 The adviser on light romance writing, Linda Jacobs, recommends first-love writing in *The Writer*, June 1974, p. 15.

Songwriter Nils Lofgren says, "Forty years from now, you're still going to have people writing about teenage love. It's the basis of human nature. . . . Teenage feelings, although they mature, remain with you always." To Paul Nelson, *Rolling Stone*, June 19, 1975, p. 20.

John Updike has written often on early love, and of his stories "The Persistence of Desire," in *Pigeon Feathers* (New York: Knopf, 1962), concerns the yearning and discomfort of first lovers remeeting years later.

162–163 John Money's observation about imprinted early love is made in collaboration with Anke A. Ehrhardt in *Man & Woman Boy & Girl* (Baltimore: The Johns Hopkins University Press, 1972), and appears on p. 196 of the Mentor edition.

His mention of the "falling in love syndrome," made in conjunction with Patricia Tucker, is in *Sexual Signatures* (Boston: Little, Brown, 1975), p. 141.

In interviews for her book *Women and Sex* (New York: Pantheon Books, 1973), psychologist Leah Cahan Schaefer found first sexual experiences set the pattern for subsequent ones primarily among women with moderate sexual drives (*McCall's*, October 1973, p. 35).

163 Snowy's dilemma is described in *The Cheerleader*, p. 272.

In her essay on "The War in the Back Seat," Alix Kates Shulman writes: "My most intense memory of adolescence is that anxious moment in the back seat of the car (one scenario, many actors), after my lipstick has been smeared, and my hair irreparably mussed, yet before my 'please stop now' has been overruled, turning a promising intimacy into an anxious struggle" (*The Atlantic*, July 1972, p. 53).

In Shulman's *Memoirs of an Ex-Prom Queen*, Sasha Davis prays that "hands would go away but leave the boys" (p. 46).

164 I read recently of a couple who remarried after being divorced for forty-one years. "A first love doesn't die easily," the seventy-eight-year-old husband explained (*National Enquirer*, July 21, 1974). The Kentucky couple's reunion was also reported by the *National Enquirer*, October 29, 1974, with a nice picture of them together.

The Smotherses were covered in *Time* and *Newsweek*, July 29, 1974, and a lot of other places. He talked of their remeeting and marriage on the *Tonight Show*, July 19, 1974.

Lee Marvin is another public figure who married an adolescent love more than two decades after the fact (though in his case she was in high school and he out, when they met). Marvin attributed their getting married to the fact that after twenty-five years of friendship, "sex had to go and raise its ugly head." This was in Carolyn See's round-up of some celebrities' recall of first love in *Today's Health*, February 1974, p. 65.

Karl and Anne Taylor Fleming's book *First Time* (New York: Simon & Schuster, 1975) goes into this subject more deeply.

164–169 I talked with Bob and Janet Lawrence on September 5, 1974.

𝒯he 𝒮igh 𝒮chool 𝒮mprint

171 Alexander Portnoy pleads for closure in *Portnoy's Complaint*, p. 77.

173 Eric Berne calls adolescence a time when the high school student must "walk down long and often lonely corridors under the critical gaze of other boys and girls, many of whom already know his weaknesses. So sometimes he sweats automatically, his hands shake, his heart pounds; girls blush, their clothes become moist, and their stomachs gurgle. In both sexes there is an assorted loosening and tightening up of various sphincters . . ." (*What Do You Say After You Say Hello?*, p. 170).

174 Dory Previn talked of high school fear during our interview.

Social critics such as Erich Fromm and David Riesman have suggested that fear is the source of conformity. In other words, those of us who most resemble a herd of contented cows may in fact be huddling for protection.

A study testing this hypothesis found that young women told to antici-
pate an electric shock gathered together more closely than groups not
expecting to be shocked. John M. Darley, "Fear and Social Comparison
as Determinants of Conformity Behavior," in Ellis D. Evans, ed., *Adolescents, Readings in Behavior and Development* (Hinsdale, Ill.: Dryden
Press, 1970), pp. 427–437.

Making the point that adolescence itself is a development disturbance,
Anna Freud writes: "Although in the childhood disorders of this nature
we are confronted usually with alterations in one or the other area of the
child's personality, in adolescence we deal with changes along the whole
line." She adds that the evolution from pregenital to genital sexual im-
pulses "involves the adolescent in dangers which did not exist before and
with which he is not accustomed to deal." In "Adolescence as a Develop-
mental Disturbance," in Gerald Caplan and Serge Lebovici, eds., *Adolescence: Psychological Perspectives* (New York: Basic Books, 1969), p. 7.

175 Accidents as the leading cause of adolescent death is cited in *Normal Adolescence*, Committee on Adolescence, Group for the Advancement of Psychiatry (New York: Charles Scribner's Sons, 1968), p. 25. This
book is an excellent summary of psychiatric perspectives on the high
school years.

The FBI's 1974 *Uniform Crime Report* showed that in 1973 Americans
under 21 committed 61.7 percent of all offenses included in their Crime
Index (what the FBI considers the seven most serious offenses—murder,
assault, rape, larceny, robbery, burglary and auto theft), and 40.8 percent
of all crimes (p. 130). Even 25 percent of Offer's "normal" population admitted at least one delinquent act (*The Psychological World of the Teenager*, p. 73).

The psychologist talking of adolescence as psychosis is Dale B. Harris,
"Work and the Adolescent Transition to Maturity," in Grinder, *Studies
in Adolescence*, p. 52. For a contrasting point of view see Offer especially
in *The Psychological World of the Teenager*.

The concept of association is basic to both the theory and practice
of memory. Those teaching memory-improvement methods emphasize the
importance of associating the unfamiliar with the familiar. See Gordon H.
Bower, "How to . . . Uh . . . Remember!" in *Psychology Today*, October
1973, and Jerry Lucas and Harry Lorayne, *The Memory Book* (New
York: Stein & Day, 1974).

The Kennedy association is as vivid for recent generations as was the
death of Franklin Roosevelt or Pearl Harbor for generations past. A Pearl
Harbor Survivors' Association still holds regular picnics on the West Coast
(*San Diego Evening Tribune*, February 14 and May 12, 1975), which seems
in the same category as the 1906 Club for San Francisco earthquake survivors, whose San Diego chapter was described in the *San Diego Union*,
April 18, 1971.

175–176 Scot Morris is a friend of mine, and was formerly an editor of
Psychology Today. His book on animal origins of human behavior is forth-
coming. He made the quoted comment to me in a conversation.

176 Dr. Pearson writes of enhanced teenage senses in *Adolescence and
the Conflict of Generations*, p. 33.

176–177   In addition to holding reunions, military units commonly produce yearbooks.
  Though an actual comparative tabulation of different kinds of reunions
would be nearly impossible, I've kept a sampling of reunion announcements to compare with those of high school classes and find military
units announce gatherings next most often (the 1st Marine Division once
did so by bumper sticker), followed by families. Families, however, probably have less need to announce their reunions in public.
  Other groups holding reunions include: elementary and college classes,
those from nursing school, the Algonquin Round Table, disassembled rock
groups, and former Securities and Exchange Commission employees.
  177–178   The comparative study of Chinese-American and Caucasian-
American students was made by Francis L. K. Hsu, Blanche G. Watrous,
and Edith M. Lord, "Culture Pattern and Adolescent Behavior," in
Grinder, *Adolescence and the Conflict of Generations,* where the quotation appears on p. 69.
  178–179   Offer writes of parents holding back their adolescent memories
on p. 62 of *The Psychological World of the Teenager.*
  179   Elizabeth Douvan and Joseph Adelson include a thorough discussion of adolescent amnesia at the outset of *The Adolescent Experience*
(New York: Wiley, 1966), in which the excerpt appears on page 4.
  The common fear of confronting one's own revived adolescent feelings
is what may make it so hard to find counselors and others willing to work
with teenagers, though this reason is rarely considered too seriously.
  In a 1958 paper, Anna Freud mentioned the amnesia for their adolescence she observed in her patients, and suggested that if other analysts'
experience corroborated hers, this might account for gaps in our understanding of this period of life. In Ruth Eissler et al., eds., *The Psychoanalytic Study of the Child,* Volume 13 (New York: International University Press, Inc., 1958), pp. 259–260.
  Her suggestion has not been paid adequate attention, possibly because
those studying this subject "objectively" can be reluctant to face even by
implication traumatic memories of their own adolescence. One set of researchers, studying a group of children from birth to maturity, could not
agree on what they were looking for after their subjects passed puberty.
This conflict grew so paralyzing that the researchers considered skipping
the subjects' adolescence entirely. "Those who looked at this particular
research crisis from the outside," writes psychologist James Anthony, "felt
that . . . the catastrophic reaction of the participants mirrored not only the
usual uncertainty of the adult with respect to adolescence but also an unconscious resistance against reactivating the basic adolescent conflicts. Some
of the investigators, who had been very much at home with the child, felt
'disoriented' when confronted with the adolescent" (p. 75 of "The Reactions of Adults to Adolescents and Their Behavior," in Caplan and Lebovici, *Adolescence: Psychological Perspectives,* pp. 54–78).
  In this excellent paper exploring adult reactions to adolescents, Dr.
Anthony also talks of parents' "reactivated adolescent" crisis. But his conclusion is not bleak, because Anthony feels that "adolescent feelings per-
sisting in the parents do not always work negatively for the adolescent

child. They can and do often lead to greater sympathy, empathy, and understanding. The parent with a better recollection of his own adolescent difficulties can use this constructively in dealing with his child and, in so doing, may be able to help himself" (ibid., p. 66).

In *How to Live with Your Teenager* (New York: McGraw-Hill, 1953), p. 17, Dorothy Baruch sets up this dicta as a poster:

By true regard for the

FEELINGS WE HAD IN OUR OWN ADOLESCENCE

we gain truer regard for

OUR ADOLESCENT'S FEELINGS

right now.

180–181   Jean Shepherd, a delightfully courageous resurrecter of adolescence, wrote the excerpted prose in the title story of *Wanda Hickey's Night of Golden Memories* (Garden City, N.Y.: Doubleday, 1971), pp. 243–244 of the Dell edition.

181   High school as a setting of American puberty rites is regularly commented upon.

George Spindler, who called high school an extended puberty rite in "The Education of Adolescents: An Anthropological Perspective" (in Evans, *Adolescents*, p. 158), adds that the major difference between high school and classic rites is that "our adolescent is providing his own rite of passage — his own initiation rite — and in other societies adults are providing it." Pointing out that our approach leads to a constantly changing set of rites, the anthropologist suggests that perhaps this is in keeping with a culture in such flux as our own.

182   Erikson's comments about adolescent modes of thought surviving socially are in his essay "Youth: Fidelity and Diversity" in Erik Erikson, ed., *The Challenge of Youth* (Garden City, N.Y.: Doubleday, 1965), p. 23 of the Anchor Books edition.

182–183   Vonnegut called high school the American core in his introduction to *Our Time Is Now*, John Birmingham, ed., on p. x.

183   Lorenz describes how he became the goslings' "mother" on pages 65, 258, and 261 of the Bantam edition of *On Aggression* (New York: Harcourt, Brace & World, 1966).

Peter Blos draws parallels between adolescence and early childhood in his *On Adolescence* (New York: The Free Press of Glencoe, 1962), p. 11, from which the quotation is excerpted.

"Imprinting" is technically a biological concept applied to species-wide behavior. When I asked my friend the physiological psychologist whether this concept might properly be applied to adolescence, she replied that since it was misapplied to early childhood, it might as well be misapplied to adolescence as well.

I've chosen to regard this problem as one primarily of vocabulary since the concept of imprinting seems valid for various phases of human learning, even if the word itself has strayed from its original moorings.

On human imprinting, see John Paul Scott, *Early Experience and the Organization of Behavior* (Belmont, Calif.: Cole Publishing Co., 1968), in which the definition of "critical period" is given on p. 69.

184   The only application I've seen of the imprinting concept to adolescence is Dr. Money's reference to first love as "an imprinting phenom-

enon" in *Man & Woman Boy & Girl*, p. 196, and Knowles's literary reference from *A Separate Peace*, p. 45. Like Vonnegut's observation, this insight of Knowles's struck a responsive chord and is commonly quoted or cited.

184–185 *Psychology Today*'s survey of "Body Image," made by Ellen Berscheid, Elaine Walster, and George Bohrnstedt, appeared in their November 1973 issue, in which the excerpt appears on p. 250.

In *Final Analysis*, Lois Gould writes, "The worst thing about ever having been fat and ugly is that it is an incurable mental condition" (pp. 47–48).

Actress Liv Ullman, who has recently become a standard of feminine beauty, recalls herself as an awkward teenager. "The problem is," she's said, "that even after you're 30 you're sometimes afraid that people will find out you're still one of the awkward ones." As told to A. Alvarez, *The New York Times Magazine*, December 22, 1974, p. 37.

One source of yearbooks' and reunions' potency is as "releaser stimuli." Looking over my own yearbook, I find strong feelings return at the mere sight of inscriptions, even before I've read them. On a broader scale, books like *The Catcher in the Rye*, or movies such as *American Graffiti*, are releaser stimuli for a culture. In a perceptive review of J. D. Salinger's novel, psychiatrist Ernest Jones suggested that the popularity of this work had less to do with its uniqueness than its universality. Dr. Jones called the book a mirror, saying, "It reflects something not at all rich and strange but what every sensitive sixteen-year-old since Rousseau has felt, and of course what each one of us is certain he has felt." *Catcher in the Rye*, he concluded, is really "a case history of all of us" (*The Nation*, September 1, 1951, p. 176).

George Lucas's movie struck such a similarly common chord that "an *American Graffiti* adolescence" has become a cliché phrase of this culture.

186 Dr. Ives Hendrick calls psychoanalysis "a second chance at adolescence" in *Facts and Theories of Psychoanalysis* (New York: Knopf, 1934, 1939, 1958). The quotation excerpted appears on p. 256, and is discussed more fully on p. 230 of the Dell edition.

Ann Landers accused a letter writer of being in high school emotionally on February 27, 1974, *San Diego Evening Tribune*.

Exorcising High School

187 Miller's epigraph is from his essay on the American theater in *Harper's*, August 1958, p. 41.

189–193 Many friends made good suggestions for this list of 101 Ways to Get High School off Your Back.

194 Hugh Hefner is quoted as calling *Playboy* an adolescent projection in *Rolling Stone* (December 20, 1973, p. 70), a point he reiterated in his interview within *Playboy*'s twentieth-anniversary issue (December 1973, p. 70). "It's been said," Hefner added, "that the boy is father to the man, but in my case, I think the boy was father to the boy."

Playboy's publisher told Bill Davidson about his adolescent timidity in *The Saturday Evening Post*, April 28, 1962. His high school years have also been covered in *The Saturday Evening Post*, April 23, 1966; *Time*, March 3, 1967; and in Frank Brady's *Hefner* (New York: Macmillan, 1974).

Betty Friedan is quoted about dating misfits in the *New York Times*, November 19, 1971. Her classmates' prediction is reported in *McCall's*, August 1973. She told Paul Wilkes of her adolescent vow in *The New York Times Magazine*, November 29, 1970, p. 27. Friedan's standing with colleagues as well as her current life-style have been widely reported. This is summed up both in Lyn Tornabene's profile of Friedan in *McCall's* (May 1971) and more skimpily in a *New York Times* profile (March 23, 1970), where the feminist leader is quoted about enjoying her second adolescence.

In her *McCall's* column on turning fifty, Ms. Friedan said that during recent experiences, "I felt more like eighteen than when I was really eighteen." Then she added (as any mature person ought), "But it's clearly ridiculous for a woman to feel like eighteen when she's going to be fifty" (August 1971, p. 56).

195 Kurt Vonnegut brings up high school regularly in his fiction. One short story in particular, "Miss Temptation," in *Welcome to the Monkey House* (New York: Delacorte, 1970), is based on the resentment of a young soldier toward a beautiful girl of the kind who snubbed him in high school.

Vonnegut once called some visitors' aspiration to be the last survivors on earth "stuck-up." Fellow Shortridge High School graduate Dan Wakefield, who was present, later observed, "I don't think I had heard the term 'stuck-up' since high school, but it seemed to apply quite nicely to the situation." In *The Vonnegut Statement*, Jerome Klinkowitz and John Somer, eds. (New York: Dell, 1973), pp. 69–70.

Vonnegut told of calling the coach in *Playboy*, July 1974, p. 66.

In a talk with Robert Scholes, the writer called Shortridge "an excellent high school which encouraged creative writing. . . ." (Klinkowitz and Somer, *The Vonnegut Statement*, p. 92), and in some unpublished remarks added, "The Shortridge experiences certainly had more to do with what I am now than any other subsequent institution."

196 Anna Freud writes about adolescent amnesia in Ruth Eissler, *The Psychoanalytic Study of the Child*, pp. 259–260.

198 The journalist who found Hefner's estate adolescently reprehensible was Sam Merrill, and his comment was made in *New Times*, August 23, 1974, p. 47.

In his *New York* report on Gay Talese's participatory sex research, Aaron Latham portrayed the writer as an arrested adolescent acting out teenage wet dreams. Just as interesting were Latham's own adolescent points of reference. Before going with Talese to a massage parlor Latham said, "I felt a high-school dance nervousness," with the visit itself "reminding me of my high school's senior prom" (*New York*, September 9, 1973, p. 45).

The famous epithet thrown at Churchill is mentioned by Dennis Bardens South, *Churchill in Parliament* (New York: A. S. Barnes, 1967), p. 274 of the 1969 American edition.

Peter Falk once said of Mike Nichols: "Mike has a lot of kid in him. His reactions can be childlike, even though he's been around. That's what makes him a good director." To Joyce Haber, *Calendar, Los Angeles Times,* January 19, 1975, p. 27.

Of Liv Ullman, Ingmar Bergman has observed, "She lives very close to her childhood — and for a creative artist this is very important" (*Newsweek*, March 17, 1975, p. 65).

Erik Erikson writes of "creative people who experience, according to their own testimony, repeated adolescences" in *Identity, Youth and Crisis* (New York: Norton, 1968), p. 183.

From Huck Finn to Holden Caulfield, adolescence has been a favorite American literary theme. Authors such as J. D. Salinger or John Knowles have written their best (some say their only) fiction by drawing on the high school of memory. In another context John Updike has written, "The lack of connection between the experiences, usually accumulated by the age of twenty, that seem worth telling about, and the sophistication needed to render them in writing, is the Unmentionable at the root of the mysterious Fall of so many auspicious beginners." In his *New Republic* review of Alan Sillitoe's *The Loneliness of the Long Distance Runner*, reprinted in *Assorted Prose* (New York: Knopf, 1965), pp. 177–178 of the Fawcett Crest edition.

Updike adds that it takes courage to write about one's boyhood, which in his own case, "funnily enough was a very innocuous boyhood." To Eric Rhode, *Vogue*, February 1, 1971, p. 185.

Roth's comment about his first eighteen years was in his essay on that topic in the *New York Times*, October 24, 1970.

199 Coppola's thought about rejection becoming art is from *Newsweek*'s cover story on him, November 25, 1974, p. 76. In his *Penthouse* profile, the director talked of a summer when he was fifteen and felt excluded by some beautiful rich kids on Long Island. This experience, Coppola told Thomas Maremaa, became "the basis for a dramatic motif that I've been playing with for years now and am still involved with" (*Penthouse*, May 1974, p. 117).

A member of Coppola's filmmaking company told me it was Coppola who advised George Lucas to make a movie about something he knew intimately. This led to *American Graffiti*. Lucas (who is supposed to resemble Terry the Toad in that movie) has said parts of him are included in every major male in *Graffiti* except for the class president, who the director says was the most difficult character to create (*New York Times*, September 19, 1973).

Lucas told Wayne Warga that *Graffiti* was his personal ten-year reunion in *Calendar, Los Angeles Times*, August 12, 1973, p. 1.

199–201 Jules Feiffer talked of reverting to adolescence in his *Playboy* interview, September 1971, p. 84.

201 After an absence of ten years, Betty Friedan was invited to lecture in her hometown. Her reaction: "The thought of coming back to Peoria

in this capacity has scared me; not for how they would receive me, but what I might revert to."

In fact she found herself moved, and proud, to be bringing home the movement she helped start (*McCall's*, January 1973, p. 147).

This actually is a pretty good way to lift the fever of high school: get invited back to give a speech. Both Charles Schulz and Alan Arkin, neither of whom were honored or even noticed at the time, have been given awards and platforms by their high schools. In Arkin's case the drill team even spelled out his name (*Holiday*, October 1966).

Journalist Sara Davidson braved a return to Teaneck High in New Jersey and reported: "One visit can instantly turn back the years. . . . The clothes were different from a decade ago when I was in high school, but the postures, the unwritten codes and manners — the gestalt is absolutely unchanged. . . . The same small groups eat together each day, always meet at the same place on the grounds and would never dream of trying, for a change, to spend an afternoon with people from another group (*Life*, February 4, 1972, p. 50).

201–202 Lyn Tornabene's intriguing *I Passed as a Teenager* (New York: Simon & Schuster, 1967) is quoted from pages 140, 219, 245, 249, 250.

202–203 Mike Mulligan (real name) is now an advertising manager for a food distributor, father of a daughter, and if anything a better friend than in high school.

203 Paula Gottschalk (real name) is now a promotion executive with CBS in New York. In a visit subsequent to our interview we watched election returns together. This time we talked hardly at all about high school. It was as if we were two people getting together rather than classmates from different crowds.